A Catalyst to Transformation

DISCIPLE

Michael Pawelke

DISCIPLE

A Catalyst to Transformation

ISBN-13: 978-1-926676-74-6

Printed by Word Alive Press
131 Cordite Road, Winnipeg, MB R3W 1S1
www.wordalivepress.ca

WORD ALIVE PRESS
Just Write!

The symbol of the eight-spoked wheel is actually an ancient symbol for Christians. *Ichthus* (ikh-thoos) or *ichthys* is a Greek word, which means fish. The Greek spelling for *ichthus* is Iota, Chi, Theta, Upsilon, and Sigma:

$$I \ X \ \Theta \ Y \ \Sigma$$

These five Greek letters represent the first letter in the words: *Jesus Christ, God's Son, Savior.* These letters are often embedded into the sign of a fish.

However, when these Greek letters, are superimposed, they create an eight-spoked wagon wheel. This symbol has been found in such places as ancient Ephesus.

TABLE OF CONTENTS

INTRODUCTION

THE POWERFUL IMPACT OF THREE FRIENDS

Look in the mirror. What determines who we become? We know that our family of origin marks us deeply and permanently. Our faith, our relationships, our education, our experiences—whether pleasant or painful—our present families, and our environmental context, all influence us significantly.

There have been three enormously impacting individuals who have shaped my life. They intersected in my life at a defining time in my teens and early twenties. Call them friends, coaches, mentors, examples, whatever you choose, these three people marked me profoundly.

Tom was the first and most pivotal. Shortly after trusting in Jesus as a young teen through the reading of a little Gideon New Testament, I started attending a church. My parents' unhappy marriage had just ended and I was now living with my mother in Toronto. While I did not know much about church, I knew that as a new follower of Jesus I should go. Tom was a lay leader in the church I began attending and he took me under his wing and befriended me. He took me out for pizza. He gave me books to read which we discussed at length. He introduced me to theology, to critical thinking, to philosophical and ideological trends. While he taught me, he also spent time with me. He listened to me. He had me over to his home. He encouraged me in my educational aspirations. When my wife Linda and I were preparing for marriage, he took me aside and had a critical "father-son chat" with me on what being a good husband looked like, as my father had died of cancer by this time. I will forever be indebted to Tom.

Bill was a passionate missionary. I spent a summer with him when I was seventeen. He had me reading and studying God's Word. He had me memorize Scripture. He taught me how to share my faith. He showed me how to prepare my testimony and share it publicly. He helped me to re-search, prepare, and deliver my first message. I watched Bill pray, zealously share his faith, love his wife as they struggled with infertility, and wrestle at times with the application of his own calling. He eventually returned to serve in England.

Jack was the first pastor who I would work with and under. He believed in me more than I believed in myself. He empowered me sooner than I felt I should have been empowered. He modeled how to love a congregation, how to care for the hurting, how to lead a staff, how to work with a board, how to be loyal, how to honour one's family, and how to stay faithful to God and to one's calling.

Tom taught me how to think biblically. Bill taught me how to repre-sent Jesus naturally and with joy. Jack taught me how to be a shepherd to a flock. They all showed me how to live, love, and follow Jesus. Essentially, they discipled me. I do not remember if any of these three individuals ever used that term to describe our relationship, but this is what they effectively did.

Discipleship is a rich word, charged with meaning, but often misunderstood. Is being a disciple like being a part of a secret society, or a university fraternity? Is it for the radically committed? Or is a disciple just another name for a Christian? Let's explore.

CHRISTIAN OR DISCIPLE?

The term *Christian* first surfaces in the New Testament in Acts 11 where it says:

> *The disciples were called Christians first at Antioch.* (Acts 11:27, NIV)

The word *Christian* is only found two more times in the New Testament (Acts 26:28; 1 Peter 4:16). Essentially a *Christian* was someone who followed Christ. They were also referred to in Scripture as *believers,* in that they placed their trust in Christ. They were also called *saved* or *redeemed,* because they were rescued from the clutches of sin, selfishness, and eternal destruction. Collectively they were referred to as the *church,* which was a term that referred to "a called out people"[1] or community, and never a building. At times, they were also called *brothers and sisters,* building on the metaphor of God's family.

However, the most frequent term used for a believer, Christ-follower, or Christian, particularly in the Gospels, is the term *disciple.* It is used 230 times in the Gospels and twenty-eight times in Acts. It is curious that the term *Christian* became the dominant identifying label when *disciple* was the word Jesus chose and the authors of the Gospels employed. If you and I trust Jesus and are following Jesus, we are *disciples!*

> *The student (disciple)[2] is not above his teacher, but everyone who is fully trained will be like his teacher.* (Luke 6:40, NIV)

The word *disciple* finds its use from a unique Greek word that means *learner, follower,* or *apprentice*.[3] The Greco-Roman world employed this word to reflect a training relationship. Before that, the Semitic world of the Hebrews had similar apprenticeship relationships. Jesus called people to become his disciples—to learn from him, to trust him, to love him, to follow him, to obey him, to emulate him, to apprentice under him—in order to make sense out of life in a relationship with God, and then reach out to others in word and action. The word *disciple* was a noun. A disciple was a person. A disciple was a person in a process and on a journey, in an accountable, apprenticeship relationship.

As human beings, we all have developmental milestones, earmarks, indicators of health and progress. We have life stages such as infancy, early childhood, play-age, school-age, adolescence, young adulthood, middle adulthood, and late adulthood. For each stage, particularly the younger ones, we look for certain motor skills, physical development, cognitive development, verbal skills, and social skills. Just as human beings grow physically, cognitively, and emotionally, so progresses our spiritual maturity. Our entry into a faith relationship with God is called being "born again" (John 3:3). This assumes a growth and development process as a believer and as a disciple. Spiritual infancy implies that there will be growth to higher levels of maturity.

Jesus later builds on this understanding and use of the word when he challenges his followers:

> *Therefore go and make disciples of all nations, baptizing them in the name of the Father and of the Son and of the Holy Spirit, and teaching them to obey everything I have commanded you. And surely I am with you always, to the very end of the age.* (Matthew 28:19-20, NIV)

This command has been notably called the Great Commission and speaks to the mission of the church. This command uses the Greek word for *disciple* to function as a verb.[4] Thus, *to disciple* a person is to aid an individual in becoming an apprentice, follower, or learner under Jesus. Understanding the word *disciple* as both a noun and a verb is meaningful and defining. A Christian is a disciple of Jesus Christ. However, a Christian is also, by definition, called to disciple others, or "make disciples."

Making a disciple involved two essential categories: (1) baptizing and (2) teaching. Baptizing was basically helping people "go public" with their faith.[5] There were no secret *disciples* at this time. When a person was baptized, it took courage, because opposition was now sure to follow. Teaching everything Jesus taught was all about helping people to submit to truth and to the transformation process of being conformed to the image of Christ. We are now going to change our thinking, our behaviour, our values, our emotions, our priorities, and our relationships. Everything will now change. Jesus calls all Christians, all disciples to become disciple-makers, reproducers, and multipliers.

Thus, a disciple begins as a new Christian. A disciple becomes a growing Christian. A disciple becomes a serving Christian. A disciple finally becomes a reproducing Christian. Discipleship, then, is a growing relationship and process. Discipleship involves accountability to that relationship and process.[6]

The Gospels (Matthew, Mark, Luke, and John) all describe the life and ministry of Jesus. In these books we see his method for discipling people. A.B. Bruce, in his classic piece *The Training of the Twelve*, notes that Jesus' approach to discipleship was progressive. Bruce observes, "The twelve arrived at their final intimate relation to Jesus only by degrees, three stages in the history of their fellowship with him being distinguished."[7] The first stage was essentially a discovery stage. The next stage was marked by intentionally following after and learning from Jesus, while the final stage was characterized by a high level of commitment to Christ's work and ministry reproduction.[8] Throughout each stage, Jesus increased the time he spent with the disciples, extended his teaching, and expanded his assignments for them.

As disciples, we are called by God to engage in the process of development and maturity.

SOMETIMES WE FAILED MISERABLY

The purpose of this book is to help appropriate the term *disciple* as both a noun and a verb in the lives of people who choose to follow Jesus. There are times when the church has done a commendable job of forming equipped, dedicated, followers of Jesus. Historically, we have seen structured and organic mentoring. We have seen the use of catechisms, spiritual orders, and training institutes. However, the church has also at times tragically floundered in establishing a straightforward plan and process for making disciples. We found ourselves juggling multiple programs and activities. We read books and curriculums, but failed to apply our lessons. We often failed to sufficiently equip the next generation with the character and qualities of Jesus. We often gained more knowledge, but little character, and even less skill. Many Christians owe their maturity to extended time, repeated and random messages and programs, unguided reading, ministry experimentation, and to relationships which came and went. Many disciples grew to maturity over time and by accident, but have no idea how to reproduce.

THE PROCESS MATTERS

This book is designed to serve as an intentional, clear, cohesive, and inclusive (though certainly not exhaustive) roadmap to embarking on the journey of being a disciple of Jesus Christ and discipling others. This book is intended to be used as a catalyst to love Jesus more, a tool to contour a life, a curriculum to shape a mind, a guide to take suitable next steps in one's faith, and a resource to multiply the qualities of a disciple in others. All of this must, however, take place in the context of a relationship. Discipleship is meant to be realized in community. Discipleship is a journey that we do not take alone.

This tool is divided into four larger sections, each reflecting a season of investigation, growth, and development. Each path contains several short chapters. These chapters are vital nuggets of truth, but in no way address the theme exhaustively. They do, however, introduce us to an essential discipleship lesson that will resurface again and again in our walk with God. Each chapter is intended to move us forward in our developmental process.

Understanding and applying these principles should affect our beliefs and behaviours. To this end, it is my deepest prayer that this material affects real life change and realizes God's kingdom objectives for and through you. We all have expectations when we enter a relationship, start a new job, read a book, attend a course, enrol in a class, or enter a training program. The following are several key learning objectives that I hope will be realized in your experience with this process.

- We will love God with our entire being, love our neighbour as we love ourselves, and have a passionate love for the work of Christ (Matthew 22:37-39; 28:19-20).
- We will be able to articulate what God has done for us as his witness (Mark 5:19; Acts 3:5).
- We will be regular participants in community worship (Hebrews 10:24-25; Acts 2:42).
- We will engage in a small group discipleship relationship (Matthew 28:19-20; Acts 2:46).

- We will publicly identify with Christ in baptism (Matthew 28:19-20).

- We will establish habits that promote spiritual growth, life transformation, and the development of Christian character. Such habits include Bible reading, meditation, prayer, service, and giving.

- We will maintain a balanced lifestyle that promotes growth mentally, physically, spiritually, and socially (Luke 2:52).

- We will engage in acts of service within the body of Christ and within the community that God has placed us (Mark 10:45; Ephesians 4:11-12).

- We will pray for service and evangelistic opportunities and seize such opportunities as they arise (Colossians 4:2-4; Acts 1:8).

- We will engage in the intentional act of making disciples with a view toward reproduction and multiplication (Matthew 28:19-20).[9]

DON'T JUST READ IT!

This resource is to be interacted with, dialogued over, and discussed in a collaborative discipleship relationship. A discipleship relationship is formed when two to twelve people engage in regular, face-to-face interactions, in which participants identify the next steps in their walk with God, cheer each other on, invite accountability for their "next steps," and pray for each other so that they become mature, multiplying disciples of Jesus Christ.[10] The number twelve is not fixed (and has nothing to do with the twelve tribes of Israel or the twelve disciples). However, any group beyond ten or twelve begins to reflect a classroom dynamic or a small assembly more than it reflects a relationship. Thus, this material will achieve the greatest transformation when the following commitments are made:

- **In Solitude:** Read through the content on your own (including all biblical passages cited) and reflect on how these truths and lessons impact your thoughts and behaviours. Be sure to process the assignments and questions in a thoughtful and personal manner. Use a journal for notes.

- **In Community:** Discuss the theme and the questions in community (with another or several others). Determine how many chapters you want to process between meetings. Tease out the implications of these themes on your beliefs and your behaviours. Truth is intended to transform our thinking and our living. This book is to be a launching pad to internal change and external action. If you are the leader/teacher, share your life and your stories. This will make truth come alive. Do not hesitate to recommend specific applications to your group members.

- **In Action:** Be sure to be thorough in your assignments and application. Learning is always reinforced by doing. When you have completed *Disciple*, determine to walk the path again with others and by doing so contribute to the continuing process of reproduction and multiplication. Further change occurs with repetition when we revisit the same themes over and over again in our spiritual lives. Remember, a disciple is both a noun and a verb. We may grow, but we never graduate.

I am a follower of Jesus and I love Jesus. I am also a pastor and I love my church. I have been engaged in the discipleship process since coming to the faith many years ago. I am both a disciple and a disciple maker. For me, being a disciple is a lifelong state, and making disciples is a lifelong calling that transcends my calling as a pastor. In this book, I have attempted to create a tool that sets us on a path toward perpetual learning and serving, that builds an initial platform and framework on which to shape a life of discipleship. I hope this resource does this for you. This book can be used in a one-to-one mentoring relationship, with one's family, or in a small group. This book can be used by followers of Christ in their local church setting, on a campus, by a parachurch ministry, in a classroom, or in a cross-cultural mission's context.

It is my prayer that this becomes a resource and catalyst to stimulate biblical discussion and personal accountability that leads to a whole-hearted love for God, to real life change, to personal godliness, and to missional exploits in advancing God's kingdom agenda. You and I are all called to be disciples! With this objective in mind, you are invited to enter the process and relationship of... *Disciple.*

Partnering together,
MICHAEL B. PAWELKE

PART ONE

The Path of Seeking

INTRODUCTION

With the exception of children who embrace faith young in life, most people go through a season of spiritual alienation, isolation, and wandering before discovering faith. You may find yourself on just suich a path. You may feel marginalized and alone. You may feel confused. You may feel a sense of futility in life. You may feel rather lost. On the other hand, you may find life to be rather uncomplicated and steady, but nevertheless you find yourself musing on the more important matters of life. Whether feeling alienated or not, you are seeking, searching, and you find yourself reflecting significantly on the person of Jesus.

Perhaps you are younger in your faith, but you still have foundational questions that have never really been addressed. The first ten themes of this book are designed to help us wrestle with real and haunting questions about life, meaning, truth, and God. These questions are not addressed exhaustively, but they are briefly highlighted through the lens of Christian perspective. These are real dilemmas and roadblocks that sometimes stump us along the way.

Jesus gave us many powerful lessons. On one occasion, he made a statement that is particularly meaningful for the path on which you may find yourself. He said:

> *Ask, and it will be given to you; seek, and you will find; knock, and it will be opened to you. For everyone who asks receives, and he who seeks finds, and to him who knocks it will be opened. Or what man is there among you who, when his son asks for a loaf, will give him a stone? Or if he asks for a fish, he will not give him a snake, will he? If you then, being evil, know how to give good gifts to your children, how much more will your Father who is in heaven give what is good to those who ask Him! (Matthew 7:7-11, NASB)*

When you ask, God is listening. When you seek, God wants you to find. As you knock, God is anxious to open. Wherever you are at in your spiritual pilgrimage, be honest with yourself and others. Most importantly, be honest with God. Ask him your questions. Seek truth. Knock on the door of understanding. God has big shoulders and listening ears.

01

Who Am I and Why Am I Here?

There is a story of a rabbi living in a Russian city a century ago. Disappointed by his lack of direction and life purpose, he wandered out into the chilly evening. With his hands thrust deep into his pockets, he aimlessly walked through the empty streets, questioning his faith in God, the scriptures, and his calling to ministry. The only thing colder than the Russian winter air was the chill within his own soul. He was so enshrouded by his own despair that he mistakenly wandered into a Russian military compound that was off-limits to civilians.

The silence of the evening chill was shattered by the bark of a Russian soldier. "Who are you and what are you doing here?"

"Excuse me?" replied the rabbi.

"I said, 'Who are you and what are you doing here?!'"

After a brief moment, the rabbi, in a gracious tone so as not to provoke the soldier, said, "How much do you get paid every day?"

"What does that have to do with you?" the soldier retorted.

With some delight, as though he had just made a discovery, the rabbi said, "I will pay you the equal sum if you will ask me those same two questions every day: Who are you and What are you doing here?"[11]

Sooner or later, in the quietness of our own self-reflection, we ask ourselves: "Who am I and what am I doing here?" It may follow a time of failure and disappointment, but it can also follow times of prosperity and success. There is something within us that cries with emptiness and discontentment, and we want more. We may need food or shelter or employment or relationship, but once these basic needs are met, we are far from content.

Why do the famous want more fame? Why do the rich want more riches? Why do the married want a younger spouse, a better-looking spouse, someone else's spouse? Why do the gainfully employed want a different job, a better job, a more prestigious job? Why do record-holders want to be faster, bigger, stronger? Why do the beautiful want more shapely curves, bigger lips, smaller noses, fuller hair, more beautiful clothes (or whatever the given culture prescribes)?

We ask, because we believe there is still something more out there. We imagine we are close, but we are still just a little short. It is out there somewhere! We know it. We feel it. We intuit it. We just cannot seem to find it, but we keep on hunting nevertheless.

The book of Ecclesiastes records the cynical wrestlings of a man who had everything but contentment. In it we read:

> He has made everything beautiful in its time. He has also set eternity in the hearts of men; yet they cannot fathom what God has done from beginning to end. (Ecclesiastes 3:11, NIV)

What the author, King Solomon, is saying, is that God has implanted into the human soul a void and a longing. Inside all of us, we know we are made for eternity, for something more, but we struggle to find it. Jesus illustrates this longing when he tells the tale of the prodigal son.

> Then He said: "A certain man had two sons. And the younger of them said to his father, 'Father, give me the portion of goods that falls to me.' So he divided to them his livelihood. And not many days after, the younger son gathered all together, journeyed to a far country, and there wasted his possessions with prodigal living. But when he had spent all, there arose a severe famine in that land, and he began to be in want. Then he went and joined himself to a citizen of that country, and he sent him into his fields to feed swine. And he would gladly have filled his stomach with the pods that the swine ate, and no one gave him anything.
>
> "But when he came to himself, he said, 'How many of my father's hired servants have bread enough and to spare, and I perish with hunger! I will arise and go to my father, and will say to him, "Father, I have sinned against heaven and before you, and I am no longer worthy to be called your son. Make me like one of your hired servants."'
>
> "And he arose and came to his father. But when he was still a great way off, his father saw him and had compassion, and ran and fell on his neck and kissed him. The son said to him, 'Father, I have sinned against heaven and in your sight, and am no longer worthy to be called your son.'
>
> "But the father said to his servants, 'Bring out the best robe and put it on him, and put a ring on his hand and sandals on his feet. And bring the fatted calf here and kill it, and let us eat and be merry; for this my son was dead and is alive again; he was lost and is found.' And they began to be merry. (Luke 15:11-24, NKJV)

It appears that this young man had come from a fine home where his parents deeply loved him. They no doubt had sought to invest values in him, cautioning and warning him of the dangers of unrestrained living. At some point, this young man thought, *What does my dad know? He is either holding out or is a fool. I am going to find what I am looking for!*

The young man then set out on his pursuit, thinking pleasure would fill his soul. The problem was that nothing he experienced gave him satisfaction. While this story illustrates the discontent, searching character of the human soul, we also learn something profoundly significant about God. God is always waiting for us with arms extended widely and with unconditional welcome. A great Christian thinker named Augustine once observed: "You have made us for yourself, and our hearts are restless until they find rest in You."

"Who am I and why am I here?" Perhaps it has something to do with our relationship with God?

ASSIGNMENT: *How do you answer the question: Who am I and why am I here?"*

DISCUSSION: *As you observe others seeking meaning, do you think their searching is bringing them satisfaction?*

—— 02 ——
Who Is Real?

Asking the questions "Who am I and why am I here?" launches us on a pilgrimage to more questions. What is real? Is there some larger meaning or purpose to reality? Is there some sort of guiding purpose to history or, for that matter, to my life? Do I matter? Philosophers and thinkers have reflected on such questions for centuries, as has every human being on some level.

DOES GOD EXIST?

All such questioning begins with the ultimate query: Does God exist? This foundational question has been tackled in various ways. There are several reasonable arguments for the existence of God.

The teleological argument is the argument of order. The apparent orderliness of the universe implies intelligent design. This is sometimes referred to as the watchmaker argument. If you find a working clock in a desert, you assume a watchmaker created it. Scientists are finding this argument increasingly compelling. From the complexity of the galaxies to the intricacies of the living cell, design appears everywhere.

The cosmological argument is the argument of causality. Everything we observe points to an original "mover." The cause/effect train eventually takes us backwards to the need for God. God is sometimes referred to as the "unmoved mover." Thus, God is often defined as the first cause, cause of all causes, yet himself uncaused. It is difficult to imagine that everything came from nothing.

The ontological argument is a more sophisticated and complex argument for the existence of God. This argument is rooted in intuition and assumes that because we can conceive of ultimate perfection, that that idea and expression of perfection must be God. The very idea of God suggests that God exists, because we cannot conceive of anything or anyone so great on our own.

The moral argument is often thought of as the argument of conscience. Human beings are distinguished from the animal kingdom in that we are gripped by a sense of ought. Right and wrong are morally intuited and when we violate our conscience, we feel guilt. The moral argument for the existence of God is rooted in the premise that this sense of moral "oughtness" is placed there by a moral designer. This argument is perhaps the most personally relevant argument. While we may work very hard at arguing for a relativistic moral framework, we nevertheless are deeply disturbed by expressions of abuse, violence, and injustice. In the core of our being, we know that abusing children, taking advantage of the poor, and enslaving humans for our benefit is a violation of our conscience. This sense of "oughtness" must come from somewhere other than our cultural upbringing.

If we do conclude that God does exist, we now have a foundation to begin to define reality, and with that an attending worldview. Constructing a worldview begins with God and builds up from there. Our worldview becomes the lens through which we interpret life and reality. However, there is also a personal side to this question.

MAKING IT PERSONAL

In 1922, Marjorie William wrote *How Toys become Real* (later titled *The Velveteen Rabbit*).[12] The novel explores the question of reality by developing a story around a young boy's relationship with his stuffed animal toys. On one occasion, the Skin Horse is speaking with the Velveteen Rabbit.

> "What is REAL?" asked the Rabbit one day, when they were lying side by side near the nursery fender, before Nana came to tidy the room. "Does it mean having things that buzz inside you and a stick-out handle?"
>
> "Real isn't how you are made," said the Skin Horse. "It's a thing that happens to you. When a child loves you for a long, long time, not just to play with, but REALLY loves you, then you become Real."
>
> "Does it hurt?" asked the Rabbit.
>
> "Sometimes," said the Skin Horse, for he was always truthful. "When you are Real you don't mind being hurt."
>
> "Does it happen all at once, like being wound up," he asked, "or bit by bit?"
>
> "It doesn't happen all at once," said the Skin Horse. "You become. It takes a long time. That's why it doesn't happen often to people who break easily, or have sharp edges, or who have to be carefully kept. Generally, by the time you are Real, most of your hair has been loved off, and your eyes drop out and you get loose in the joints and very shabby. But these things don't matter at all, because once you are Real you can't be ugly, except to people who don't understand."[13]

Indeed the question of ultimate reality is one that explores the objective realities outside of us. When we believe in God, it begins to help us navigate other questions about objective reality. Meaning is created by context, and when our life exists in the context of God, it has the potential for meaning. The question of meaning becomes intensely personal when we explore our place in what is real. We want to think and feel like our life somehow matters. Reality does exist outside of us, but somehow it "becomes" more real when we activate something called faith and enter into a relationship with our creator.

In the New Testament book of Hebrews, the author explores:

> Now faith is being sure of what we hope for and certain of what we do not see... And without faith it is impossible to please God, because anyone who comes to him must believe that he exists and that he rewards those who earnestly seek him. (Hebrews 11:1, 6, NIV)

The question "What is real?" is abstract and philosophical, but it is also intensely personal and relevant. The question must be wrestled with in our mind, but it is also grappled with in our personal longings for relationship, meaning, and purpose. Such inquiries begin to surface the need for something called faith. Now the question becomes, "What will I believe in?"

ASSIGNMENT: *Do you believe there is a real, objective world out there? Do you believe in God?*

DISCUSSION: *Describe moments when you have felt most alive and like you lived in a world of meaning and purpose. Do these experiences point you to something larger?*

—————— 03 ——————
Can I Know If Anything Is True?

The exploration of truth invites the passionate pursuits of humanity. To some, truth is like a gem to be discovered, while to others truth is perceived to be fluid, unpredictable, and relative. In Western contexts, we frequently hear statements like: "It doesn't really matter what you believe, so long as you are sincere," or "There is no such thing as truth," or "What's true for you may be different for me." Regardless of the historical or cultural context, the question of truth is pivotal.

There was a time when much of the world believed in objective, absolute truth, and that this came from God. Then the Enlightenment gave us reason as our final authority and we began to assess what we thought was true. Our present, post-modern world has moved us still further in our evaluation and left us with a truth void and we find ourselves tumbling into a vortex of ambiguity and doubt. Nothing is certain.

WAYS OF LOOKING AT TRUTH

The following are some of the current perspectives on the nature of truth:

- Truth does not exist. There are no absolutes. This is the post-modern creed; all ideas are relative. There is no such thing as fixed objective reality.

- Truth is determined by the individual. I create my own truth. Protagoras taught this with the premise being that "man is the measure of all things."[14]

- Truth is determined by the community. This is expressed in new forms of tribalism, and mini-communities. Gangs and small homogenous people groups reflect this.

- Truth is determined by culture. Here, "mankind" is the measure of all things.

- Truth is determined by the situation. Joseph Fletcher coined the term "situational ethics."[15] Here, "the end justifies the means" and critical questions need to be asked: "What is the greatest good for the greatest number" and "What is the most loving thing?"

- Truth is determined by what feels good or brings pleasure. Epicurus[16] developed this and his thinking would shape hedonistic expression, as well as modern existentialism.

- Truth is determined by moderation. Aristotle taught that we should avoid extremes of all kinds and seek to balance conflicting ideas.[17]

- Truth is determined by the strong. Frederick Nietzsche would be a definer of this view where "might is right."[18]

While we will not here explore all of the issues for each of these positions, some general questions beg to be addressed. What do we do when "truths" collide? Who distinguishes between "reform" and "regression"? An example of this may be found in the reforms history, witnessed with changes to women's rights, child labour, and slavery. Are the changes much of the world has experienced related to sexual values really advancements and reforms, or could these be regressions? These changes still suggest a value system at work, and yet we have failed to identify how that value system is defined or should work.

An honest relativistic, post-modern philosophical position would press us to moral chaos, because no single moral position could be objectively defended as superior to another. These are significant questions that must be tackled when we have no objective standard for truth. Perhaps there is another way to look at truth.

JESUS ON TRUTH

Jesus said some very provocative and controversial things about truth. During his trial before the Roman Governor Pontius Pilate, Jesus explains,

> *Everyone on the side of truth listens to me.* (John 18:38, NIV)

Pilate responds with a haunting question:

> *What is truth?* (John 18:39, NIV)

Jesus earlier spoke of the liberating power of truth when he instructed his disciples:

> *If you hold to my teaching, you are really my disciples. Then you will know the truth, and the truth will set you free.* (John 8:31-32, NIV)

According to Jesus, the existence of truth was implicit and this truth must be believed, embraced, internalized, and applied. When truth is internalized, truth acts as an agent of freedom. Truth has a power to change the way we think.

However, the most controversial statement Jesus ever made about truth was in the Gospel of John when he stated:

> *I am the way and the truth and the life. No one comes to the Fa-*
> *ther except through me.* (John 14:6, NIV)

While people speak of truth and its implications, Jesus' statement was significant in that no one had ever claimed to be the embodiment of truth before. Truth, in Jesus' understanding, existed, was objective, could be known, and he was the embodiment of it.

A BIBLICAL VIEW OF TRUTH

The premise that Jesus operated with is that truth is determined by God. Because God is a personal God, he longs to know and be known. He thus chose to reveal himself through creation, through prophets and teachers, through reason, through sensory input, and through intuition. The premise is further built on the following key assumptions:

- Truth is an expression of the very nature of God. This is why Jesus said: "I am the truth." Truth therefore exists objectively outside of us, because God is outside of us.
- Truth has been revealed to humanity and thus can be known. We may not be able to know everything about truth because of our finite minds, but we can truly know some truth.
- Truth, as it is given in the Bible, transcends history and culture. What was true in Jesus' day is still true today because it is an expression of the person and character of God.
- Truth is for our benefit. Truth is designed to "set us free" from mental and spiritual bondage.
- Truth is given to human beings, who are made in God's image. Humans are moral creatures.

MORAL TRUTH

The Bible is a testimony of truth. It describes truth about God, about ultimate reality, about our world, and how we should live. While the philosophical view of relativism rejects the existence of absolute truth, the premise of the Bible is that it contains and has revealed absolute, objective truth to us. Moral truth is given to us to show us how to live. While moral truth peppers the pages of the Bible, the giving of the Ten Commandments to the people of Israel in Exodus 20 is a clear and succinct embodiment of biblical, moral truth.

> *And God spoke all these words, saying:*
>
> *"I am the Lord your God, who brought you out of the land of Egypt, out of the house of bondage.*
>
> *"You shall have no other gods before Me.*
>
> *"You shall not make for yourself a carved image—any likeness of anything that is in heaven above, or that is in the earth beneath, or that is in the water under the earth; you shall not bow down to them nor serve them. For I, the Lord your God, am a jealous God, visiting the iniquity of the fathers upon the children to the third and fourth generations of those who hate Me, but showing mercy to thousands, to those who love Me and keep My commandments.*
>
> *"You shall not take the name of the Lord your God in vain, for the Lord will not hold him guiltless who takes His name in vain.*
>
> *"Remember the Sabbath day, to keep it holy. Six days you shall labor and do all your work, but the seventh day is the Sabbath of the Lord your God. In it you shall do no work: you, nor your son, nor your daughter, nor your male servant, nor your female servant, nor your cattle, nor your stranger who is within your gates. For in six days the Lord made the heavens and the earth, the sea, and all that is in them, and rested the seventh day.*

Therefore the Lord blessed the Sabbath day and hallowed it.

"Honor your father and your mother, that your days may be long upon the land which the Lord your God is giving you.

"You shall not murder.

"You shall not commit adultery.

"You shall not steal.

"You shall not bear false witness against your neighbor.

"You shall not covet your neighbor's house; you shall not covet your neighbor's wife, nor his male servant, nor his female servant, nor his ox, nor his donkey, nor anything that is your neighbor's." (Exodus 20:1-17, NKJV)

The Bible contains further details on moral truth. Jesus himself spoke of the commandments as the foundation of moral truth; however, Jesus then takes them a step further. The Ten Commandments essentially address moral behaviour, but Jesus interprets the commandments and then challenges us with the view that morality is something internal and of the mind (see Matthew 5). Moral truth is about moral behaviour and moral thinking.

ASSIGNMENT: *Do you believe in fixed, unchanging, objective truth? If not, what do you believe? Are there difficulties with this position?*

DISCUSSION: *Discuss why you think each commandment was given.*

04

Does God Care?

While as human beings we wrestle with concepts and ideas, eventually these ideas are fleshed out in our everyday emotions and experiences. We may conclude that God does exist, that he has revealed himself, and that we may know some true things about him. However, we ultimately want to know if this matters to us personally. Does God care about me?

Jesus understood the anxieties and fears of human beings and he sought to change our thinking from fear to faith, from anxiety to trust, from feelings of being abandoned to feelings of acceptance and being cared for. In Matthew 6, Jesus taught:

> *Therefore I tell you, do not be anxious about your life, what you will eat or what you will drink, nor about your body, what you will put on. Is not life more than food, and the body more than clothing? Look at the birds of the air: they neither sow nor reap nor gather into barns, and yet your heavenly Father feeds them. Are*

you not of more value than they? And which of you by being anx-
ious can add a single hour to his span of life? And why are you
anxious about clothing? Consider the lilies of the field, how they
grow: they neither toil nor spin, yet I tell you, even Solomon in all
his glory was not arrayed like one of these. But if God so clothes
the grass of the field, which today is alive and tomorrow is thrown
into the oven, will he not much more clothe you, O you of little
faith? Therefore do not be anxious, saying, "What shall we eat?"
or "What shall we drink?" or "What shall we wear?" For the Gen-
tiles seek after all these things, and your heavenly Father knows
that you need them all. But seek first the kingdom of God and his
righteousness, and all these things will be added to you.

Therefore do not be anxious about tomorrow, for tomorrow
will be anxious for itself. Sufficient for the day is its own trouble.
(Matthew 6:25-34, ESV)

God is not described as a distant philosophical abstraction; rather he is
called "Father." The use of this image is intentional, because the picture of
a father should stir an image of care and love. God cares enough to be involved with us.

If we were to think of the antithesis of love, we might suggest anger or
hostility. However, anger and love can actually coexist. They are both real
human emotions that we can experience simultaneously. The real antithesis of love is indifference and apathy. When someone can witness human
tragedy and declare, "So what?" or "I don't care," they are reflecting the
tragic erosion of what it means to be a human being made in the image of
God. On the other hand, God does care. He is concerned, and this concern
leads to active involvement in our lives. The psalmist reflected with wonder:

Sing to God, sing praises to His name; Extol Him who rides on
the clouds, By His name YAH, And rejoice before Him. A father
of the fatherless, a defender of widows, Is God in His holy habita-

tion. God sets the solitary in families; He brings out those who are bound into prosperity; But the rebellious dwell in a dry land. O God, when You went out before Your people, When You marched through the wilderness, Selah. The earth shook; The heavens also dropped rain at the presence of God; Sinai itself was moved at the presence of God, the God of Israel. You, O God, sent a plentiful rain, Whereby You confirmed Your inheritance, When it was weary. Your congregation dwelt in it; You, O God, provided from Your goodness for the poor. (Psalm 68:4-10, NKJV)

The God of the Bible should not be described in deistic terms of lack of involvement and unconcern. God sees us in our need, in our distress, in our shortage, in our aloneness, and he enters and acts. The God of the Bible does care and he wants us to know that he cares. His book is a love letter devoted to communicating this message. However, his care for us is real and evidenced every day. Amidst our disappointments, we need to observe the expressions of grace and kindness that come from the hand and heart of God.

ASSIGNMENT: *Reflect on a time when you believed that God was showing you that he cared. What did God do?*

DISCUSSION: *Discuss a time when you felt that God did not care. Is there another possible explanation for what was going on?*

05

Why Is There Suffering?

We all shudder at the sight of human tragedy and disaster, whether it is caused by natural means or is the result of physical illness. The question of suffering is never more relevant than when we go through it ourselves in loss, disappointment, or adversity. We find ourselves in somewhat of a quandary when we want to believe in a God who cares, but then are perplexed with the reality and presence of pain and suffering. This has caused some to ask, "Is God good?" Others have asked, "Is God powerful?" assuming that pain and suffering nullifies either God's goodness or his power, or both. The Bible presents a series of prospective roles that pain and suffering can have. Exploring these will help us process our pain and our attending questions.

WE BROKE IT

First, pain and suffering are ultimately a result of the recklessness of humanity itself. This is the most comprehensive reason, although it is the least satisfying reason. The Genesis account describes the wonder of a human being's relationship with God, but it also describes God's expectations and guidelines for enjoying that relationship.[19] Man in his pride chose to deviate from God's ideal, and in so doing set into motion a whole inventory of consequences, including physical illness and death, emotional issues such as shame, fear, guilt, and insecurity, along with relational fallout evidenced in home and work life (Genesis 3). In fact, the consequences further reached the order of nature itself (Romans 8:22). The world mankind lives in is broken because mankind broke it. These consequences are real and painful. We are often tempted to blame God for our disappointments, but the inescapable reality is that all our disappointments are the ultimate result of our own folly. This does not bode well for our tormented minds and aching hearts, but we must reconcile ourselves to this effect.

However, the Bible does cite additional purposes and reasons for why pain and suffering may take place. These finer nuances require some level of careful reflection. They also point to the wonder and grace of God, in that God is able to take pain and use it to accomplish his redemptive purposes. The following biblical stories illustrate these creative workings of God.

Poor Judgment

Some pain and suffering is the result of our specific acts of foolishness or poor judgment. The story of Eli is a tragic story of a father who, although he loved and served God, was a negligent and weak father.

> *Eli's sons were wicked men; they had no regard for the Lord.* (1 Samuel 2:12, NIV)

Specific acts of immorality and injustice are cited, and the text further comments:

> *The sin of the young men was very great in the Lord's sight, for they were treating the Lord's offering with contempt.* (1 Samuel 2:17, NIV)

Eli, fully aware of this, does nothing and tragedy befalls him and his sons, resulting in their deaths. The point of this story is that there are times when we are experiencing the direct results of our own personal wrongdoing. Illegal activity will result in legal or criminal consequences. Immoral living will invite moral fallout. Abusing our bodies will lead to health implications. In such cases, we would be wise to reflect on these consequences, and make the appropriate corrections.

STRATEGIC PURPOSES

Some pain and suffering has strategic purpose. Perhaps the most gripping biblical story illustrating this is the account of Joseph (Genesis 37-50). Joseph was a man of integrity and honour. He had the affections of his parents, but the jealousy of his siblings. Following a horrendous betrayal by his own brothers, Joseph is sold into slavery and carried off to Egypt. In Egypt, he is unjustly accused of rape, is imprisoned, and then forgotten. In time, he is released and moved into a position of great influence and respect in the government. When his family faces the prospects of famine, his brothers come to Egypt in humility seeking food. Not knowing that the brothers must stand before their own betrayed kin, they make a frightening discovery to which Joseph responds with curious grace and remarkable wisdom. The final chapter of Genesis paints an amazing picture.

> *When Joseph's brothers saw that their father was dead, they said, "It may be that Joseph will hate us and pay us back for all the evil that we did to him." So they sent a message to Joseph, saying,*

"Your father gave this command before he died, 'Say to Joseph, Please forgive the transgression of your brothers and their sin, because they did evil to you.' And now, please forgive the transgression of the servants of the God of your father." Joseph wept when they spoke to him. His brothers also came and fell down before him and said, "Behold, we are your servants." But Joseph said to them, "Do not fear, for am I in the place of God? As for you, you meant evil against me, but God meant it for good, to bring it about that many people should be kept alive, as they are today. So do not fear; I will provide for you and your little ones." Thus he comforted them and spoke kindly to them. (Genesis 50:15-21, ESV)

Somehow amidst all the pain and suffering which Joseph endured, there was a purpose unfolding. Maturity, faith, and a greater perspective allowed Joseph to see this.

SHAPING CHARACTER

Some pain and suffering is for the purpose of shaping and developing our character. The Apostle Paul apparently was struck with some kind of "thorn in his flesh," from which he pleaded for God to deliver him. God simply declines the prayer request, and Paul is given the insight to understand the reason. Paul reflects:

So to keep me from becoming conceited because of the surpassing greatness of the revelations, a thorn was given me in the flesh, a messenger of Satan to harass me, to keep me from becoming conceited. Three times I pleaded with the Lord about this, that it should leave me. But he said to me, "My grace is sufficient for you, for my power is made perfect in weakness." Therefore I will boast all the more gladly of my weaknesses, so that the power of Christ may rest upon me. For the sake of Christ, then, I am content with weaknesses, insults, hardships, persecutions, and ca-

lamities. For when I am weak, then I am strong. (2 Corinthians 12:7-11, ESV)

When we find ourselves in such a dilemma, James invites us to ask God for wisdom. He declares:

> *My brethren, count it all joy when you fall into various trials, knowing that the testing of your faith produces patience. But let patience have its perfect work, that you may be perfect and complete, lacking nothing. If any of you lacks wisdom, let him ask of God, who gives to all liberally and without reproach, and it will be given to him.* (James 1:2-5, NKJV)

We may need wisdom to be able to see how pain is shaping our character. Ask God to show you how your character may be strengthened as a result of the difficult experience you are going through.

GRASPING SOMETHING STILL GREATER AND MORE MYSTERIOUS

There is one final observation that should be made about pain and suffering. There are times when our pain and heartaches occur to remind us of the very divine prerogatives of God. The principle is illustrated in the perplexing story of the life of Job. We are told that Job loved God and was viewed as righteous in the community. However, he experienced unimaginable loss as he buried all his children and lost his health and wealth. The book of Job records extensive probing into this question: "What is the purpose of suffering?" Various theories are presented by Job's friends, but in the end God reveals himself in splendour and awe. Job is left humbled and yet having had his mind stretched. He responds with new insight and acceptance:

> *Then Job answered the Lord and said:*
> *"I know that You can do everything, And that no purpose of*

Yours can be withheld from You.

You asked, 'Who is this who hides counsel without knowledge?' Therefore I have uttered what I did not understand, Things too wonderful for me, which I did not know.

Listen, please, and let me speak; You said, 'I will question you, and you shall answer Me.'" (Job 42:1-4, NKJV)

ASSIGNMENT: *As you look at pain and suffering in this world, can you see some of these categories at work? Identify them.*

DISCUSSION: *As you reflect on your own suffering, what do you think you can learn from these hard times?*

06

How Does Christianity Differ from Other Religions?

Most of the Western world has been deeply impacted by pluralism. Pluralism is a term used to describe the acceptance of all religious worldviews and ideologies as equally valid. In a pluralistic society, differing religious expressions are encouraged to coexist in harmony. There is some value in operational pluralism, in that we must learn how to live amidst the plurality of religious views. However, one of the assumptions of philosophical pluralism is that no religion is truer than the other. Rather, all distinguishing features are diluted. "They all teach the same thing and will lead to the same place," it is suggested. Jesus, however, declared something very different with clarity and conviction. He said:

> *I am the way and the truth and the life. No one comes to the Father except through me.* (John 14:6, NIV)

While Jesus' approach embodies grace and respect for the human will, he nevertheless presented an unquestionably exclusive view to religious truth and the path to God. Jesus' words fly in the face of modern pluralistic thought, creating tensions and stirring questions. On what basis can Jesus make such a claim? Ultimately we must ask, how does the God of the Bible differ from other religious perspectives?

ISLAM

Before examining Jesus' claim more closely, it is helpful for us to have an essential grasp of some of the other world religions. Understanding Islam is critical, as it is one of the three great western religions and is rapidly growing. Judaism, Christianity, and Islam are all monotheistic religions and all three claim Abraham as a pivotal figure. Muslims claim their ancestry is rooted in Abraham and his son Ishmael. Isaac and Ishmael were Abraham's two sons. Through Isaac came the Jewish line; through Ishmael came the Arab line. Islam means "submission" or "surrender" to the will of the one God, Allah. However, the word "islam" is derived from the word "salam," which primarily "peace." Thus, a central theme of Islam is that "perfect peace comes when one's life is surrendered to God."

While Muslims claim Abraham as their father, its historic roots began in 610 A.D. when a man from Mecca (in Arabia) named Muhammad encountered several divine revelations from an angel, who he claimed was Gabriel. Over the next twenty-three years, he continued to receive these revelations and he recorded them in what is now referred to as the *Koran (Qur'an).*

There are five basic tenets of Islam:

- There is only one God and his name is Allah.
- Muhammad was the last of the great prophets. Jewish

prophets and Jesus were predecessors.

- The *Koran* was the last of the sacred books, which also include the Torah, Psalms, and the Gospels of Jesus.
- "Life on earth" is a test to prepare people for eternal life.
- The "final judgment" will usher faithful Muslims to an eternal Heaven and infidels to Hell.

Then there are the five pillars of Islam:

- The profession of Faith—"There is no God but Allah, and Muhammad is his prophet."
- Prayer—five times a day facing Mecca.
- Give alms—two and a half percent of what they possess.
- Fasting—during the month of Ramadan.
- Pilgrimage to Mecca—if possible, at least once in their lifetime.

It should be observed that there are different sects of Islam. There is the "Sunni" group, of which there are some eight hundred million all over the world. They are viewed as more liberal by "Shiites." "Shiites" are more orthodox and often more militant. Shiites primarily reside in Iran, Iraq, and Palestine. However, regardless of their camp, Islam is cohesive in its emphasis on Monotheism, the Koran, Allah, Muhammad, and on earning heaven through submission to Allah. Islam is exclusionary in that it claims to be the only way to God.

HINDUISM

Hinduism is essentially a polytheistic religion, with deities ranging from one thousand to thirty-three million gods. The gods Vishnu, Shiva, and Krishna would be among the better known gods; however, the only absolute manifestation is Brahman. Thus, Hinduism is most often referred to as polytheistic, but it does have a hierarchy of deities, with Brahman as the ultimate absolute reality at the top. Hinduism also reflects religious pantheism in its perspectives on reality and matter.

In Brahman, says Krishna (a lesser god), the distinctions between good and evil break down. That which appears as evil is only a lesser reality. In the end, all life, all good, all evil, flow from god and back to him or it. This fatalism is the root of some of the views of the eternality of good and evil. Hinduism is often ambiguous and perplexing. Divine beings are impersonal and transcendent.

Foundational to Hinduism is the law of the Karma or the law of the deed. This concept is the sowing and reaping of life. One sows in this life and reaps in the next life. Hindus also believe in reincarnation. One of the social results of the law of the Karma is the infamous "caste system." Little social concern is demonstrated between castes because people are at their level because they are reaping for past wrongdoings. Incarnations can take various forms, animal or human. The goal is to move up in each incarnation. A Hindu achieves a kind of "release" by meditation, discipline, or devotion.

BUDDHISM

Buddhism is a variation of Hinduism. Buddha was a Hindu before he rejected some of Hinduism's fundamental doctrines. Buddhism was founded in India in 528 B.C. by a wealthy prince named Gautama, who was born in what is now Nepal. On his twenty-ninth birthday, he abandoned his palace, his wife, and child and started to search for the cause of suffering and the source of peace and happiness. He became an ascetic, followed the way of two yoga masters, and at age thirty-five entered into a seven-week period of meditation under a fig tree. At the end of this fast, he encountered his way, "in a flash," and became "Buddha," the enlightened one. Life's problems were no longer an enigma to him. Enlightenment was centrally about the elimination of desire.

Buddha's four noble truths were:

- The truth of suffering.
- The cause of suffering.
- The cessation of suffering.
- The truth of the way to remove suffering.

Buddha sought to remove much of the supernatural beliefs of Hinduism: the gods, the complicated rituals, magic prayers, and superstitious beliefs. His solution did retain the law of the Karma and reincarnation. Buddha believed that there are many cycles of reincarnation by which a person could ultimately achieve "Nirvana," which is enlightenment. Nirvana is a state of mind and being. In Nirvana, the individual ceases to exist. It is not so much religious experience or a connection with a deity; it is a uniting with some kind of impersonal ultimate reality. Buddhism, in the end, is also an impersonal form of pantheism. All matter and reality is god, and god is in all matter. While Brahman was impersonal in the Hindu religion, Nirvana was even less so. Nirvana was a state.

THE SAME OR DIFFERENT?

There certainly are more religious perspectives we could explore, however these three global forces wield enormous influence. We now return to the question: How does the God of the Bible differ from other religious worldviews? The following would be a general description of some of the central differences.

- The nature of God: Islam believes in one god. God is personal, but we are left with an impression of harshness, justice, and a lack of compassion. While forgiveness is cited, it is not emphasized. Hinduism believes in many gods, yet the ultimate reality is an impersonal pantheistic view of god called Brahman. Buddhism is more of a pantheistic philosophy than a religion. Again, god is impersonal in Buddhism. The God of the Bible is transcendent, imminent, and personal. God is holy, but also loving, and offers grace and forgiveness.

- The problem of evil: Islam believes in moral goodness and evil. Hinduism and Buddhism have a sense of moral oughtness in the law of the Karma, however good and evil ultimately blur in Brahman (Hinduism) or Nirvana (Buddhism). Thus, a clear demarcation between good and evil is vague in both Hinduism and Buddhism. The Bible holds to a very clear differentiation between good and evil, with good finally triumphing over evil.

- The matter of forgiveness and the path toward salvation: On this point, Islam and Christianity differ greatly. In Islam, forgiveness is conditionally offered, but there is not the same kind of assurance of forgiveness. Furthermore, Allah has no basis on which to forgive. Hinduism and Buddhism leave wrongdoing to be worked off through the cycle of reincarnation. Christianity emerges from beside these other religions with emphasis on justice and compassion. Jesus' death on the cross served as a legal act to atone for the wrongdoings of humanity. Essentially, Jesus was punished and died for those who deserved to be punished and die. Forgiveness is activated by faith, not human effort. At the risk of oversimplification, all world religions suggest that human beings can somehow earn or merit "salvation" (or its equivalent). Christianity exposes mankind's depravity head on and declares that divine initiative is needed. God, motivated by love, sent Jesus to die for us.

> When we believe in Jesus and his work, we enter into a
> new and living relationship with God.

The foundational premise of pluralism meets with difficulty here. These world religious forces are all very different. All claim some sense of exclusivity. If we are going to explore the merits of one religious ideology over another, we must appreciate that they are mutually incompatible from a religious perspective. Indeed, we do have to live with operational tolerance, but we must also acknowledge their radical differences.

Christianity may be accepted or rejected, but it cannot be accepted as equal with, or the same as, other world religious expressions. Whether we are happy about it or not, Jesus presented an exclusive solution to an inclusive problem.

ASSIGNMENT: *Why are Jesus' claims so bold? Why are they so offensive? Why might they also be inviting?*

DISCUSSION: *If there is one truth, what does this do to the way you think, believe, and live?*

07

Why Am I So Broken and Confused?

The ancient Greek sage Socrates challenged us with the aphorism, "Know thyself."[20] Introspection and self-reflection is not one of the qualities that Western society extols. We have learned effective ways of living in denial, medicating our pain, and distracting ourselves from really grappling with who we are and our deeper issues. The honest person who looks inward for any length of time will eventually see qualities that are deeply disturbing. Usually the darkest qualities surface when we are in relationships. The paradox is that, while we need relationship, it is here that we are most prone to self-destruction.

What is it that we see in ourselves? We express selfishness, self-righteousness, hypocrisy, greed, lust, pride, lack of compassion, fickleness, anger, hate, and indifference. Indeed, we can also see nobility, virtue, love, grace, compassion, courage, and integrity, but all too often we see duplicity, which leaves us confused. What am I?

The Bible describes human beings as uniquely wonderful creatures who have been made in, and reflect "the image of God" (Genesis 1:27). The psalmist asks:

> *What is man that you are mindful of him... You made him a little lower than the heavenly beings and crowned him with glory and honor.* (Psalm 8:4-5, NIV)

And yet, following our tragic "fall from grace," everything changed around us and inside us. The Bible describes with brutal honesty what human beings had become.

> *For even though they knew God, they did not honor Him as God or give thanks, but they became futile in their speculations, and their foolish heart was darkened.*
>
> *Professing to be wise, they became fools, and exchanged the glory of the incorruptible God for an image in the form of corruptible man and of birds and four-footed animals and crawling creatures.*
>
> *Therefore God gave them over in the lusts of their hearts to impurity, so that their bodies would be dishonored among them.*
>
> *For they exchanged the truth of God for a lie, and worshiped and served the creature rather than the Creator, who is blessed forever. Amen.*
>
> *For this reason God gave them over to degrading passions; for their women exchanged the natural function for that which is unnatural, and in the same way also the men abandoned the natural function of the woman and burned in their desire toward one another, men with men committing indecent acts and receiving in their own persons the due penalty of their error.*
>
> *And just as they did not see fit to acknowledge God any longer, God gave them over to a depraved mind, to do those things which are not proper, being filled with all unrighteousness, wickedness, greed, evil; full of envy, murder, strife, deceit, malice;*

they are gossips, slanderers, haters of God, insolent, arrogant, boastful, inventors of evil, disobedient to parents, without understanding, untrustworthy, unloving, unmerciful; and although they know the ordinance of God, that those who practice such things are worthy of death, they not only do the same, but also give hearty approval to those who practice them. (Romans 1:21-32, NASB)

This same New Testament epistle, Romans, later draws on numerous Old Testament passages and further observes:

As it is written: "None is righteous, no, not one; no one understands; no one seeks for God. All have turned aside; together they have become worthless; no one does good, not even one. Their throat is an open grave; they use their tongues to deceive. The venom of asps is under their lips. Their mouth is full of curses and bitterness. "Their feet are swift to shed blood; in their paths are ruin and misery, and the way of peace they have not known. There is no fear of God before their eyes. "(Romans 3:10-18, ESV)

These passages are hard to read and can be even harder to accept. However, for the honest person who looks inward long enough and is truly seeking to apply Socrates' challenge, the conclusion is that yes, we are broken and confused. We are selfish and self-serving. We want to create our own universe in which we can act the way we please and not be accountable to anyone. However, the cost for such thinking and behaviour is high. Just as there are cause and effect relationships in the natural world, there are similar cause and effect relationships in the spiritual world.

Living life that is a distortion of God's intended path invites consequences. Unresolved anger leads to deep seated bitterness. Uncontrolled lust can lead to all kinds of sexual addictions and attending health risks. Greed can lead to a life of ongoing dissatisfaction and discontentment. Unlimited eating can lead to overeating and additional health concerns. To

envision guilt, dissatisfaction, self-image issues, and emotional issues mani-
festing themselves as a result of such thoughtless and undisciplined pursuits is to be expected. When we seek to self-medicate our pain with yet
another counterfeit, we only complicate our lives further with additional
coping strategies that fill us for a moment and then leave us wanting.

Alas, we are a broken and confused lot.

ASSIGNMENT: *How does your brokenness display itself?*

DISCUSSION: *What does thinking of yourself as "sinful" do to you? Why do
we not like to think and speak this way? What does our sin do to our relationship with our creator?*

—— 08 ——
Can God Forgive Me?

Guilt is an unwelcome companion that walks with all of us. Regret is the ghost that haunts us. The prospect of forgiveness is an inviting and attractive concept, but can we really experience it? Can God forgive me? Whether our sins and failures are measured as socially destructive or personally damaging, too often we feel like our wrongdoings cannot be pardoned. Jesus understands this and places no limits on his forgiveness.

On one occasion, Jesus was a guest at the home of a well-known community leader who was held in high regard. However, all the guests at this function were not deemed as such. The story unfolds this way:

> *One of the Pharisees asked him to eat with him, and he went into the Pharisee's house and took his place at the table. And behold, a woman of the city, who was a sinner, when she learned that he was reclining at table in the Pharisee's house, brought an alabaster flask of ointment, and standing behind him at his feet, weeping,*

she began to wet his feet with her tears and wiped them with the hair of her head and kissed his feet and anointed them with the ointment. Now when the Pharisee who had invited him saw this, he said to himself, "If this man were a prophet, he would have known who and what sort of woman this is who is touching him, for she is a sinner." And Jesus answering said to him, "Simon, I have something to say to you." And he answered, "Say it, Teacher."

"A certain moneylender had two debtors. One owed five hundred denarii, and the other fifty. When they could not pay, he cancelled the debt of both. Now which of them will love him more?" Simon answered, "The one, I suppose, for whom he cancelled the larger debt." And he said to him, "You have judged rightly." Then turning toward the woman he said to Simon, "Do you see this woman? I entered your house; you gave me no water for my feet, but she has wet my feet with her tears and wiped them with her hair. You gave me no kiss, but from the time I came in she has not ceased to kiss my feet. You did not anoint my head with oil, but she has anointed my feet with ointment. Therefore I tell you, her sins, which are many, are forgiven—for she loved much. But he who is forgiven little, loves little." And he said to her, "Your sins are forgiven." Then those who were at table with him began to say among themselves, "Who is this, who even forgives sins?" And he said to the woman, "Your faith has saved you; go in peace." (Luke 7:36-50, ESV)

This story implies that the woman was a promiscuous woman, and as such, in the mind of orthodox Jews, did not deserve Jesus' attention. Jesus, however, corrects the faulty self-righteousness of this religious leader and assures the woman that God has a heart to forgive those who seek it.

Perhaps the most celebrated story of forgiveness is the pardon that King David experienced. David was a man of great virtue and zeal. His heart for God was renowned. His loyalty to King Saul and to God was exemplary. However, he allowed his passions to carry him away and he capitulated to adultery. When David is confronted, he immediately is afflicted by his own sense of guilt and pleads for the mercy and grace of God. The following passages for the Psalms reflect both David's heart, and God's willingness to forgive.

> How blessed is he whose transgression is forgiven, Whose sin is covered! How blessed is the man to whom the Lord does not impute iniquity, and in whose spirit there is no deceit! When I kept silent about my sin, my body wasted away. Through my groaning all day long. For day and night Your hand was heavy upon me; my vitality was drained away as with the fever heat of summer. Selah. I acknowledged my sin to You, and my iniquity I did not hide; I said, "I will confess my transgressions to the Lord"; and You forgave the guilt of my sin. Selah. (Psalm 32:1-5, NASB)

> Be gracious to me, O God, according to Your lovingkindness; according to the greatness of Your compassion blot out my transgressions. Wash me thoroughly from my iniquity and cleanse me from my sin. For I know my transgressions, and my sin is ever before me. Against You, You only, I have sinned and done what is evil in Your sight, so that You are justified when You speak and blameless when You judge. Behold, I was brought forth in iniquity, and in sin my mother conceived me. Behold, You desire truth in the innermost being, and in the hidden part You will make me know wisdom. Purify me with hyssop, and I shall be clean; wash me, and I shall be whiter than snow. Make me to hear joy and gladness, let the bones which You have broken rejoice. Hide Your face from my sins and blot out all my iniquities. Create in me a clean heart, O God, and renew a steadfast spirit within me. (Psalm 51:1-10, NASB)

> For as high as the heavens are above the earth, so great is His lovingkindness toward those who fear Him. As far as the east is from

the west, so far has He removed our transgressions from us. Just
as a father has compassion on his children, so the Lord has com-
passion on those who fear Him. (Psalm 103:11-13, NASB)

Forgiveness is possible. We can recapture a sense of having a clean soul, but we must confess to experience this grace. The next two chapters further explain the basis on which we can experience authentic and enduring forgiveness.

He who conceals his sins does not prosper, but whoever confesses
and renounces them finds mercy. (Proverbs 28:13, NIV)

ASSIGNMENT: *What do you do with your feelings of guilt?*

DISCUSSION: *What does the thought of forgiveness do for you? Why does confession make us feel better?*

09

Who Is Jesus?

Who is Jesus? Was he just a man? Was he God? Before we ask ourselves what we believe, we should first ask ourselves, what did Jesus say about his own identity? If we focus on one Gospel account, the Gospel of John, we will observe a number of self-declared statements.

JESUS' CLAIMS

I am the bread of life. (John 6:35, NIV)

In this statement, Jesus was claiming to be the source of spiritual life. Jesus also said:

I am the light of the world. (John 8:12, NIV)

In this passage, he is claiming to be the source of spiritual knowledge and truth. Jesus said:

I am the gate. (John 10:7, 9, NIV)

Jesus thereby claimed to be the path that leads to eternal life with God. Jesus further stated:

I am the good shepherd. (John 10:11, 14, NIV)

Jesus here was essentially saying, "I am your caring leader who is willing to sacrifice his life for you." Jesus then later stated:

I am the resurrection and the life. He who believes in me will live, even though he dies; and whoever lives and believes in me will never die. (John 11:25, NIV)

In these powerful words, Jesus was announcing that he was the source of spiritual, eternal life and the giver of that life. While we have looked at this next verse, it bears review. Jesus boldly said:

I am the way and the truth and the life. No one comes to the father except through me (John 14:6, NIV).

In this controversial passage, Jesus asserts that he is the way for man to find God, the truth by which man discovers ultimate reality in God, and the life by which man lives in God and God lives in man. Theologians have sought to explain away such passages by suggesting that Jesus was not claiming a divine identity. Such arguments are unfounded and misguided. Jesus knew exactly what he was saying when he provoked a hostile response from the religious elite of his day.

In John 8, Jesus has a heated debate with the Pharisees. As Jesus defended his actions and his claims, he concluded with a simple statement:

I tell you the truth... before Abraham was born, I am! (John 8:58, NIV)

Some further background will make this episode more meaningful. Jesus earlier had told the audience (followers and sceptics, including some Pharisees) that he was the light of the world. He tells them:

> *If you hold to my teaching, you are really my disciples. Then you will know the truth, and the truth will set you free.* (John 8 32, NIV)

The Pharisees respond by saying they are already free, being Abraham's descendants. Jesus then serves them with a stinging challenge. He says that they were descendants of Abraham in ethnicity, but not in faith. Jesus then accuses them of having a different father (John 8:44-45). "We are not illegitimate children," the Pharisees argue, implying that Jesus was born illegitimately (recall how Jesus' mother was pregnant before she and Joseph were married). The argument heats up further and Jesus claims not only to know Abraham personally and experientially, but he does so by using a very meaningful term: "I am," which is the name of God. "I am" describes absolute eternal existence, not simply existence prior to Abraham. It is a claim to the Yahweh of the Old Testament ("I am who I am," in Exodus 3:14).

The Pharisees understood exactly what Jesus was saying, as indicated by their response. They wanted to punish him by stoning him for this blasphemous claim (John 8:59). The inescapable point here is that Jesus claimed to be God. He claimed divinity. Jesus understood what he was saying and the Jews understood what he said.

THE EARLY CHURCH CLAIMS

The early church also believed that Jesus was God. The book of Hebrews bares this out. Hebrews is full of Old Testament imagery and references. A dominant word in this book is the word "better." This book is essentially all about Christ and how he was the "better" plan when compared to the "good" plan that Judaism offered. The book begins with a description of the supremacy of Christ:

> *God, who at various times and in various ways spoke in time past to the fathers by the prophets, has in these last days spoken to us by His Son, whom He has appointed heir of all things, through whom also He made the worlds; who being the brightness of His glory and the express image of His person, and upholding all things by the word of His power, when He had by Himself purged our sins, sat down at the right hand of the Majesty on high, having become so much better than the angels, as He has by inheritance obtained a more excellent name than they.* (Hebrews 1:1-4, NKJV)

Through laws, institutions, ceremonies, kings, judges, prophets, and divine circumstances, God has spoken and revealed himself. The final and ultimate revelation has been the person of his Son. Thus a divine relationship is identified. To the Jewish mind, the son and the father were both different and equal. This Son is the heir of all things and was instrumental in and at creation. That is a prerogative of God. So we have the Son involved in a divine act. Jesus is attributed a divine nature. He is the radiance of God's glory (God's character) and the "exact representation of his being." The image employed here is that of comparing a coin to its original die, in the same way that the Son is the exact expression of the divine essence of God himself. One directly corresponds to the other.

Finally, Hebrews teaches that Jesus is also superior to angels, which again was no small matter to the Jewish readers. Angels were viewed with high regard, respect, and power. They were frequently the agents of God's messages and activities (miracles and judgments alike). Jesus, however, as supreme Lord, is also above the angels and the angels are subordinate to him.

The early church believed that Jesus was God.

ASSIGNMENT: *Who do you believe Jesus was?*

DISCUSSION: *Does it really matter what we believe about Jesus?*

10

How Can I Become a
Follower of Jesus Christ?

FAITH

The New Testament repeatedly invites would-be disciples of Christ to be-lieve, trust, place faith in, and follow Christ. Jesus assures,

> *I tell you the truth, whoever hears my word and believes him who sent me has eternal life and will not be condemned; he has crossed over from death to life.* (John 5:24, NIV)

The Gospel writer also declares:

> *Yet to all who received him, to those who believed in his name, he gave the right to become children of God.* (John 1:12, NIV)

Faith is the foundational quality that God looks for in us. It is faith that essentially "establishes" us in our connection with God. Hebrews 11 lists numerous men and women who were in relationship with God and did momentous things for God because of their faith. Faith requires an object. The object of their faith was God. However, with the coming of Jesus, the work of God took on greater significance, and the object of our faith became even clearer.

WHAT DID JESUS DO?

Faith is the key. The object of our faith is God. But it must be asked, "What exactly are we to believe?" We may believe that Jesus is God, but so what? What is it that Jesus has done that is so significant? The Old Testament prophesied the Messiah's (Jesus) work some seven hundred years before Jesus came.

> But he was pierced for our transgressions, he was crushed for our iniquities; the punishment that brought us peace was upon him, and by his wounds we are healed. We all, like sheep, have gone astray, each of us has turned to his own way; and the Lord has laid on him the iniquity of us all. (Isaiah 53:5-6, NIV)

Jesus was placed in a position of sacrifice on behalf of others. The New Testament further explains this.

> For Christ died for sins once for all, the righteous for the unrighteous, to bring you to God. He was put to death in the body but made alive by the Spirit. (1 Peter 3:18, NIV)

> God made him who had no sin to be sin for us, so that in him we might become the righteousness of God. (2 Corinthians 5:21, NIV)

The point of these verses is that Jesus traded down and became a sacrifice. He became a substitute. He took the place of another. He took the place of you and me, so that we could trade up from our state of brokenness into a state of relationship with God. The key concept here is that of sacrifice and substitution. Jesus' goal in all of this was to restore us to our intended relationship with God, as well as to restore our moral character, which was the original reflection of the image of God in us.

In this section (The Path of Seeking), we have explored the themes that God exists, God cares, God loves, God forgives, truth exists, truth can be known, man is broken, man is confused, man is sinful, Jesus is unique, and Jesus is God. If we believe that man is broken and sinful and deserving of punishment, and we believe that man cannot merit his own salvation, then we need God to do something for us. If God really cares and loves humanity, it seems reasonable that God would take initiative to rescue humanity.

Jesus was this rescuer. Jesus came to earth as the sinless Son of God. Jesus then died on the cross for the sins of humanity as a legal act of payment. Romans 6 states:

> The wages of sin is death, but the gift of God is eternal life in Christ Jesus our Lord. (Romans 6:23, NIV)

Humanity deserves death. However, the book of Romans further states:

> But God demonstrated his own love for us in this: While we were still sinners, Christ died for us. (Romans 5:8, NIV)

God in his holiness and justice satisfied his own justice requirements by having his own Son sacrifice his life on our behalf. Because God is just, wrongdoing had to be addressed and atoned for. The atoning for wrongdoing was the payment or sacrifice of Jesus' life. God is then the initiator of the rescue. God is the provider. God is the problem solver, and human beings are the receivers.

How can I become a follower of Christ? If we review John 5:24, we read:

> I tell you the truth, whoever hears my word and believes him who

sent me has eternal life and will not be condemned; he has crossed over from death to life. (John 5:24, NIV)

We begin as followers of Christ when we believe, when we trust. In this step of faith, we are accepting or believing that someone (Jesus) did something for us (died on the cross), and we are embracing that truth (personally). Believing in Jesus requires that we stop believing in ourselves and our own foolish coping strategies. We must choose to believe something different. This change of thinking is called repentance. While not elegant or sophisticated, Jesus calls us to repent—to change our mind about what we believe and how we live.

"The time has come," he said. "The kingdom of God is near. Repent and believe the good news!" (Mark 1:15, NIV)

MAKING IT PERSONAL

An episode from the life of Charles Blondin may help us here. A huge crowd was watching the famous tightrope walker, Blondin, cross Niagara Falls one day in 1860. He crossed it numerous times—a 1,000 foot trip, 160 feet above the raging waters. He asked the crowd if they believed he could take one person across. All assented. Then he approached one man and asked him to get on his back and go with him. The man refused. Mental assent or even verbal assent is not real belief. The real question became, "Do you trust Blondin... really trust him?"[21]

Belief is all about trust. When we trust Jesus with the eternal destiny of our souls, this is not a mere assent of the mind. It is an expression of trust at its deepest level. We should note that it is not the strength of our faith that saves us; it is the object of our faith that saves us. Jesus is that object. Jesus is worthy of that trust. When we trust Christ (who he is and what he has done for us), we receive a guarantee from God. Promises matter:

And this is the testimony: God has given us eternal life, and this life is in his Son. He who has the Son has life; he who does not have the Son of God does not have life. (1 John 5:11-12, NIV)

Once we make this step of faith, we need not fear that God will give up on us or change his mind. We are now in the grip of God's hands. We are forgiven. We enjoy a new relationship of peace with God and we have been given the gift of eternal life. Eternal life begins the moment we believe and knows no end. While Heaven will become our future dwelling place, our restored relationship with God has begun and will never end. Romans 8 offers a wonderful promise:

Who shall separate us from the love of Christ? Shall tribulation, or distress, or persecution, or famine, or nakedness, or peril, or sword?...

Yet in all these things we are more than conquerors through Him who loved us. For I am persuaded that neither death nor life, nor angels nor principalities nor powers, nor things present nor things to come, nor height nor depth, nor any other created thing, shall be able to separate us from the love of God which is in Christ Jesus our Lord. (Romans 8:35-39, NKJV)

A disciple of Christ is someone who has acknowledged his brokenness and sin and has seen the wonder of God's love in the sacrificial death of Jesus, the Son of God. A disciple is someone who has turned from her broken ways, has placed her trust in Jesus, and has now begun the path of following Jesus. The Bible calls the solution of God "the Gospel." Gospel means "good news." The good news that we are called on to believe can be summarized like this:

THE GOSPEL AND OUR RESPONSE

- The Gospel is the Person of Christ (he is God; he is

man)—We believe!

- The Gospel is the Work of Christ (he sacrificed his life as an atonement for sin)—We believe and say thank you!
- The Gospel is the Reign of Christ (he is Lord and King of the Kingdom of God)—We repent of our old ways; we believe and we follow in obedience.

Conversion is a step of faith. Following Jesus begins an inner decision of the heart and mind. It is this inner step of faith that results in salvation. In the New Testament, this act of faith it is reflected and publicly declared in an outward symbol called baptism.[22] It should be understood that baptism is not a work that saves us, but only a symbol of the work of God in us.

In trusting Christ, the journey of the disciple has begun and the process of transformation has been launched.

ASSIGNMENT: *Have you made this step of faith? If not, what is holding you back? If you have, describe the process and experiences that led you to this point of faith. Share it.*

DISCUSSION: *How would most people describe the core message of the Christian faith? Do most people really understand the Gospel?*

PART TWO

The Path of Discovering

INTRODUCTION

Once we embrace Jesus in faith, we find ourselves in a whole new relationship and reality. We experience the gift of eternal life (John 5:24), which is in part a promise of duration, but equally a promise that we now share life with the Eternal One. We now enjoy peace in our relationship with God (Romans 5:1), and we enjoy forgiveness (Ephesians 1:7). Forgiveness is not a thing to ponder lightly. Jesus paid dearly for us to experience this forgiveness.

Unfortunately, there have always been some who have identified with Christ in a moment of fear and anxiety and have done so to alleviate their apprehension of the future. They have missed the wonder that God has forgiven us, given us eternal life so that we can be in relationship with God and can begin to discover the reason why we have been placed on this earth. God wants to dwell with us in community. God wants to help us grow. God wants to change us and shape us into what we were meant to be. God then wants to use us to make a difference in our world by serving our broken communities and presenting a message of hope.

The path that you have embarked on is one of new beginnings. Indeed, Jesus calls this the act of being born again. He said:

> *I tell you the truth, no one can see the kingdom of God unless he is born again.* (John 3:3, NIV)

With the dawning of this new faith, we begin the path toward spiritual discovery and grounding. The Apostle Paul states:

> *So then, just as you received Christ Jesus as Lord, continue to live in him, rooted and built up in him, strengthened in the faith as you were taught, and overflowing with thankfulness.* (Colossians 2:6-7, NIV)

It should be our desire to become "rooted and built up in him." The following steps take us on a path of new faith discoveries and spiritual grounding. This path can be understood by considering the parallel path of human development. In the same way infants grow into children, so we move from spiritual infancy through spiritual childhood. Savour each step.

— 11 —

Discovering a New Source of Truth

Christians are people of the Book. The word Bible is a Latin word which means "holy book." It is this book that records the interactions of God with our world and the revelation of the person of God with his creation. The Old Testament reflects a great reverence for God's Word. Psalm 119 describes some of this sense of wonder, passion, and respect.

> *Blessed are the undefiled in the way, Who walk in the law of the Lord!*
> *Blessed are those who keep His testimonies, Who seek Him with the whole heart!*
> *They also do no iniquity; They walk in His ways.*
> *You have commanded us To keep Your precepts diligently.*
> *Oh, that my ways were directed To keep Your statutes!*
> *Then I would not be ashamed, When I look into all Your commandments.*
> *I will praise You with uprightness of heart, When I learn Your*

righteous judgments.

I will keep Your statutes; Oh, do not forsake me utterly!

*How can a young man cleanse his way? By taking heed according
to Your word.*

*With my whole heart I have sought You; Oh, let me not wander
from Your commandments!*

*Your word I have hidden in my heart, That I might not sin against
You*

*Blessed are You, O Lord! Teach me Your statutes. With my lips I
have declared All the judgments of Your mouth.*

*I have rejoiced in the way of Your testimonies, As much as in all
riches.*

I will meditate on Your precepts, And contemplate Your ways.

I will delight myself in Your statutes; I will not forget Your word.
(Psalm 119:1-16, NKJV)

*Teach me, O Lord, the way of Your statutes, And I shall keep it to
the end.*

*Give me understanding, and I shall keep Your law; Indeed, I shall
observe it with my whole heart.*

*Make me walk in the path of Your commandments, For I delight
in it.*

Incline my heart to Your testimonies, And not to covetousness.

*Turn away my eyes from looking at worthless things, And revive
me in Your way.*

*Establish Your word to Your servant, Who is devoted to fearing
You.*

*Turn away my reproach which I dread, For Your judgments are
good.*

*Behold, I long for Your precepts; Revive me in Your
righteousness.* (Psalm 119:33-40, NKJV)

*You have dealt well with Your servant, O Lord, according to Your
word. Teach me good judgment and knowledge, For I believe*

Your commandments. (Psalm 119:65-66, NKJV)

Oh, how I love Your law! It is my meditation all the day.
You, through Your commandments, make me wiser than my
enemies; For they are ever with me.
I have more understanding than all my teachers, For Your
testimonies are my meditation.
I understand more than the ancients, Because I keep Your
precepts.
I have restrained my feet from every evil way, That I may keep
Your word.
I have not departed from Your judgments, For You Yourself have
taught me.
How sweet are Your words to my taste, Sweeter than honey to my
mouth!
Through Your precepts I get understanding; Therefore I hate
every false way. (Psalm 119:97-105, NKJV).

God's Word was understood as an authoritative revelation from God. It was to be listened to, taught, and applied as a rule for life. 2 Timothy 3 and 4 offers a foundational understanding of the role of the Bible in the life of the believer. The Apostle Paul is instructing a younger church leader and in the process encourages Timothy to maintain a high view of the Scripture.

Teach me Your statutes. With my lips I have declared All the
judgments of Your Now you followed my teaching, conduct, pur-
pose, faith, patience, love, perseverance, persecutions, and suffer-
ings, such as happened to me at Antioch, at Iconium and at Ly-
stra; what persecutions I endured, and out of them all the Lord
rescued me! Indeed, all who desire to live godly in Christ Jesus
will be persecuted. But evil men and impostors will proceed from
bad to worse, deceiving and being deceived. You, however, con-
tinue in the things you have learned and become convinced of,

knowing from whom you have learned them, and that from childhood you have known the sacred writings which are able to give you the wisdom that leads to salvation through faith which is in Christ Jesus. All Scripture is inspired by God and profitable for teaching, for reproof, for correction, for training in righteousness; so that the man of God may be adequate, equipped for every good work. (2 Timothy 3:10-17, NASB)

I solemnly charge you in the presence of God and of Christ Jesus, who is to judge the living and the dead, and by His appearing and His kingdom: preach the word; be ready in season and out of season; reprove, rebuke, exhort, with great patience and instruction. For the time will come when they will not endure sound doctrine; but wanting to have their ears tickled, they will accumulate for themselves teachers in accordance to their own desires, and will turn away their ears from the truth and will turn aside to myths. But you, be sober in all things, endure hardship, do the work of an evangelist, fulfill your ministry. (2 Timothy 4:1-5, NASB)

Paul desperately wanted Timothy to understand the power, authority, and effectiveness of God's Word when it is believed and applied. Notice how Paul says that Scripture is "God-breathed." The Bible finds its source in God himself. The Scriptures are useful for teaching (new information), rebuking (pointing out erroneous beliefs, values, or behaviours), correcting (replacing the erroneous with the truth), and training in righteousness (effecting real transformation in our lives).

ASSIGNMENT: *Re-examine the passages in this chapter and make a list of all the things that the Bible does for us and to us.*

DISCUSSION: *What are the implications of having a source of truth, a source of knowledge?*

— 12 —

Discovering How to Interact with This New Truth

As Christians, one of the most important disciplines to adopt is that of interacting with and applying the Bible. The Scriptures were never intended to be held in the hands of the religious elite. The Scriptures were given to people of faith in order to have it effect real life change. The following is an outline that we can use to read God's Word in an active manner with a view to application. The goal is not to learn more content, but to learn in such a way that it transforms our thinking and our behaviour.

Essentially, interacting with the Bible is the process of observing the interactions of God with humanity (observation), seeking to understand the transferable truths or principles that are true of all time and with all people (interpretation), and responding to these truths (application).

OBSERVATION (What does the Bible say?)

Ask: Who?

         What?

         When?

         Where?

Note: Grammatical clues

         Repetition

         Comparisons and contrasts

         Climax

         Cause and effect

         Question and answer

         Illustrations

         Key words

INTERPRETATION (What does the Bible mean?)

Ask: What does it mean?

         Why?

         What are the implications?

         What is the significance of the facts observed?

         Is the meaning clear?

         Are there other options?

         Is this interpretation consistent with other passages?

Note: Seek to discover the principle or truth that transcends time.

APPLICATION (What does the Bible mean to me?)

Ask: So what?

         How does this relate to my life?

Note: Meditate... think/reflect on what you have read.

Look for something... new to understand

to find comfort in

to praise God for

to be sorry for

to avoid or correct

to put into practice

to pray for

to think differently about

Make plans

Share your discovery with someone.

ASSIGNMENT: *If you have not yet started to do so, set a time each day to read a portion of God's Word. Start with the New Testament. After reading, ask and answer the three key questions (What does the passage say? What does the passage mean? What does the passage mean to me?), and record your notes in your journal.*

DISCUSSION: *Discuss the benefits of a systematic Bible reading plan. For practice, choose a passage from the Bible and work through each of the three questions together.*

13

Discovering God

The present post-modern Western context of relativism, pluralism, religious tolerance, and political correctness has set the stage for a kind of neo-paganism. It is current, chic, adaptable, versatile, inoffensive, and very personal. Just make up your own kind of god, one that will fit your personal worldview and morality. We do not want an interfering god. We do not want a meddling god. We just want a god to be there when we need him. This may not be the case in every cultural context, but the greater question we want to wrestle with is: What is God like? Our view of God will shape our views of life, meaning, morality, the arts, and just about every other thing imaginable.

How can we know what God is like? We have been given four resources to help us with this immense inquiry. First, we have been given intuition. These are innate ideas that have been placed within us. These intuitive ideas, along with our conscience, collaborate to help us understand something about God. Romans 1:18-32 speaks to this in greater detail. Second, empirical evidence also tells us something about God. Romans 1 bares this out as well. Third, reason is another tool. Anselm's ontological argument for the existence of God helps us to form an image of God who is the sum total of all perfection. The final and ultimately most significant resource is revelation. Through divine revelation (the Bible), we learn that God is a personal being with mind, emotion, and will. This defines God as a personal and relational being. Personal, relational beings desire relationship. Therefore, it is conceivable to envision God revealing himself to human beings.

Some of these attributes and qualities of God are "incommunicable," absolute and transcendent. This means that they are beyond our ability to fully comprehend. We can know God truly, but just not exhaustively. Other qualities are "communicable," relative to us and imminent, and may also be found in human beings.

A helpful way of understanding the person of God, along with his incommunicable and communicable attributes, may be through reflecting upon an old childhood prayer that many of us have learned: "God is great. God is good. Let us thank Him for our food. Amen."

God Is Great

God is self-existing. He possesses life in the absolute sense. He does not depend on it from anyone or anything else.

> *For as the Father has life in himself, so he has granted the Son to have life in himself.* (John 5:26, NIV)

God is spirit. This defines his simplicity of essence. He is uncompounded and indivisible.

> *God is spirit, and his worshipers must worship in spirit and in*

truth. (John 4:24, NIV)

God is a unity. God is one in essence, yet three in subsistence or per-sons.[23]

> *Hear, O Israel: The Lord our God, the Lord is one.* (Deuteronomy 6:4, NIV)

God is infinite. God is without termination and finiteness. There are no limitations to God. This verse also describes the eternity of God. He is free from the succession of time.

> *Before the mountains were born or you brought forth the earth and the world, from everlasting to everlasting you are God.* (Psalm 90:2, NIV)

God is immutable. He is unchanging and unchangeable.

> *I the Lord do not change. So you, O descendants of Jacob, are not destroyed.* (Malachi 3:6, NIV)

> *Every good and perfect gift is from above, coming down from the Father of the heavenly lights, who does not change like shifting shadows.* (James 1:17, NIV)

God is omnipresent. God is everywhere (but not in everything).

> *Where can I go from Your Spirit? Or where can I flee from Your presence? If I ascend into heaven, You are there; If I make my bed in hell, behold, You are there. If I take the wings of the morning, And dwell in the uttermost parts of the sea, Even there Your hand shall lead me, And Your right hand shall hold me. If I say, "Surely the darkness shall fall on me," Even the night shall be light about me; Indeed, the darkness shall not hide from You, But the night shines as the day; The darkness and the light are both alike to You.* (Psalm 139:7-12, NKJV)

God is omniscient. God knows everything that can be known.

O Lord, You have searched me and known me. You know my sitting down and my rising up; You understand my thought afar off. You comprehend my path and my lying down, And are acquainted with all my ways. For there is not a word on my tongue, But behold, O Lord, You know it altogether. You have hedged me behind and before, And laid Your hand upon me. Such knowledge is too wonderful for me; It is high, I cannot attain it. (Psalm 139:1-6, NKJV)

God is omnipotent. God is all-powerful.

Then I heard what sounded like a great multitude, like the roar of rushing waters and like loud peals of thunder, shouting: "Hallelujah! For our Lord God Almighty reigns." (Revelation 19:6, NIV)

God is sovereign. God is the supreme and ultimate ruler of all.

In him we were also chosen, having been predestined according to the plan of him who works out everything in conformity with the purpose of his will, in order that we, who were the first to hope in Christ, might be for the praise of his glory. And you also were included in Christ when you heard the word of truth, the Gospel of your salvation. Having believed, you were marked in him with a seal, the promised Holy Spirit, who is a deposit guaranteeing our inheritance until the redemption of those who are God's possession—to the praise of his glory. (Ephesians 1:11-14, NIV)

GOD IS GOOD

God is love. God's character seeks the highest good in the expression of his will.

But because of his great love for us, God, who is rich in mercy,

> *made us alive with Christ even when we were dead in transgres-*
> *sions—it is by grace you have been saved.* (Ephesians 2:4-5, NIV)

God is just. God is fair. God will address sin, evil, and injustice. Implied in this is God's righteousness.

> *Your throne, O God, will last for ever and ever; a scepter of justice*
> *will be the scepter of your kingdom.* (Psalm 45:6, NIV)

God is truth. God is the embodiment of truth. There is congruity and consistency within God. He is the ultimate expression of that which is real.

> *Jesus answered, "I am the way and the truth and the life. No one*
> *comes to the Father except through me."* (John 14:6, NIV)

God is free. God is independent from his creation.

> *Who has understood the mind of the Lord, or instructed him as*
> *his counselor? Whom did the Lord consult to enlighten him, and*
> *who taught him the right way? Who was it that taught him*
> *knowledge or showed him the path of understanding?* (Isaiah
> 40:13-14, NIV)

God is holy. God is morally healthy. There is nothing evil in God.

> *This is the message we have heard from him and declare to you:*
> *God is light; in him there is no darkness at all.* (1 John 1:5, NIV)

God is full of grace and mercy. Grace is the expression of unmerited favour, while mercy is the withholding of punishment. Both of these grow out of God's limitless love.

> *The Word became flesh and made his dwelling among us. We*
> *have seen his glory, the glory of the One and Only, who came*
> *from the Father, full of grace and truth. John testifies concerning*
> *him. He cries out, saying, "This was he of whom I said, 'He who*
> *comes after me has surpassed me because he was before me.'*

"From the fullness of his grace we have all received one blessing after another. For the law was given through Moses; grace and truth came through Jesus Christ. (John 1:14-17, NIV)

GETTING IT STRAIGHT

Does God care if we get it straight? The Scriptures explain how important it is to know God correctly. Consider the first three commandments:

I am the Lord your God, who brought you out of Egypt, out of the land of slavery.

You shall have no other gods before me.

You shall not make for yourself an idol in the form of anything in heaven above or on the earth beneath or in the waters below. You shall not bow down to them or worship them; for I, the Lord your God, am a jealous God, punishing the children for the sin of the fathers to the third and fourth generation of those who hate me, but showing love to a thousand generations of those who love me and keep my commandments.

You shall not misuse the name of the Lord your God, for the Lord will not hold anyone guiltless who misuses his name. (Exodus 20:2-7, NIV)

The first three commandments are all about getting it straight. The first commandment is all about making the one true God our first and highest relationship. No person, no passion, no career, no activity, no sport, no elixir, nothing should rival God. The second commandment is all about making it absolutely clear who the true God is. He is the God of Abraham, Isaac, and Jacob, the God who delivered Israel from slavery in Egypt. He is not a manmade idol. He is not an idea. He is a person with a name. He is jealous and he is protective of his identity and his relationships. The third commandment is all about showing the one true God appropriate respect.

This has been a very brief introduction to the nature of God. We will delve deeper in future chapters, as we explore God as a Triune being of Father, Son, and Holy Spirit.

ASSIGNMENT: *Make a list of all the ways that God is great. Make a similar list of all the ways that God shows that he is good.*

DISCUSSION: *It has been said that "people become like the God they worship." How is this true for Christians? How is this true for people who worship "idols" (of all kinds)?*

14

Discovering the Role of Faith

Faith requires an object. Faith is trusting God. Faith is the foundation to our relationship with God. The Bible instructs us to love God, to obey God, to fear God, and to serve God. Everything about our relationship with God begins with faith. Consider the words of the Apostle Paul from Romans 4.

> What then shall we say was gained by Abraham, our forefather according to the flesh? For if Abraham was justified by works, he has something to boast about, but not before God. For what does the Scripture say? "Abraham believed God, and it was counted to him as righteousness." Now to the one who works, his wages are not counted as a gift but as his due. And to the one who does not work but believes in him who justifies the ungodly, his faith is counted as righteousness. (Romans 4:1-5, ESV)

Abraham trusted God, believed God, and this was "credited to him as righteousness." This means that God considered Abraham legally justified in his eyes. Faith was the operative means that established this relationship. Romans 4 continues with the story of Abraham to assure us that his faith was apart from circumcision and the law, both of which were so important to the Jews. Paul then continues his examination of the faith of Abraham:

> That is why it depends on faith, in order that the promise may rest on grace and be guaranteed to all his offspring—not only to the adherent of the law but also to the one who shares the faith of Abraham, who is the father of us all, as it is written, "I have made you the father of many nations"—in the presence of the God in whom he believed, who gives life to the dead and calls into existence the things that do not exist.
>
> In hope he believed against hope, that he should become the father of many nations, as he had been told, "So shall your offspring be." He did not weaken in faith when he considered his own body, which was as good as dead (since he was about a hundred years old), or when he considered the barrenness of Sarah's womb. No distrust made him waver concerning the promise of God, but he grew strong in his faith as he gave glory to God, fully convinced that God was able to do what he had promised. That is why his faith was "counted to him as righteousness." But the words "it was counted to him" were not written for his sake alone, but for ours also. It will be counted to us who believe in him who raised from the dead Jesus our Lord, who was delivered up for our trespasses and raised for our justification. (Romans 4:16-25, ESV)

Abraham believed God. Paul then compares this act with how we come into a relationship with God. We too believe. We believe in and trust the God who raised Jesus from the dead. This justifies us and declares us righteous. The author of Hebrews adds further insight to the role of faith:

> Now faith is the assurance of things hoped for, the conviction of things not seen. For by it the people of old received their commendation. By faith we understand that the universe was created

by the word of God, so that what is seen was not made out of things that are visible.

By faith Abel offered to God a more acceptable sacrifice than Cain, through which he was commended as righteous, God commending him by accepting his gifts. And through his faith, though he died, he still speaks. By faith Enoch was taken up so that he should not see death, and he was not found, because God had taken him. Now before he was taken he was commended as having pleased God. And without faith it is impossible to please him, for whoever would draw near to God must believe that he exists and that he rewards those who seek him. By faith Noah, being warned by God concerning events as yet unseen, in reverent fear constructed an ark for the saving of his household. By this he condemned the world and became an heir of the righteousness that comes by faith.

By faith Abraham obeyed when he was called to go out to a place that he was to receive as an inheritance. And he went out, not knowing where he was going. By faith he went to live in the land of promise, as in a foreign land, living in tents with Isaac and Jacob, heirs with him of the same promise. For he was looking forward to the city that has foundations, whose designer and builder is God. By faith Sarah herself received power to conceive, even when she was past the age, since she considered him faithful who had promised. Therefore from one man, and him as good as dead, were born descendants as many as the stars of heaven and as many as the innumerable grains of sand by the seashore.

These all died in faith, not having received the things promised, but having seen them and greeted them from afar, and having acknowledged that they were strangers and exiles on the earth. For people who speak thus make it clear that they are seeking a homeland. If they had been thinking of that land from which they had gone out, they would have had opportunity to return. But as it is, they desire a better country, that is, a heavenly one. Therefore God is not ashamed to be called their God, for he has prepared for them a city.

By faith Abraham, when he was tested, offered up Isaac, and he who had received the promises was in the act of offering up his only son, of whom it was said, "Through Isaac shall your offspring be named." He considered that God was able even to raise him from the dead, from which, figuratively speaking, he did receive him back. By faith Isaac invoked future blessings on Jacob and Esau. By faith Jacob, when dying, blessed each of the sons of Joseph, bowing in worship over the head of his staff. By faith Joseph, at the end of his life, made mention of the exodus of the Israelites and gave directions concerning his bones.

By faith Moses, when he was born, was hidden for three months by his parents, because they saw that the child was beautiful, and they were not afraid of the king's edict. By faith Moses, when he was grown up, refused to be called the son of Pharaoh's daughter, choosing rather to be mistreated with the people of God than to enjoy the fleeting pleasures of sin. He considered the reproach of Christ greater wealth than the treasures of Egypt, for he was looking to the reward. By faith he left Egypt, not being afraid of the anger of the king, for he endured as seeing him who is invisible. By faith he kept the Passover and sprinkled the blood, so that the Destroyer of the firstborn might not touch them.

By faith the people crossed the Red Sea as on dry land, but the Egyptians, when they attempted to do the same, were drowned. By faith the walls of Jericho fell down after they had been encircled for seven days. By faith Rahab the prostitute did not perish with those who were disobedient, because she had given a friendly welcome to the spies.

And what more shall I say? For time would fail me to tell of Gideon Barak, Samson, Jephthah, of David and Samuel and the prophets—who through faith conquered kingdoms, enforced justice, obtained promises, stopped the mouths of lions, quenched the power of fire, escaped the edge of the sword, were made strong out of weakness, became mighty in war, put foreign armies to flight. Women received back their dead by resurrection. Some were tortured, refusing to accept release, so that they might rise again to a better life. Others suffered mocking and flogging, and even chains and imprisonment. They were stoned, they were sawn in two, they were killed with the sword. They went about in skins of sheep and goats, destitute, afflicted, mistreated—of whom the world was not worthy—wandering about in deserts and mountains, and in dens and caves of the earth.

And all these, though commended through their faith, did not receive what was promised, since God had provided something better for us, that apart from us they should not be made perfect. (Hebrews 11:1-40, ESV)

Here, the author of Hebrews identifies numerous major and minor biblical figures. What unites them all in their relationship with God and their bold living was their faith. What is particularly noteworthy is the quality that faith trusts God, not only for the positive things of life, but also in the painful and disappointing affairs of life.

James too stresses the role of faith. However, James makes it very clear that faith is not just a mental attitude. Faith lives; faith acts; faith works. Thus, we come into a relationship with God by faith, and not works. However, our faith is a faith that acts. Our deeds are the fruit of our faith, not our motivation for salvation.

What good is it, my brothers, if someone says he has faith but does not have works? Can that faith save him? If a brother or sister is poorly clothed and lacking in daily food, and one of you says to them, "Go in peace, be warmed and filled," without giving them the things needed for the body, what good is that? So also faith by itself, if it does not have works, is dead.

But someone will say, "You have faith and I have works." Show me your faith apart from your works, and I will show you my faith by my works. You believe that God is one; you do well.

Even the demons believe—and shudder! Do you want to be shown, you foolish person, that faith apart from works is useless? Was not Abraham our father justified by works when he offered up his son Isaac on the altar? You see that faith was active along with his works, and faith was completed by his works; and the Scripture was fulfilled that says, "Abraham believed God, and it was counted to him as righteousness"—and he was called a friend of God. You see that a person is justified by works and not by faith alone. And in the same way was not also Rahab the prostitute justified by works when she received the messengers and sent them out by another way? For as the body apart from the spirit is dead, so also faith apart from works is dead. (James 2:14-26, ESV)

ASSIGNMENT: *What do you need to trust God for in your life right now?*

DISCUSSION: *Discuss the difference between trusting God and demanding of God?*

───── 15 ─────

Understanding a Faith That Loves

Jesus was once asked which was the greatest commandment. In his response, he gave a compound answer. He said:

> *"Love the Lord your God with all your heart and with all your soul and with all your mind." This is the first and greatest commandment. And the second is like it: "Love your neighbor as yourself." All the Law and the Prophets hang on these two commandments.* (Matthew 22:37-40, NIV)

Our first priority ought to be that of love: loving God and loving others. Jesus' answer is packaged in a way that implies that the expression of love for God and people are two parts of the same commandment. Love is fundamentally a relationship of devotion, self-giving, and of willing the best for another.

THE ULTIMATE PRIORITY

Jesus knew that other interests, other options, other worries, other cares, and other stressors would distract us, causing us to get our priorities out of line. So Jesus addressed the theme of priorities by testing it against a great antagonist: worry. This lesson is given to us in Matthew 6:19-32. Jesus employs the metaphor of treasure, the metaphor of sight, and the metaphor of slavery as he speaks to the affluent about their tendency to worry. Then he speaks to the needy as well and talks about their anxiety over having enough food, over their health and lifespan, and over their need for clothing (all very real and very legitimate concerns). Jesus tells us that both the affluent and the needy worry. So, after identifying the issue of worry, Jesus then transitions to the subject of priorities, and states:

> But seek first his kingdom and his righteousness, and all these things will be given to you as well. (Matthew 6:33, NIV)

When we make Christ and his kingdom purposes our primary focus, all our other needs are secondary, even our need for food, clothing, and health. When our love relationship with Jesus is so intimate, real, vital, alive, and cherished, every stress, every need, and every other matter pales in significance and falls in line.

We all live by priorities. For many of us, they have become automatic, habitual, and almost involuntary. We have perhaps never thought that much about our priorities and we likely have never written them down, but we have them. We make choices everyday based on our priorities.

The following exercise may help us with our priorities:

- Assess your present priorities. Here is where we simply need to do the hard work of asking ourselves what priorities shape our decisions. The "enemy" of the best is often the good. A good opportunity may keep us from a great opportunity. Similarly, a good priority may distract us from a great one.

- Adjust your priorities. Stephen Covey, in his classic work *The Seven Habits of Highly Effective People,* identifies this concept as a life-defining principle. He simple calls this, "First things first."[24] C.S. Lewis said, "Put first things first and we get second things thrown in: Put second things first and we lose both first and second things."[25]

- Plan to live with your new priorities. The key word here is plan. Again, planning requires a little time, a pen, some paper, and a calendar. Good intentions go nowhere without a plan. You've no doubt heard the axiom, "Fail to plan and you plan to fail." Isaiah 32:8 says: *"But the noble man makes noble plans, and by noble deeds he stands."*

- Decide to live with your new priorities. Decision-making is all about the capacity of our will. It is all about making good decisions and repeating good decisions. This is the heart of self-discipline.

THE ULTIMATE VIRTUE

The Apostle Paul spoke of how this quality of love was the ultimate virtue to be expressed by a follower of Christ. He said:

> *If I speak with the tongues of men and of angels, but do not have love, I have become a noisy gong or a clanging cymbal. If I have the gift of prophecy, and know all mysteries and all knowledge; and if I have all faith, so as to remove mountains, but do not have love, I am nothing. And if I give all my possessions to feed the poor, and if I surrender my body to be burned, but do not have love, it profits me nothing.*
>
> *Love is patient, love is kind and is not jealous; love does not brag and is not arrogant, does not act unbecomingly; it does not*

seek its own, is not provoked, does not take into account a wrong
suffered, does not rejoice in unrighteousness, but rejoices with
the truth; bears all things, believes all things, hopes all things, en-
dures all things. Love never fails; but if there are gifts of prophecy,
they will be done away; if there are tongues, they will cease; if
there is knowledge, it will be done away. (1 Corinthians 13:1-8,
NASB)

But now faith, hope, love, abide these three; but the greatest of
these is love. (1 Corinthians 13:13, NASB)

Unless we have love in our speech, we have nothing. Unless we have
love in our knowledge, we have nothing. Unless we have love in our actions, we have nothing. Love is the foundational virtue.

THE ULTIMATE PURSUIT

Human beings pursue love. Proverbs states:

What a man desires is unfailing love. (Proverbs 19:22, NIV)

When we express love, we are realizing a deep longing. When we apply
this pursuit, we find personal meaning and fulfillment. Love says something
to God. Love says something to others. Love does something inside of us.

THE ULTIMATE APOLOGETIC

Love is a powerful apologetic for the Christian faith. Jesus challenged his
disciples with:

A new command I give you: Love one another. As I have loved
you, so you must love one another. By this all men will know that
you are my disciples, if you love one another. (John 13:34-35,
NIV)

Clearly, love can be obeyed and applied, which implies that love is far more than an emotion. However, the lesson also drives home the reality that love is a powerful apologetic before a critical and cynical world. When Christians apply this, the world will know what real Christianity is!

THE ULTIMATE EXAMPLE

The love we are called to express was first modelled by Jesus himself. The Apostle John makes this observation:

> *Beloved, let us love one another, for love is from God; and every-one who loves is born of God and knows God. The one who does not love does not know God, for God is love. By this the love of God was manifested in us, that God has sent His only begotten Son into the world so that we might live through Him. In this is love, not that we loved God, but that He loved us and sent His Son to be the propitiation for our sins. Beloved, if God so loved us, we also ought to love one another.* (1 John 4:7-11, NASB)

ASSIGNMENT: *Do you love God... really love God? How do you show it? How do you think you could fan the flames of your passion and devotion for God?*

DISCUSSION: *Discuss culture's emphasis on love as an emotion. How is bib-lical love very different?*

16

Understanding a Faith That Follows

While faith is foundational to our relationship with God, and love is the desired heart that God wants from us, Jesus invites us into this relationship with a simple appeal: "Come, follow me." Mark 1 describes the first interactions that Jesus had with Simon, Andrew, James, and John, who all became disciples and ultimately apostles of Jesus.

> *Now after John was put in prison, Jesus came to Galilee, preaching the Gospel of the kingdom of God, and saying, "The time is fulfilled, and the kingdom of God is at hand. Repent, and believe in the Gospel."*
>
> *And as He walked by the Sea of Galilee, He saw Simon and Andrew his brother casting a net into the sea; for they were fishermen. Then Jesus said to them, "Follow Me, and I will make you become fishers of men." They immediately left their nets and followed Him.*
>
> *When He had gone a little farther from there, He saw James*

the son of Zebedee, and John his brother, who also were in the
boat mending their nets. And immediately He called them, and
they left their father Zebedee in the boat with the hired servants,
and went after Him. (Mark 1:14-20, NKJV)

This invitation to follow Jesus was the invitation to apprentice under
Jesus as a disciple. This would imply spending significant time with Jesus:
listening, learning, applying, copying, and obeying. Such was the method of
teachers and rabbis of both Greco-Roman and Semitic peoples. Jesus, however, significantly raises the bar of expectation for his followers. After
spending several months in community with the disciples, Jesus declares:

If anyone would come after me, he must deny himself and take up
his cross daily and follow me.(Luke 9:23, NIV)

Jesus here challenges his followers that a disciple is one who has done
three things:

- They have denied themselves. This is all about surrender.
  A follower of Jesus willingly surrenders his goals and aspirations. This does not mean the individual has relin-
  quished all thoughts, motivations, and intentions. But it
  does mean that all these are made secondary to the will
  and plans of God. We are no longer at the centre of our
  own universe; God is.
- They have taken up their cross. This is all about sacrifice.
  The cross implied death and the disciples needed to understand this. The message here is that our devotion
  knows no limits. As disciples of Christ, we need to be willing and prepared to die for Jesus and his cause. This defines radical devotion in very specific terms: "willing to
  die."
- They have chosen to follow Christ in service. Discipleship

is ultimately expressed in a life of routine obedience and service. Implied is the principle that the spiritual life is a process. It is a conformance and a transformation into the image of Christ, and we do this one step at a time as we follow Jesus.[26]

We follow Jesus to be like Jesus. Luke 6:40 clarifies this goal.

> *A student is not above his teacher, but everyone who is fully trained will be like his teacher.* (Luke 6:40, NIV)

Our end goal is to look like Jesus, act like Jesus, and reflect the virtues of Jesus. This happens when we intentionally follow Jesus. As radical and demanding a message as this is, the end result is not that we lose our own life, but that we actually find it. Jesus said:

> *Anyone who loves his father or mother more than me is not worthy of me; anyone who loves his son or daughter more than me is not worthy of me; and anyone who does not take his cross and follow me is not worthy of me. Whoever finds his life will lose it, and whoever loses his life for my sake will find it.* (Matthew 10:37-39, NIV)

Becoming like Jesus is the objective of our discipleship relationship and the process in which we are presently engaged. Keep following.

ASSIGNMENT: *What should following Jesus look like in the cultural and societal context you live in? Think about our use of time, our use of money, our use of abilities, and our ambitions.*

DISCUSSION: *Are there areas of surrender, sacrifice, or service that you are not yet ready to give up?*

── 17 ──
Understanding a Faith That Prays

Prayer is simply conversing with God. It may be an expression of worship and gratitude. It may be a confession and a request for forgiveness. It may be a plea or a request. It may be an expression of our confusion and perplexing questions. There are examples of such prayers throughout the Scripture. Jesus gave us a wonderful model prayer to use as a pattern for prayer. In Matthew 6:9-13, Jesus invites:

> *In this manner, therefore, pray: Our Father in heaven, Hallowed be Your name. Your kingdom come. Your will be done On earth as it is in heaven. Give us this day our daily bread. And forgive us our debts, As we forgive our debtors. And do not lead us into temptation, But deliver us from the evil one. For Yours is the kingdom and the power and the glory forever. Amen.* (Matthew 6:9-13, NKJV)

In this prayer, Jesus invites us to worship God, requests God's leadership in our world, seeks God's provision, and seeks God's forgiveness and strength to resist temptation. The subject of prayer, however, surfaces all kinds of questions. Does praying really matter? Do my prayers change God's mind? A study of these passages will help us round out our understanding.

PRAYER BRINGS INTIMACY

I am the true vine, and My Father is the vinedresser. Every branch in Me that does not bear fruit He takes away; and every branch that bears fruit He prunes, that it may bear more fruit. You are already clean because of the word which I have spoken to you. Abide in Me, and I in you. As the branch cannot bear fruit of itself, unless it abides in the vine, neither can you, unless you abide in Me.

I am the vine, you are the branches. He who abides in Me, and I in him, bears much fruit; for without Me you can do nothing. If anyone does not abide in Me, he is cast out as a branch and is withered; and they gather them and throw them into the fire, and they are burned. If you abide in Me, and My words abide in you, you will ask what you desire, and it shall be done for you. By this My Father is glorified, that you bear much fruit; so you will be My disciples. (John 15:1-8, NKJV)

PRAY BRINGS HELP

Is anyone among you suffering? Then he must pray Is anyone cheerful? He is to sing praises. Is anyone among you sick? Then he must call for the elders of the church and they are to pray over him, anointing him with oil in the name of the Lord; and the prayer offered in faith will restore the one who is sick, and the Lord will raise him up, and if he has committed sins, they will be forgiven him.

Therefore, confess your sins to one another, and pray for one another so that you may be healed. The effective prayer of a righteous man can accomplish much.

Elijah was a man with a nature like ours, and he prayed earnestly that it would not rain, and it did not rain on the earth for three years and six months. Then he prayed again, and the sky poured rain and the earth produced its fruit. (James 5:13-18, NASB)

PRAYER IS SOMETIMES A STRUGGLE THAT BRINGS ALIGNMENT

Genesis records a fascinating wrestling match between God and a man. The story is about the selfish, deceptive, and cunning work of Jacob as he tricks his brother, Esau, and lies to his own father, Isaac, in order to receive his father's blessing and a greater inheritance as the succeeding patriarch. As the eldest, Esau should have received this role and a double portion of Isaac's inheritance, but this was all snatched away. The story begins in Genesis 25. Jacob was a schemer. In fact, the name Jacob means "trickster." He cheats his brother twice. Following the second deception, where he steals the blessing and legal inheritance that is due Esau, Esau is so enraged that the only thoughts to console his fury are thoughts of taking Jacob's life. Jacob sees the wrath in his brother's eyes and flees for his life. He flees some five hundred miles, back to Mesopotamia, the land of his mother's relatives. There he marries and has many children.

In Genesis 32, we read of how Jacob, after years of separation from Esau, prepares to once again meet him. Understandably, Jacob is afraid, and I believe even remorseful. He has experienced the sting of betrayal himself several times by his father-in-law, Laban, and his heart is now much more attuned to justice, fairness, and integrity. Jacob sees his brother's four hundred men advancing. He formulates a plan and prays. He plans further, and prays still more.

> *So Jacob was left alone, and a man wrestled with him till day-*
> *break. When the man saw that he could not overpower him, he*
> *touched the socket of Jacob's hip so that his hip was wrenched as*
> *he wrestled with the man. Then the man said, "Let me go, for it is*
> *daybreak."*
>
> > *But Jacob replied, "I will not let you go unless you bless me."*
> > *The man asked him, "What is your name?"*
> > *"Jacob," he answered.*
> > *Then the man said, "Your name will no longer be Jacob, but*
> > *Israel, because you have struggled with God and with men and*
> > *have overcome."* (Genesis 32:24-28, NIV)

Jacob is even given a new name, Israel. Israel means "he who persists with God."

The prophet Hosea comments on the wrestlings of Jacob and identifies it as prayer that reflected a struggle between Jacob and God.

> *In the womb he grasped his brother's heel; as a man he struggled*
> *with God. He struggled withthe angel and overcame him; he wept*
> *and begged for his favor.* (Hosea 12:3-4, NIV)

Jacob wanted to be blessed. Jacob was tired of living on the run. Jacob was tired of the family division. Jacob wanted a brother back. Jacob was also tired of the deception and difficulties with Laban, his father-in-law. Jacob finally wanted to be used by God, to be blessed by God. He wanted, hungered for, passionately longed for a fresh sense of relationship and destiny.

While this story raises questions about prayer, it illustrates a powerful truth: life is often a wrestling match. We wrestle at work, we wrestle at home, we wrestle with our spouse, we wrestle with our kids, we wrestle with our parents, we wrestle with our neighbours, we wrestle with our church, we wrestle with our country, we wrestle with decisions, we wrestle with temptation, we wrestle with ourselves, and we wrestle with God.

In those wrestling matches, God must win. We must learn to submit. But we can win, too. This story is telling us that God longs to see in us a hunger for him. He wants us to have a determination and devotion that we will not easily give up. And this struggle, this wrestling match, is one aspect of this communication we call "prayer." Prayer is often a struggle, a wrestling match.

A Military Image

The Scriptures offer yet another helpful insight to this communication called prayer. Think of the imagery of Spiritual warfare.

> *Finally, be strong in the Lord and in the strength of his might. Put on the whole armor of God, that you may be able to stand against the schemes of the devil. For we do not wrestle against flesh and blood, but against the rulers, against the authorities, against the cosmic powers over this present darkness, against the spiritual forces of evil in the heavenly places. Therefore take up the whole armor of God, that you may be able to withstand in the evil day, and having done all, to stand firm. Stand therefore, having fastened on the belt of truth, and having put on the breastplate of righteousness, and, as shoes for your feet, having put on the readiness given by the Gospel of peace. In all circumstances take up the shield of faith, with which you can extinguish all the flaming darts of the evil one; and take the helmet of salvation, and the sword of the Spirit, which is the word of God, praying at all times in the Spirit, with all prayer and supplication. To that end keep alert with all perseverance, making supplication for all the saints, and also for me, that words may be given to me in opening my mouth boldly to proclaim the mystery of the Gospel, for which I am an ambassador in chains, that I may declare it boldly, as I*

ought to speak. (Ephesians 6:10-20, ESV)

Ephesians 6 tells us that our struggle is not with flesh and blood, but with greater powers, unseen powers, spiritual powers, very real powers, both good and evil. This match is not realized in physical spheres, but rather is spiritual spheres. It is won in prayer.

We sometimes struggle with faith and doubt. Jacob knew the promise to the patriarchs, but he doubted. While he prayed, he also struggled. The same is true in our lives. We struggle with our will and with God's will. However, in the end, when we can submit to the divine purposes and plans of God, a meaningful alignment takes place, and we find ourselves at peace.

Prayer is a wonderful avenue of communing with God, but in it we also learn how to submit to the divine purposes of God.

ASSIGNMENT: *Someone has created a helpful little acrostic using the word ACTS: Adoration, Confession, Thanksgiving, and Supplication. Prepare a prayer section in your journal using this acrostic. Begin to use it daily.*

DISCUSSION: *What is causing you to wrestle with God these days?*

— 18 —

Understanding a Faith
That Is Grateful and Worships

Religion, properly understood, begins with worship. God's heart is broken when our worship becomes empty religious rituals. What is God looking for in worship?

When we say "I love you" to someone, we expect a response. Hopefully, we will hear the reply, "I love you, too." When we give a gift, we expect a response. A "thank you" is nice to hear. So when God shows himself to us in his splendour, in his wonder, and in his glory, it seems consistent or understandable that God expects a response. That response is what we call worship. The two words *revelation* and *response* sum it up. God reveals; we respond. God acts; we respond. God gives; we respond. God teaches; we respond. God corrects; we respond. God reminds; we respond.

Our response may be: praise and wonder (like so many of the psalmists), gratitude and thanksgiving (like the forgiven prostitute who wept at

Jesus' feet), brokenness and confession (like some other psalms), or obedience and sacrifice (as Romans 12:1-2 states).

Soren Kierkegaard was a Danish theologian who served God from 1813-1855. He said the problem with the modern church was that God is the prompter, the pastor is the performer/actor, and the church is the audience. With this approach, the congregation has become spectators, the entertained, and the consumers. What *should* be reflected is that the pastor/worship leader is to be the prompter, the church should be the performers/actors, and God should be the intended audience.[27] God is to receive our worship.

Leitourgia is the word for worship used in the Greek New Testament. It is from this word that we get the word liturgy. Liturgy means "the work of the people."

JESUS EXPLAINS WORSHIP

> *The woman said to Him, "Sir, I perceive that You are a prophet. Our fathers worshiped in this mountain, and you people say that in Jerusalem is the place where men ought to worship."*
>
> *Jesus said to her, "Woman, believe Me, an hour is coming when neither in this mountain nor in Jerusalem will you worship the Father. You worship what you do not know; we worship what we know, for salvation is from the Jews. But an hour is coming, and now is, when the true worshipers will worship the Father in spirit and truth; for such people the Father seeks to be His worshipers. God is spirit, and those who worship Him must worship in spirit and truth."* (John 4:19-24, NASB)

Mount Gerizim was sacred to the Samaritans, as this was where Abraham met Melchizedek. Jesus explains how a crisis or a change is coming. The temple will be destroyed, a new era will begin, and worship will no longer be temple-focused. To "worship in spirit" is not simply outward and done in the right place by someone with the right position. Authentic worship is the antithesis to all externals of place, time, or circumstance.

The necessity of strictly spiritual worship is rooted in the very nature of God, for God is Spirit. "Spirit and truth" is all about sincerity and authenticity (the real thing, the true thing). It speaks of rendering such homage to God that the entire heart enters into the act, and doing this in full harmony with the truth of God as revealed in His Word. Such worship, therefore, will not only be spiritual instead of physical, inward instead of outward, but it will also be directed to the true God as set forth in Scripture. A humble and sincere heart and a correct understanding of God are both needed.

So, if worship is a response, God is looking for an internal heart response, not an external form. The issues of music style, order, décor, length, and service timing all pale in light of that which really matters. So when the worship leaders prompt the people of God with the truth of God, we all collectively respond and God, as the audience of one, is honoured and glorified.

What is God looking for in worship? He is not looking for hollow, empty religious activities! He is not looking for big offerings and the temptation to brag that may go with it. He is not looking for a particular music style. God is looking for a response to a revelation of his greatness and goodness. Keep style and taste in delicate perspective. We have different styles, and will seek to continue to honour these style tastes. But let's be gracious with each other.

Allow yourself to be able to see God, hear God, and then respond to God.

> *Ascribe to the Lord the glory due his name; worship the Lord in the splendor of his holiness.* (Psalm 29:2, NIV)

> *I have seen you in the sanctuary and beheld your power and your*

glory. (Psalm 63:2, NIV)

May they sing of the ways of the Lord, for the glory of the Lord is great. (Psalm 138:5, NIV)

Holy, holy, holy is the Lord Almighty; the whole earth is full of his glory. (Isaiah 6:3, NIV)

Yours, O Lord, is the greatness and the power and the glory and the majesty and the splendor for everything in heaven and earth is yours. Yours, O Lord, is the kingdom; you are exalted as head over. all (1 Chronicles 29:11, NIV)

Worship is realized in community. In the Old Testament, the Jews gathered for worship. In the New Testament, the early church chose to meet on the first day of the week (Sunday, in remembrance of Christ's resurrection) to worship. The value of worshipping together was deeply cherished, and should be.

Therefore, brothers, since we have confidence to enter the holy places by the blood of Jesus, by the new and living way that he opened for us through the curtain, that is, through his flesh, and since we have a great priest over the house of God, let us draw near with a true heart in full assurance of faith, with our hearts sprinkled clean from an evil conscience and our bodies washed with pure water.

Let us hold fast the confession of our hope without wavering, for he who promised is faithful. And let us consider how to stir up one another to love and good works, not neglecting to meet together, as is the habit of some, but encouraging one another, and all the more as you see the Day drawing near. (Hebrews 10:19-25, ESV)

ASSIGNMENT: *What do you like and dislike in worship? Do your likes and dislikes really matter?*

DISCUSSION: *When you come to worship, do you come with an attitude seeking entertainment, or do you prepare your heart to hear from God and to respond to God? In what ways is corporate worship the same as personal worship? In what ways do these differ?*

19

Understanding a Faith
That Serves and Gives

A man once came to Jesus seeking to justify himself. He knew that he did not love all people, but he did love some people. Jesus tells a story.

> And behold, a lawyer stood up to put him to the test, saying, "Teacher, what shall I do to inherit eternal life?" He said to him, "What is written in the Law? How do you read it?" And he answered, "You shall love the Lord your God with all your heart and with all your soul and with all your strength and with all your mind, and your neighbor as yourself." And he said to him, "You have answered correctly; do this, and you will live."
>
> But he, desiring to justify himself, said to Jesus, "And who is my neighbor?" Jesus replied, "A man was going down from Jerusalem to Jericho, and he fell among robbers, who stripped him and beat him and departed, leaving him half dead. Now by chance a priest was going down that road, and when he saw him he passed

by on the other side. So likewise a Levite, when he came to the
place and saw him, passed by on the other side. But a Samaritan,
as he journeyed, came to where he was, and when he saw him, he
had compassion. He went to him and bound up his wounds,
pouring on oil and wine. Then he set him on his own animal and
brought him to an inn and took care of him. And the next day he
took out two denarii and gave them to the innkeeper, saying,
'Take care of him, and whatever more you spend, I will repay you
when I come back.' Which of these three, do you think, proved to
be a neighbor to the man who fell among the robbers?" He said,
"The one who showed him mercy." And Jesus said to him, "You
go, and do likewise." (Luke 10:25-37, ESV)

The road from Jerusalem to Jericho crosses a rocky seventeen mile stretch of terrain with all kinds of caves and hiding places along the way, perfectly suitable for thieves to hide in, in anticipation of an easy robbery. Sure enough, in this story, a robbery occurs. A priest (someone who should care for people) happens upon the situation and amazingly does nothing. Soon, a Levite (someone who should care for people) also passes by and does nothing. Finally, a Samaritan comes upon the victimized person. Samaritans were half-Jew and half-Gentile, and were prejudiced against by conscientious Jews. However, this Samaritan helps with the robbed and abused person, and even leaves money behind for future stabilization. This act of kindness costs the Samaritan. He served; he gave.

Jesus asks the self-righteous man who came to question him, which one was the neighbour? The Jewish Priest? The Jewish Levite? Or the rejected stranger who was a Samaritan? The answer is self-evident. Jesus tells this story to describe what a true citizen of the kingdom of God looks like. Such citizens are servants. Such individuals have an eye to the needs around them and take the initiative to serve and give, even when it costs them.

Whether we live in a prosperous nation or a needy nation, there is poverty and social injustice that may be readily identified. We see physical needs, educational needs, psychological needs, domestic needs, and health needs. Individually, we cannot meet all needs, but we can meet some needs. Together, however, we can meet many of these global issues. Throughout the history of the church, the church was often the first to bring relief to crises, the first to build hospitals and schools, the first to press for social and justice reform.

This is what a disciple looks like. We serve. We give.

> *He has showed you, O man, what is good. And what does the Lord require of you? To act justly and to love mercy and to walk humbly with your God.* (Micah 6:8, NIV)

ASSIGNMENT: *What are some needs that you see in your relational spheres and what could you do about their needs?*

DISCUSSION: *In light of our ever-shrinking global context, how might we define "neighbour"? What can you do about the needs of people you will likely never meet? Think of some very specific situations and determine to do something about it.*

20

Understanding a Faith That Tells

Global pandemics are always of concern to health officials. One of the many concerns is the availability of a vaccine or related medication. Some countries would seek to stockpile medication. Some poorer countries are very worried. Some countries are suggesting that, when there is an outbreak, patent laws may be disregarded and pharmaceutical companies given permission to mass-produce medications that may be used to save lives. The argument, of course, is that the saving of lives takes precedence over patent laws.

Imagine for a moment that you are in a position of authority. You have the information and the power to help save lives. Do you remain silent? Do you act? If you act, what will you do?

The parallel of this hypothetical situation with the message and mission of the church is neither minor nor insignificant. God has given us "the message of reconciliation," as 2 Corinthians 5:19 calls it. Essentially, God has given us the antidote to the disease of the soul. We have been healed, and we can now help others find healing and find God. This is "evangelism." Evangelism is the proclamation of the Good News.

Recall what Jesus said to his disciples just before his ascension to be with his Father in Heaven.

> *Therefore go and make disciples of all nations, baptizing them in the name of the Father and of the Son and of the Holy Spirit, and teaching them to obey everything I have commanded you. And surely I am with you always, to the very end of the age.* (Matthew 28:19-20, NIV)

The New Testament reinforces this theme. Peter, appeals:

> *But in your hearts set apart Christ as Lord. Always be prepared to give an answer to everyone who asks you to give the reason for the hope that you have. But do this with gentleness and respect, keeping a clear conscience, so that those who speak maliciously against your good behavior in Christ may be ashamed of their slander.* (1 Peter 3:15-16, NIV)

In Peter's epistle, we learn that we need three simple but vital matters in order to do the work of evangelism. We need dedication, training, and a strategy.

DEDICATION

Dedication is needed. Peter tells us to "set apart," or sanctify Christ in our lives. This is the appropriation of the reign and rule of Christ in our lives. This begins with understanding the role of motivation. People are motivated intrinsically (internally) and extrinsically (from outside). Character-based people "do the right thing" and then feel good about it afterwards, while emotionally-based people "wait to feel right" about it and then do it (that is, if the feeling ever comes).

Our motivation should grow out of gratitude for what Christ has done for us, as well as authentic care and compassion for those who have not embraced faith in Christ and are still trying to navigate the challenges of life in isolation and alienation from God.

TRAINING

Peter also challenges us to be prepared to "give an answer" for our faith. This suggests that we need to expose ourselves to suitable training to help us share our faith in our cultural context. We need to be able to tell our story, tell the story of Jesus, and be able to answer some foundational questions about faith, competing faiths, and other worldviews.

STRATEGY

The final quality Peter cautions us with is the need for a strategy. Our strategy should reflect a gentle style as Jesus himself was always gracious with those who were lost, and more direct with the Pharisees. We should also reflect a respectful attitude, as God respects the human will. Our outreach initiatives should also always be an extension of our reputation. Scandals, hypocrisy, and inconsistencies destroy our platform. While every missional context will require unique, strategic adaptation of methods, Jesus modelled a simple strategy which we can follow.

First, Jesus showed that he cared. When we care, people listen. When we care, we build a platform of credibility from which we can communicate the essence of the Gospel. Our hope and prayer in this communication is that people will, in time, embrace the message of the Gospel. Invariably this is a process. Evangelism takes time. Evangelism takes place in the context of a relationship. Any strategy should take these critical realities into consideration.

Ours is a faith that tells. This telling should become as natural as breathing.

ASSIGNMENT: *In Colossians 4:2-4, Paul invites us to pray for clarity and opportunities to share our faith. Who are some people for whom you can pray? Add them to your prayer journal and start looking for opportunities to share.*

DISCUSSION: *As you think of these three areas (dedication, training, strategy), which area do you need to give most attention to right now?*

—— 21 ——
Assurance That God Cares for Us

Doubt is a powerful and destructive force. To assure is to "put beyond all doubt." When we feel doubt, we hesitate, we question (with a leaning toward a negative answer), we lack confidence, we disbelieve, and we distrust. But when we are assured of something, we become confident, we act secure, we function with optimism, and we decide with freedom and conviction.

One of the things that we are prone to question, especially after a failure or capitulating to sin, is: Does God still love and care for me? The following parables of Jesus describe the all-out pursuit of a lost sheep and a lost coin. The last parable in this triplet describes a father patiently waiting for the return of his lost son.

> Then all the tax collectors and the sinners drew near to Him to hear Him. And the Pharisees and scribes complained, saying, "This Man receives sinners and eats with them." So He spoke this

parable to them, saying: "What man of you, having a hundred sheep, if he loses one of them, does not leave the ninety-nine in the wilderness, and go after the one which is lost until he finds it? And when he has found it, he lays it on his shoulders, rejoicing. And when he comes home, he calls together his friends and neighbors, saying to them, 'Rejoice with me, for I have found my sheep which was lost!' I say to you that likewise there will be more joy in heaven over one sinner who repents than over ninety-nine just persons who need no repentance.

"Or what woman, having ten silver coins, if she loses one coin, does not light a lamp, sweep the house, and search carefully until she finds it? And when she has found it, she calls her friends and neighbors together, saying, 'Rejoice with me, for I have found the piece which I lost!' Likewise, I say to you, there is joy in the presence of the angels of God over one sinner who repents."

Then He said: "A certain man had two sons. And the younger of them said to his father, 'Father, give me the portion of goods that falls to me.' So he divided to them his livelihood. And not many days after, the younger son gathered all together, journeyed to a far country, and there wasted his possessions with prodigal living. But when he had spent all, there arose a severe famine in that land, and he began to be in want. Then he went and joined himself to a citizen of that country, and he sent him into his fields to feed swine. And he would gladly have filled his stomach with the pods that the swine ate, and no one gave him anything.

"But when he came to himself, he said, 'How many of my father's hired servants have bread enough and to spare, and I perish with hunger! I will arise and go to my father, and will say to him, "Father, I have sinned against heaven and before you, and I am no longer worthy to be called your son. Make me like one of your hired servants."'

"And he arose and came to his father. But when he was still a great way off, his father saw him and had compassion, and ran and fell on his neck and kissed him. And the son said to him, 'Fa-

ther, I have sinned against heaven and in your sight, and am no longer worthy to be called your son.'

"But the father said to his servants, 'Bring out the best robe and put it on him, and put a ring on his hand and sandals on his feet. And bring the fatted calf here and kill it, and let us eat and be merry; for this my son was dead and is alive again; he was lost and is found.' And they began to be merry.

"Now his older son was in the field. And as he came and drew near to the house, he heard music and dancing. So he called one of the servants and asked what these things meant. And he said to him, 'Your brother has come, and because he has received him safe and sound, your father has killed the fatted calf.'

"But he was angry and would not go in. Therefore his father came out and pleaded with him. So he answered and said to his father, 'Lo, these many years I have been serving you; I never transgressed your commandment at any time; and yet you never gave me a young goat, that I might make merry with my friends. But as soon as this son of yours came, who has devoured your livelihood with harlots, you killed the fatted calf for him.'

"And he said to him, 'Son, you are always with me, and all that I have is yours. It was right that we should make merry and be glad, for your brother was dead and is alive again, and was lost and is found.'" (Luke 15:1-31, NKVJ)

These three stories drive a powerful and personal message to all people. God cares. God cares for lost, confused, wandering, even rebellious souls. This passage is most often cited to communicate God's heart for people who do not yet know him. However, if this is how God feels about his wayward children, would it make sense that God feels any less for those who are already a part of his family.

While doubts descend from time to time, we must lock on to the promise of God that we are the object of his love and care. Peter encourages us:

Cast all your anxiety on him because he cares for you. (1 Peter 5:7, NIV)

ASSIGNMENT: *When are you most tempted to question God's love and care for you?*

DISCUSSION: *Does how you feel about God's care change the fact of God's care?*

———— 22 ————

Assurance That God Forgives Us

We can rest in the assurance that God cares for us and is willing to forgive us. However, we ought not to perceive that we have a passive role in maintaining our relationship with God. While we have the promise of forgiveness, we have a responsibility to take steps in appropriating that forgiveness from God, and from others.

SEEK FORGIVENESS

> If we confess our sins, he is faithful and just and will forgive us
> our sins and purify us from all unrighteousness. (1 John 1:9, NIV)

First, let's seek to understand forgiveness and what it is in theological terms. Forgiveness is the legal act whereby God removes the charges that were held against the sinner through making the proper satisfaction or atonement for those sins. There are several Greek words used to describe forgiveness. One is *charizomai*, which is related to the word grace and means "to forgive out of grace."[28] This word is used in the context of cancelling a debt (Colossians 2:13). The context emphasizes that our debts were nailed to the cross, with Christ's atonement freely forgiving the sins that were charged against us.

The most common word for forgiveness is *aphiemi*, which means "to let go, release" or "send away." The noun form is used in Ephesians 1:7, where it stresses that the believer's sins have been forgiven or sent away through the riches of God's grace as revealed in the death of Christ. Forgiveness forever solves the problem of sin in the believer's life—all sins past, present, and future (Colossians 2:13). This is distinct from the daily cleansing from sin that is necessary to maintain fellowship with God (1 John 1:9).

Forgiveness is man-ward. Man had sinned and needed to have his sins dealt with and removed. Forgiveness, then, is possible only because God is a God of grace, who is willing to act on his grace and extend grace, mercy, and forgiveness to us.

How is forgiveness activated? When we seek it, or confess. Confess literally means to agree with God. So, when we are confessing a matter, we are saying to God, "God, I agree with you; I have sinned; I have blown it; I have been wrong and you are right."

Agreeing with God certainly also involves regret or remorse. It is not just academic; it is personal. We have hurt someone; we have hurt God. Psalm 38 is instructive here:

> *I confess my iniquity; I am troubled by my sin.* (Psalm 38:18, NIV)

When we blow it, and we know it, and we admit it, usually most of us feel regret and a level of shame. We feel guilty. This is normal and correct. But it is not the only emotion we should feel. We should feel badly, truly badly because we have disappointed and hurt our heavenly father.

While the initial thrust is on our seeking forgiveness from God, the same principle is true for human relationships. When we hurt others, we need to seek their forgiveness, too. And the same principles are at work. We are acknowledging, agreeing, admitting that we have done wrong. We have remorse. We see the pain we have caused.

ACCEPT FORGIVENESS

While this principle may be implied, it needs to be highlighted. While we may feel badly, and in fact seek forgiveness, we may not accept it for ourselves. We may not believe we have been forgiven. We may choose to continue to punish ourselves.

Not accepting forgiveness is to remain in a prison cell, but the door is unlocked and open. If God says we are forgiven, then we are forgiven. If the friend you wronged forgives you, then accept the forgiveness. If your spouse forgives you, then accept the forgiveness.

There is an episode in Jesus' ministry which beautifully illustrates the need to accept forgiveness. The situation was that Jesus was a guest at an influential man's community gathering. There were all kinds of people there, including a woman who was known for her promiscuous lifestyle. She placed herself at Jesus' feet and was worshipping and wiping his feet with her tears.

> *One of the Pharisees asked him to eat with him, and he went into the Pharisee's house and took his place at the table. And behold, a woman of the city, who was a sinner, when she learned that he was reclining at table in the Pharisee's house, brought an alabaster flask of ointment, and standing behind him at his feet, weeping, she began to wet his feet with her tears and wiped them with the hair of her head and kissed his feet and anointed them with the ointment. Now when the Pharisee who had invited him saw this,*

he said to himself, "If this man were a prophet, he would have known who and what sort of woman this is who is touching him, for she is a sinner." And Jesus answering said to him, "Simon, I have something to say to you." And he answered, "Say it, Teacher."

"A certain moneylender had two debtors. One owed five hundred denarii, and the other fifty. When they could not pay, he cancelled the debt of both. Now which of them will love him more?" Simon answered, "The one, I suppose, for whom he cancelled the larger debt." And he said to him, "You have judged rightly." Then turning toward the woman he said to Simon, "Do you see this woman? I entered your house; you gave me no water for my feet, but she has wet my feet with her tears and wiped them with her hair. You gave me no kiss, but from the time I came in she has not ceased to kiss my feet. You did not anoint my head with oil, but she has anointed my feet with ointment. Therefore I tell you, her sins, which are many, are forgiven—for she loved much. But he who is forgiven little, loves little." And he said to her, "Your sins are forgiven." Then those who were at table with him began to say among themselves ,"Who is this, who even forgives sins?" And he said to the woman, "Your faith has saved you; go in peace." (Luke 7:36-50, ESV)

Simon, the host, was appalled at Jesus' interaction and care for this woman. Why wasn't he rebuking her and sending her away? "Jesus, where is your sense of discretion?" he must have wondered. However, Jesus was revelling in her response. Jesus says to Simon, "I tell you, her many sins have been forgiven—for she loved much. But he who has been forgiven little loves little." This woman has accepted forgiveness and could not help worshipping and expressing gratitude.

GRANT FORGIVENESS

> *Bear with each other and forgive whatever grievances you may have against one another. Forgive as the Lord forgave you.* (Colossians 3:13, NIV)

> *Then Peter came to Jesus and asked, "Lord, how many times shall I forgive my brother when he sins against me? Up to seven times?" Jesus answered, "I tell you, not seven times, but seventy-seven times.* (Matthew 18:21-22, NIV)

The principle is essentially simple. We grant forgiveness because we have experienced forgiveness. Further, forgiveness knows no limits. Since Jesus has paid the price for our sins, forgiveness is possible. Ask for it. Since Jesus has paid the price for our sins and offers to forgive us, we should accept his forgiveness. Since Jesus has forgiven us, we should grant it. If we do not, bitterness and resentment will haunt us. Alcoholics Anonymous tells us that resentment is the number one offender. They teach that it destroys more alcoholics than any other cause or factor. But resentment doesn't just affect alcoholics, of course; resentment is the result of any number of spiritual diseases. This is important to understand, since we don't just suffer from mental and physical illnesses, but spiritually ones as well.

Practically, we must ask, how do I forgive someone who maliciously wounded me? Archibald Hart suggests, "Forgiveness is surrendering my right to hurt you for hurting me."[29] Forgiveness means letting go. Forgiveness means releasing. Forgiveness is not forgetting. We may forgive and forget, but forgetting is not how we forgive. Forgiveness is a choice. If it can be commanded, it can be obeyed. Forgiving is so difficult because it pulls at our sense of justice. We want justice (or revenge) for offenses against us. Neil Anderson has observed, "Forgiveness is agreeing to live with the consequences of another person's sin."[30] The reality is that we are going to live with the consequences of another's sins regardless of our attitude. The question is, will we do so with a spirit of bitterness or a spirit of forgiveness?

All forgiveness is substitutionary, because no one really forgives without bearing the consequences of the other's sin, just as Christ did for us.

ASSIGNMENT: *What past sin or reoccurring vice is robbing you of joy? Confess it and move forward.*

DISCUSSION: *Is there a person who has hurt you deeply that you have not forgiven? How is this affecting you?*

— 23 —

Assurance That God Keeps Us

There is a theme in Scripture that is both surprising and comforting. It is the theme that God calls selfish human beings into relationship and then promises to keep us in that eternal relationship. We come to faith because of God's sovereign and benevolent care, and He similarly keeps us by his grace. Paul's teaching in Ephesians and Romans is insightful.

> *Blessed be the God and Father of our Lord Jesus Christ, who has blessed us in Christ with every spiritual blessing in the heavenly places, even as he chose us in him before the foundation of the world, that we should be holy and blameless before him. In love he predestined us for adoption as sons through Jesus Christ, according to the purpose of his will, to the praise of his glorious grace, with which he has blessed us in the Beloved. In him we have redemption through his blood, the forgiveness of our trespasses, according to the riches of his grace, which he lavished upon us, in all wisdom and insight making known to us the mys-*

tery of his will, according to his purpose, which he set forth in Christ as a plan for the fullness of time, to unite all things in him, things in heaven and things on earth.

In him we have obtained an inheritance, having been predestined according to the purpose of him who works all things according to the counsel of his will, so that we who were the first to hope in Christ might be to the praise of his glory. In him you also, when you heard the word of truth, the Gospel of your salvation, and believed in him, were sealed with the promised Holy Spirit, who is the guarantee of our inheritance until we acquire possession of it, to the praise of his glory. (Ephesians 1:3-14, ESV)

The first part of Ephesians focuses on what we as believers have in Christ. In this section of Scripture, we discover the following:

WE HAVE BEEN CHOSEN

Before creation, God in his sovereignty elected, chose, predestined us to be his children. This is wonderful and confusing. It is a wonder in that it is like being adopted as a child; it comforts us to know we were chosen. It is, however, somewhat confusing as we wonder about the role of human responsibility and choice. In Christ, we are to now live holy lives out of a motive of love. We are assured that as his children we enjoy intimacy and relationship. Our response is praise and worship.

WE HAVE BEEN REDEEMED

To be redeemed carries the concept of "to buy, purchase or pay a price for something," or "to purchase out of the market." The implication is that Jesus has purchased us out of the marketplace of sin. The word can also mean, "to loose or set free from bondage or slavery." How did Christ accomplish this? He did so when he shed his blood as a sacrifice and substitute on our behalf (see also Hebrews 9:12-14, 22; 10:4). Certain qualifications had to be realized. The redeemer had to be related to the one being redeemed. The redeemer had to be able to pay the price, and the redeemer had to be willing. Jesus satisfied these requirements and forgiveness was thus able to be extended.

WE HAVE BEEN SEALED

Our sealing speaks of ownership. Like a signet ring on a letter, we bear God's family name. This concept also speaks of security and protection, as well as of being a certification that something is genuine. We are not imposters. We rightfully belong to God. This seal is a deposit guaranteeing our inheritance. It is a down payment of more to come, which will find its ultimate expression in heaven.

GOD HAS CALLED US AND HE WILL KEEP US

Paul, in Romans 8, further explains the work of God in our lives and on our behalf. Paul affirms the calling and election of God (as he did in Ephesians 1), but he adds a further message of hope and comfort: that God also keeps us in His grip.

> And we know that all things work together for good to those who love God, to those who are the called according to His purpose. For whom He foreknew, He also predestined to be conformed to the image of His Son, that He might be the firstborn among many brethren. Moreover whom He predestined, these He also called; whom He called, these He also justified; and whom He justified, these He also glorified.
>
> What then shall we say to these things? If God is for us, who can be against us? He who did not spare His own Son, but delivered Him up for us all, how shall He not with Him also freely give

us all things? Who shall bring a charge against God's elect? It is
God who justifies. Who is he who condemns? It is Christ who
died, and furthermore is also risen, who is even at the right hand
of God, who also makes intercession for us. Who shall separate us
from the love of Christ? Shall tribulation, or distress, or persecu-
tion, or famine, or nakedness, or peril, or sword? As it is written:
"For Your sake we are killed all day long; We are accounted as
sheep for the slaughter."

Yet in all these things we are more than conquerors through
Him who loved us. For I am persuaded that neither death nor life,
nor angels nor principalities nor powers, nor things present nor
things to come, nor height nor depth, nor any other created thing,
shall be able to separate us from the love of God which is in
Christ Jesus our Lord. (Romans 8:28-39, NKJV)

Because nothing in the entire universe is outside of God's control, nothing in the entire universe can separate us from his enduring love. God has called us and he will keep us.

ASSIGNMENT: *When you think that God has chosen you from before time, how does this affect you? When you think that God has you in the grip of His love, how does this affect you?*

DISCUSSION: *Discuss why so many Christians seem to lack the assurance of their salvation.*

—— 24 ——
Assurance That God Disciplines Us

Although none of us enjoyed being disciplined as children, we know that discipline was ultimately for our own good. Loving parents do employ discipline. This is no less true of our relationship with God the Father. The writer of Hebrews states:

> *And you have forgotten that word of encouragement that addresses you as sons:*
>
> *"My son, do not make light of the Lord's discipline, and do not lose heart when he rebukes you, because the Lord disciplines those he loves, and he punishes everyone he accepts as a son."*
>
> *Endure hardship as discipline; God is treating you as sons. For what son is not disciplined by his father? If you are not disciplined (and everyone undergoes discipline), then you are illegitimate children and not true sons. Moreover, we have all had human fathers who disciplined us and we respected them for it. How much more should we submit to the Father of our spirits*

and live! Our fathers disciplined us for a little while as they
thought best; but God disciplines us for our good, that we may
share in his holiness. No discipline seems pleasant at the time, but
painful. Later on, however, it produces a harvest of righteousness
and peace for those who have been trained by it. (Hebrews 12:5-
11, NIV)

There are times in our lives when we have a deaf ear to the Spirit's whispers in our lives. There are times when we hear a truth, read a truth, and even proclaim a truth, that we ourselves are not living up to. This is hypocrisy, and while it may be common in the human condition, it disappoints God. God has as his goal the transformation of our character and behaviour, and our conformation to the image of his Son. Thus, God will use discipline if such is needed to gain our attention and turn us back to the right path. This expression of love was evidenced in a number of situations in the Bible.

CASE STUDY: DAVID AND THE CHILDREN OF ISRAEL IN THE WILDERNESS

The children of Israel were turned away from their first opportunity to enter the Promised Land when they doubted God and recoiled in fear at the prospect of the challenges they would have to face upon entry into Canaan. Following Israel's miraculous deliverance from the bondage of Egypt, Moses commissioned spies on a reconnaissance mission to the land of Canaan.

They proceeded to come to Moses and Aaron and to all the con-
gregation of the sons of Israel in the wilderness of Paran, at
Kadesh; and they brought back word to them and to all the con-
gregation and showed them the fruit of the land.
Thus they told him, and said, "We went in to the land where
you sent us; and it certainly does flow with milk and honey, and

this is its fruit.

"Nevertheless, the people who live in the land are strong, and the cities are fortified and very large; and moreover, we saw the descendants of Anak there.

"Amalek is living in the land of the Negev and the Hittites and the Jebusites and the Amorites are living in the hill country, and the Canaanites are living by the sea and by the side of the Jordan."

Then Caleb quieted the people before Moses and said, "We should by all means go up and take possession of it, for we will surely overcome it."

But the men who had gone up with him said, "We are not able to go up against the people, for they are too strong for us."

So they gave out to the sons of Israel a bad report of the land which they had spied out, saying, "The land through which we have gone, in spying it out, is a land that devours its inhabitants; and all the people whom we saw in it are men of great size.

"There also we saw the Nephilim (the sons of Anak are part of the Nephilim); and we became like grasshoppers in our own sight, and so we were in their sight." (Numbers 13:26-33, NASB)

It was because of the people's unbelief that they were disciplined and had to wander in the wilderness until an entire generation died. The book of Hebrews highlights this period of discipline by God and links it to King David's season of discipline.

Therefore God again set a certain day, calling it Today, when a long time later he spoke through David, as was said before: 'Today, if you hear his voice, do not harden your hearts.' (Hebrews 4:7, NIV).

This was a quote which David made in Psalm 95.

Come, let us bow down in worship, let us kneel before the Lord our Maker; for he is our God and we are the people of his pasture,

the flock under his care. Today, if you hear his voice, do not
harden your hearts as you did at Meribah, as you did that day at
Massah in the desert, where your fathers tested and tried me,
though they had seen what I did. (Psalm 95:6-9, NIV)

The tragic event that David was speaking to was recorded in Exodus 17 when the people complained to God about their lack of water in the dessert. God was leading them to what ultimately would be the safety and prosperity of the Promised Land, but the people doubted, argued, and in the end capitulated to fear and said no. When God spoke, they refused to listen. When Nathan confronted David with his sin of adultery, David was instantly broken. David knew he was being disciplined by God and his mind went to this period in Israel's history. David wanted those who came after him to reflect on Israel and his experience.

CASE STUDY: MOSES

While Moses was a man of immense integrity and humility, he lost his temper at a critical time and thus found himself disqualified to lead the people into the Promised Land. While this was a disappointment to Moses, he willingly accepted this discipline from God with a humble heart.

And the Lord spoke to Moses, saying, "Take the rod; and you and
your brother Aaron assemble the congregation and speak to the
rock before their eyes, that it may yield its water. You shall thus
bring forth water for them out of the rock and let the congrega-
tion and their beasts drink."

So Moses took the rod from before the Lord, just as He had
commanded him; and Moses and Aaron gathered the assembly
before the rock. And he said to them, "Listen now, you rebels;
shall we bring forth water for you out of this rock?"

Then Moses lifted up his hand and struck the rock twice with
his rod; and water came forth abundantly, and the congregation

and their beasts drank.

But the Lord said to Moses and Aaron, "Because you have not believed Me, to treat Me as holy in the sight of the sons of Israel, therefore you shall not bring this assembly into the land which I have given them."

Those were the waters of Meribah, because the sons of Israel contended with the Lord, and He proved Himself holy among them. (Numbers 20:7-13, NASB)

ASSIGNMENT: *Do you think of discipline as "punishment" or as "loving correction"?*

DISCUSSION: *How do we distinguish discipline from the routine hard times of life that come our way?*

25

Assurance That God
Calls Us and Uses Us

In William J. Bennett's book, *The Book of Virtues*, the inspiring legend of bravery and purposefulness of St. George is retold by J. Berg Esenwein and Marietta Stockard:

> Long ago, when the knights lived in the land, there was one knight whose name was Sir George. He was not only braver than all the rest, but he was so noble, kind, and good that the people came to call him Saint George.
>
> No robbers ever dared to trouble the people who lived near his castle, and all the wild animals were killed or driven away, so the little children could play even in the woods without being afraid.
>
> One day St. George rode throughout the country. Every-where he saw the men busy at their work in the fields, the women

singing at work in their homes, and the little children shouting at their play.

"These people are all safe and happy. They need me no more," said St. George.

"But somewhere perhaps there is trouble and fear. There may be someplace where little children cannot play in safety, some woman may have been carried away from her home—perhaps there are even dragons left to be slain. Tomorrow I shall ride away and never stop until I find work which only a knight can do."

Early the next morning St. George put on his helmet and all his shining armor, and fastened his sword at his side. Then he mounted his great white horse and rode out from his castle gate. Down the steep, rough road he went, sitting straight and tall, and looking brave and strong as a knight should look.

On through the little village at the foot of the hill and out across the country he rode. Everywhere he saw rich fields filled with waving grain, everywhere there was peace and plenty.

He rode on and on until at last he came into a part of the country he had never seen before. He noticed that there were no men working in the fields. The houses which he passed stood silent and empty. The grass along the roadside was scorched as if a fire had passed over it. A field of wheat was all trampled and burned.

St. George drew up his horse, and looked carefully about him. Everywhere there was silence and desolation. "What can be the dreadful thing which has driven all the people from their homes? I must find out, and give them help if I can," he said.

But there was no one to ask, so St. George rode forward until at last far in the distance he saw the walls of a city. "Here surely I shall find someone who can tell me the cause of all this," he said, so he rode more swiftly toward the city.

Just then the great gate opened and St. George saw crowds of people standing inside the wall. Some of them were weeping, all of them seemed afraid. As St. George watched, he saw a beautiful maiden dressed in white, with a girdle of scarlet about her waist, pass through the gate alone. The gate clanged shut and the maiden walked along the road, weeping bitterly. She did not see St. George who was riding quickly toward her.

"Maiden, why do you weep?" he asked as he reached her side.

She looked up at St. George sitting there on his horse, so straight and tall and beautiful. "Oh, Sir Knight!" she cried, "ride quickly from this place. You know not the danger you are in!"

"Danger!" said St. George. "Do you think a knight would flee from danger? Besides, you, a fair girl, are here alone. Think you a knight would leave you so? Tell me your trouble that I may help you."

"No! No!" she cried, "hasten away. You would only lose your life. There is a terrible dragon near. He may come at any moment. One breath would destroy you if he found you here. Go! Go quickly!"

"Tell me more of this," said St. George sternly. "Why are you here alone to meet this dragon? Are there no men left in your city?"

"Oh," said the maiden, "my father, the King, is old and feeble. He has only me to help him take care of his people. This terrible dragon has driven them from their homes, carried away their cattle, and ruined their crops. They have all come within the walls of the city for safety. For weeks now the dragon has come to the very gates of the city. We have been forced to give him two sheep each day for his breakfast.

"Yesterday there were no sheep left to give, so he said that unless a young maiden were given him today he would break down the walls and destroy the city. The people cried to my father to save them, but he could do nothing. I am going to give myself to the dragon. Perhaps if he has me, the Princess, he may spare our people."

"Lead the way, brave Princess. Show me where this monster

may be found."

When the Princess saw St. George's flashing eyes and great, strong arm as he drew forth his sword, she felt afraid no more. Turning, she led the way to a shining pool.

"There's where he stays," she whispered. "See, the water moves. He is waking."

St. George saw the head of the dragon lifted from the pool. Fold on fold he rose from the water. When he saw St. George he gave a roar of rage and plunged toward him. The smoke and flames flew from his nostrils, and he opened his great jaws as if to swallow both the knight and his horse.

St. George shouted and, waving his sword above his head, rode at the dragon. Quick and hard came the blows from St. George's sword. It was a terrible battle.

At last the dragon was wounded. He roared with pain and plunged at St. George, opening his great mouth close to the brave knight's head.

St. George looked carefully, then struck with all his strength straight down through the dragon's throat, and he fell at the horse's feet—dead.

Then St. George shouted for joy at his victory. He called to the Princess. She came and stood beside him.

"Give me the girdle from about your waist, O Princess," said St. George.

The Princess gave him her girdle and St. George bound it around the dragon's neck, and they pulled the dragon after them by that little silken ribbon back to the city so that all of the people could see that the dragon could never harm them again.

When they saw St. George bringing the Princess back in safety and knew that the dragon was slain, they threw open the gates of the city and sent up great shouts of joy.

The King heard them and came out from his palace to see why the people were shouting. When he saw his daughter safe he was the happiest of them all.

"O brave knight," he said, "I am old and weak. Stay here and
help me guard my people from harm."

"I'll stay as long as ever you have need of me," St. George answered.[31]

Sir George's piercing reflection is soul impacting: "But somewhere perhaps there is trouble and fear. There may be someplace where little children cannot play in safety, some woman may have been carried away from
her home—perhaps there are even dragons left to be slain. Tomorrow, I
shall ride away and never stop until I find work which only a knight can
do." Sir George was gripped with a sense of mission, a sense of destiny, a
sense of call.

God longs for every one of us to live our lives with a sense of call. That
is, an invitation to purpose. Such a purpose transcends vocation, geogra-
phy, and even circumstances. It is all about doing what we were built to do.

> For it is by grace you have been saved, through faith—and this
> not from yourselves, it is the gift of God—not by works, so that
> no one can boast. For we are God's workmanship, created in
> Christ Jesus to do good works, which God prepared in advance
> for us to do. (Ephesians 2:8-10, NIV)

GOD CALLS US INTO RELATIONSHIP

Paul assures us that we have been invited into a relationship with God
solely and completely because of the grace of God. No one has any impressive "works" to claim as being worthy or meritorious before God. No one
can boast. God is gracious and he has offered to us a free gift of salvation.
(Ephesians 2:8-9)

GOD CALLS US INTO MISSION

God's gracious gift does not stop with salvation. In his grace, he also invites us into partnership in the work of God (Ephesians 2:10). Paul says, "We" (people of faith; adopted by God) are his "workmanship." This is the Greek work *poiema*, from which we derive the word poem. Thus, we are individual works of poetry. We are individual works of art. We are all unique masterpieces.

We are "created" (creation of life is a work only God can do) "in Christ" for the purpose of doing "good works." These unique, purposeful works were "prepared in advance for us to do." What is in view here is that our job descriptions were all pre-purposed and pre-designed. In fact, what is suggested here is a kind of pre-engineering, the way furniture is sometimes boxed for home assembly.

Every believer is called into a relationship with God and into a purposeful calling to be used by God. God wants to use us, regardless of our family or origin, regardless of our intellectual capacity, regardless of our physical appearance, regardless of our natural abilities. God calls us and wants to use us.

It should be a major goal for every believer to discover this personal sense of mission and give themselves wholly to this fulfillment. This will be explored further in future chapters.

ASSIGNMENT: *What do you think your purpose or calling might be? What steps will you take to either discover your calling or refine your calling?*

DISCUSSION: *Discuss the connection between meaning and motivation. How does a sense of mission give you energy?*

26

Assurance That God Strengthens Us and Matures Us

Spiritual growth leading to maturity is an anticipated process in the life of the believer. God is the one who strengthens. However, this does not occur automatically, and not with us passively standing by. Paul addresses this theme numerous times, with the Epistle to the Philippians being one of these passages.

> *Therefore, my dear friends, as you have always obeyed—not only in my presence, but now much more in my absence—continue to work out your salvation with fear and trembling, for it is God who works in you to will and to act according to his good purpose.*
>
> *Do everything without complaining or arguing, so that you may become blameless and pure, children of God without fault in a crooked and depraved generation, in which you shine like stars in the universe as you hold out the word of life—in order that I*

may boast on the day of Christ that I did not run or labor for nothing. But even if I am being poured out like a drink offering on the sacrifice and service coming from your faith, I am glad and re-joice with all of you. So you too should be glad and rejoice with me. (Philippians 2:12-18, NIV)

GOD STRENGTHENS US

Paul acknowledges the obedience and faithful practices of the Philippians (2:12), and then invites them to "continue to work out your salvation." Literally, he is asking them to "carry out to completion," like a student "working out" a math problem. They were to do so with fear and trembling; that is, with a healthy respect and deep reverence for God. Paul's essential point is that they were to be conscientious, diligent, intentional, and thoughtful in their efforts to grow, change, mature, and in this case to adopt and exhibit this virtue of selflessness (which was the focus of Philippians 2:1-11).

However, Paul takes an interesting turn in verse 13, where he assures them that it is, after all, God who "works in you, to will and act according to his good purpose." Initially, maturity is made our responsibility, but in the next breath we discover that maturity is God's work. This is somewhat paradoxical. Paul is talking about this mysterious, radical, counter-intuitive virtue of selfishness and he knows what the Philippian believers are going to ask: How? Paul's answer: It is a mysterious combination and interface of the human and the divine.

This cooperative working may be described this way. When I work out, God works through; when I start, God finishes; when I put in the effort, God supplies the energy.

Throughout the remainder of this chapter, Paul tells believers to work on their attitude (don't grumble and complain because you didn't get your own way). Then, Paul tells believers to work on their reputation (amidst a polluted environment). Finally, Paul tells believers to work on their testimony, using the imagery of stars. Stars shine individually and as clusters, creating beauty and drawing attention.

GOD MATURES US

If anyone else thinks he has reasons to put confidence in the flesh, I have more: circumcised on the eighth day, of the people of Israel, of the tribe of Benjamin, a Hebrew of Hebrews; in regard to the law, a Pharisee; as for zeal, persecuting the church; as for legalistic righteousness, faultless.

But whatever was to my profit I now consider loss for the sake of Christ. What is more, I consider everything a loss compared to the surpassing greatness of knowing Christ Jesus my Lord, for whose sake I have lost all things. I consider them rubbish, that I may gain Christ and be found in him, not having a righteousness of my own that comes from the law, but that which is through faith in Christ—the righteousness that comes from God and is by faith. I want to know Christ and the power of his resurrection and the fellowship of sharing in his sufferings, becoming like him in his death, and so, somehow, to attain to the resurrection from the dead.

Not that I have already obtained all this, or have already been made perfect, but I press on to take hold of that for which Christ Jesus took hold of me. Brothers, I do not consider myself yet to have taken hold of it. But one thing I do: Forgetting what is behind and straining toward what is ahead, I press on toward the goal to win the prize for which God has called me heavenward in Christ Jesus.

All of us who are mature should take such a view of things. And if on some point you think differently, that too God will make clear to you. Only let us live up to what we have already attained.

Join with others in following my example, brothers, and take note of those who live according to the pattern we gave you. For, as I have often told you before and now say again even with tears, many live as enemies of the cross of Christ. Their destiny is destruction, their god is their stomach, and their glory is in their shame. Their mind is on earthly things. But our citizenship is in heaven. And we eagerly await a Savior from there, the Lord Jesus Christ, who, by the power that enables him to bring everything under his control, will transform our lowly bodies so that they will be like his glorious body. (Philippians 3:4-21, NIV)

We all want to see change take place in our lives. We want to see healthy, mature progress to our character and behaviour. What does "spiritual maturity" look like? When you think of a "holy man" or a "holy woman" what images come to your mind? Spiritual maturity has been described as "a grown-up relationship with the Holy Spirit."[32] To be a "grown-up" implies, time, health, seasoning, life experiences, and perspective—good perspective, even wisdom. That is why we sometimes will say of a young person, "They are very mature for their age," and why we also sometimes say of adults, "You are acting very childish and immature."

In Philippians 3, Paul addresses the theme of the believer's motivation and maturity. In the earlier section of Chapter 3, Paul vulnerably shares his personal story and how he once lived a morally-driven life. However, it was a desperately unfulfilled life. He offers the timeless principle that self-focused motivation leaves us wanting, but a Christ-focused motivation leaves us satisfied. Paul used to be driven by the thought that he could earn God's attention and God's reward of heaven. Paul, in the end, discovered that such attempts made in his own strength left him empty. However, when he met Christ, he was introduced to a simple but radically life-altering motivation of wanting to know and serve Christ. Now his motivation was rooted in relationship.

Paul explains this difficult concept passionately, assertively, and intensely. Knowing this is a little heady and abstract, Paul moves into application mode and helps us understand how to live with a mature motivation. Paul addresses some helpful arenas of application.

First, maturity is measured by one's motivation. Verse 15 speaks to the mature and we are challenged to "take such a view;" namely, to follow Paul's example. Second, Paul explains how maturity is measured by integrity. Verse 16 delineates how when we come into a relationship with Christ we are positionally, judicially, and legally declared righteous. Paul's point is this: if we are viewed as righteous, we should live righteously. We should live with integrity. Integrity is an agreement between what we say we believe and how we actually live. Third, Paul says that maturity is sustained by following godly examples (3:17-19). Lastly, Paul tells us that maturity is sustained by remembering where you are going. We are reminded that our citizenship is in heaven, from the time we first believed (3:20-21).

John Newton once said, "I have ever to confess, with sorrow, that I am far from being what I ought to be, and far from what I wish to be, but also—Bless be God's name—to testify that I am far, very far from what I once was." Maturity is not arrival, but it is a grown-up relationship with Christ. Change is a lifelong process, so let's keep growing. Let's keep doing our part, and God will do his part.

ASSIGNMENT: *What needs to change in your life? What steps are you prompted to make that will invite the strength of God so that you can see change take place in your life?*

DISCUSSION: *Why are there so many believers who have been Christians for many years, but lack spiritual maturity?*

—————— 27 ——————
Discovering a New Community

The word "church" creates a host of diverse images. To some, a church is a building. To others, church is the church, an institution. To still others, church is equivalent to a one-hour worship assembly (often unfortunately perceived as irrelevant and boring). Some have happy memories of "church," some have tragic memories, while many have no idea what "church" does or should look like.

The church is essentially the community of believers. The church is an abstract, theological community in that it is made up of all believers, from all places, and all times, living and dead. However, the church expresses itself locally as well. Perhaps the best description of the church in action is found in Acts 2.

> They devoted themselves to the apostles' teaching and to the fellowship, to the breaking of bread and to prayer. Everyone was filled with awe, and many wonders and miraculous signs were

done by the apostles. All the believers were together and had eve-
rything in common. Selling their possessions and goods, they gave
to anyone as he had need. Every day they continued to meet to-
gether in the temple courts. They broke bread in their homes and
ate together with glad and sincere hearts, praising God and enjoy-
ing the favor of all the people. And the Lord added to their num-
ber daily those who were being saved. (Acts 2:42-47, NIV)

This is a wonderful and inspiring paragraph in Scripture. It speaks of worship and devotion. It reflects selfless mission and compassion. It tells about spiritual growth and training. It describes internal harmony as well as external reputation, resulting in growth and expansion. This passage does not define the church, but it does describe its activities. If we were to define the church, we might employ something simple and straightforward, such as: The church is a spiritual community organized to do God's will.

A SPIRITUAL COMMUNITY

The word "church" is a Greek word that simply means "called out ones" (*ecclesia*). It is a people, a community, a gathering. When we place our trust in Christ, we became part of this community. Children obviously gather within the community, but the hope and expectation is that they will one day make the intentional decision to follow Jesus themselves. The same is hoped for friends and spiritual seekers. However, at its core, the church is a spiritual community, not a country club. It is a spiritual community that is free to join. It is a spiritual community that welcomes all who want to discover faith. It has no ethnic boundaries. It is not the same as Israel, and yet it is not uniquely gentile. It is a spiritual community for people of all ethnic, cultural, and economic backgrounds. It was never understood as a building. It was always people. In fact, in the writings of Paul, we have the church most often described as a "body," a living community.[33]

ORGANIZED

The word "organization" can be a rich, meaningful word, but it can also create images of hollow structure, empty traditions, legalistic rules. All organizations risk becoming institutionalized over time. Unfortunately, the history of the church is no exception. Being aware of this propensity should help safeguard against institutionalism, and we should not fear being organized.

As an organized community, the church does have structure. It requires leadership. It has a mission. It initiates plans. It gathers to meet for worship and education. We may debate the nature and parameters of that organizational structure, but four or five people having lattes at a coffee shop once every few months does not constitute a church.

TO DO GOD'S WILL

The church has a mission, a purpose, a reason. This purpose is embodied in two great statements: The Great Commandment and the Great Commission.

> *Hearing that Jesus had silenced the Sadducees, the Pharisees got together. One of them, an expert in the law, tested him with this question: "Teacher, which is the greatest commandment in the Law?"*
>
> *Jesus replied: "'Love the Lord your God with all your heart and with all your soul and with all your mind.' This is the first and greatest commandment. And the second is like it: 'Love your neighbor as yourself.' All the Law and the Prophets hang on these two commandments"* (Matthew 22:34-40).
>
> *Then Jesus came to them and said, "All authority in heaven and on earth has been given to me. Therefore go and make disciples*

of all nations, baptizing them in the name of the Father and of the
Son and of the Holy Spirit, and teaching them to obey everything
I have commanded you. And surely I am with you always, to the
very end of the age." (Matthew 28:18-20, NIV)

The Acts 2 church reflected these qualities: a spiritual community organized to do God's will. In this community, we find friendship, encouragement, ministry, care, and challenge. We become a part of something larger, and more meaningful. We have a community, a family with which to face the challenges of life and offer service to a needy world.

ASSIGNMENT: *What could you do to increase your participation in your local church?*

DISCUSSION: *Why do some believers not value the church?*

PART THREE

The Path of Maturing

INTRODUCTION

As we round corners, trek hills and valleys, and navigate the paths before us, we find ourselves becoming more and more comfortable with the journey. Our faith becomes more real, more passionate, and more robust. God becomes less of a philosophical being and more of a Father. The Bible increasingly becomes our indispensible roadmap and guide. And to make the journey ever interesting, God brings people into our lives to walk the path together in community.

This is the path of spiritual growth and maturity. It may be likened to a season of spiritual adolescence leading to spiritual adulthood. We are processing our faith, spiritual truths, and life experiences. Our beliefs are increasingly becoming convictions that we own ourselves. The Apostle Paul stresses the significance of growth and stable maturity when he reminds the leaders at the church of Ephesus of their primary responsibility of discipleship. He says:

And He gave some as apostles, and some as prophets, and some

*as evangelists, and some as pastors and teachers, for the equip-
ping of the saints for the work of service, to the building up of the
body of Christ; until we all attain to the unity of the faith, and of
the knowledge of the Son of God, to a mature man, to the measure of the stature which belongs to the fullness of Christ.*

*As a result, we are no longer to be children, tossed here and
there by waves and carried about by every wind of doctrine, by
the trickery of men, by craftiness in deceitful scheming; but
speaking the truth in love, we are to grow up in all aspects into
Him who is the head, even Christ, from whom the whole body,
being fitted and held together by what every joint supplies, according to the proper working of each individual part, causes the
growth of the body for the building up of itself in love.* (Ephesians
4:11-16, NASB)

We mature in community and we are equipped to serve as a part of the
body of Christ. The result is that we are further grounded in our faith.
Along this path we will glean an overview of the theme of Scripture. We
will explore the major theological themes that link truths together as a system. Finally, we will investigate and reflect more deeply on our inner life
and the role of character.

Stay the course.

28

The Nature of the Bible

We began our reflections on the Bible in Chapter 11 as we explored our new source of truth. In this study, we will seek to drill down deeper. The Bible continues to be the world's bestseller, a text of immense personal, religious, and cultural influence, and a work that defies human explanation in that it was written over 1500 years by at least forty different authors and yet reflects an incredible unity of theme and purpose. Understanding the role of the Bible in the Christian faith is absolutely pivotal.

REVELATION

Epistemology is the study of knowledge. How do we come to know things? We can do so through empirical study or through rational inquiry. We may also reflect on intuition or innate ideas. All of these approaches introduce a host of complex philosophical questions. The foundational presupposition that Christianity is based on is the assumption that an infinite and yet personal God would want to make himself known. Revelation then is reasonable. For an all-powerful supernatural being to reveal himself is not incongruent or unreasonable. The content of this revelation becomes a source of information. Indeed, faith is still required, but it is a reasonable faith.

Thus, the Christian faith and its foundational beliefs are rooted in the view that God has revealed truth to us so that we may know true things about him. The Bible describes how God has revealed himself through nature, direct revelation, visions, dreams, miracles, supernatural events, prophecies, prophets, circumstances, pain, joy, intuition, the faith community, inspired text, and ultimately through Jesus Christ. It is the inspired text that we want to explore here, as it is this "text" or "truth" that we can objectively interact with and under which bring our lives into accountability.

INSPIRATION

The view that God has revealed himself is a theme that runs throughout the Scriptures. Throughout the Old Testament, we repeatedly read phrases like: "This is what the Lord God Almighty says..." or "The Word of the Lord came to me..." However, the concept of inspiration is addressed specifically in a few key texts.

> *All Scripture is inspired by God and profitable for teaching, for reproof, for correction, for training in righteousness; so that the man of God may be adequate, equipped for every good work.* (2 Timothy 3:16-17, NASB)

> *But know this first of all, that no prophecy of Scripture is a matter of one's own interpretation, for no prophecy was ever made by an act of human will, but men moved by the Holy Spirit spoke from God.* (2 Peter 1:20-21, NASB)

The word often translated as "inspired" is the Greek word *theopneus-tos* and means "God-breathed," and thus sourced in God.[34] The Bible claims to be inspired, sourced in God, and therefore true and trustworthy. Jesus, speaking of his Father in heaven, said, "Your word is truth" (John 17:17). A good definition of the inspiration of the Bible would be: God superintending human authors so that they wrote the original autographs, in their own style, infallibly.[35] In the act of inspiration, God is communicating truth to his servant. That servant is then recording truth onto papyrus, but with his own style. This is why, for example, the writing style of John differs significantly from the writing style of Paul. Both are still true and inspired, but reflect stylistic distinction. Finally, even though we can have a high degree of trust in our present versions and translations, we should acknowledge that what was "inspired" were the original texts in the original language. This is why it is helpful to trace the etymology of a word to its original usage, or why we continue to value Biblical scholars who interact with the original languages. Understanding the text in its original setting and language may breathe significant insight.

AUTHORITY

2 Timothy 3:16-17 both implies and states that because the Word of God is inspired, it is therefore authoritative. The Bible should rightfully have a place over our thinking, feelings, and behaviours. The Bible should guide and define our morality, our ethics, and our theology. As disciples, we must devote ourselves to reading, interacting, meditating, memorizing, and ultimately submitting to the authority of the Bible in our lives. This begins with the routine discipline of spending time in God's Word.

ALL TRUTH IS GOD'S TRUTH

While we embrace the truthfulness and reliability of the Bible, we need not avoid other sources of inquiry. The sciences, be they hard or soft, can offer insight to understanding our world. Philosophical inquiry, reason, logic, and empirical analysis can all breathe insight into our pursuits to comprehend and explain how our world works. The Bible is not intended to be an exhaustive revelation of truth; thus, truth may come from other sources. However, because we do believe that the Bible is true, we ought to bring other data under the scrutiny of the Biblical text and theme. The Bible ought to be our ultimate authority.

ASSIGNMENT: *The Appendix at the back of this book has a list of the following Bible verses: Romans 3:23, Romans 5:8, Romans 6:23, John 3:16, John 1:12, Luke 9:23, 2 Corinthians 5:17, John 5:24, Ephesians 2:8-10, Romans 12:1-2; 2 Timothy 3:16-17; Psalm 119:9-11; Philippians 4:6-7; 1 Peter 5:7; Isaiah 26:3; Matthew 22:37-39, Matthew 28:19-20, 1 Corinthians 10:31, John 13:34-35, and Mark 10:45. Set a goal of reading, meditating, and memorizing one per week, while being careful to review the verses you have already committed to memory. This is a large assignment that will take time; however, once these verses are inside of us, they will prove life transforming.*

DISCUSSION: *Discuss the nature of the authority of Scripture over such matters as morality, philosophy, art, and science. How should we handle conflict between these?*

29

The Content and Themes of the Bible

One of the objectives of this book is to get us into God's Word. Each theme that we have examined has been significantly rooted in the teachings of Scripture. The Bible is our anchor. Christians are a people of "The Book" (which is what the word *Bible* means). While we have discussed how to study a passage of Scripture, eventually we must learn how to interact with the Bible in its entirety, in its context, and in its relationship to other books within the Bible. Too often, those who are new in the faith start reading in Genesis, but before long discover that the Bible is not assembled chronologically. People, places, and events are spoken of, with the assumption that the reader understands what is going on. The result is often confusion and discouragement. The following is designed to be a basic overview of the Bible and its attending themes. Please read this material several times and discuss your questions.

THE TESTAMENTS OF THE BIBLE

- There are 66 books that make up the Bible, which is divided into the Old Testament and the New Testament. These books are written by numerous authors over a period of 1500 years.
- There are 39 books in the Old Testament which address creation, the early history of human beings, the history of Israel, as well as wisdom literature.
- There are 27 books in the New Testament which address the life of Jesus Christ, the development of the early church, as well as many early writings of early church leaders.

THE OLD TESTAMENT BOOKS OF THE BIBLE

The 39 Old Testament books include the following classifications:

- Books of the Law (often called the Pentateuch, written by Moses)
  1. Genesis (creation; early humanity; the establishment of Israel)
  2. Exodus (the bondage and deliverance of Israel from Egypt; the giving of the law)
  3. Leviticus (details surrounding the law; the character of God)
  4. Numbers (details surrounding the law; Israel's wanderings in the wilderness)
  5. Deuteronomy (rehearsing the law; recapitulation of Israel's wanderings)
- Books of History (from Israel's entry into the promised land through the Kings)
  1. Joshua (Israel enters the Promised Land of Canaan;

conflict in the land)

2. Judges (Israel conquering Canaan; Israel's cycles of failure and restoration)

3. Ruth (tender story of family loyalty; inclusion of a Gentile in the people of God)

4. 1 Samuel (Israel's first king; the rise of David; conflict between David and Saul)

5. 2 Samuel (David's coronation as king; conflict in David's life and kingdom)

6. 1 Kings (rise of Solomon; the kingdom divides into two, Israel and Judah)

7. 2 Kings (the decline and captivities of the two divided kingdoms)

8. 1 Chronicles (retracing the rise of David as king)

9. 2 Chronicles (retracing the rise of Solomon as king; kings of Judah)

10. Ezra (the restoration of Israel following the Babylonian captivity)

11. Nehemiah (the rebuilding of the walls of Jerusalem following the captivity)

12. Esther (during the reign of Persian king Xerxes, a noble queen saves Israel)

- Books of Poetry or Wisdom (poems; songs; proverbs; stories with wise lessons)

1. Job (the tragic story of Job and his exploration of the problem of suffering)

2. Psalms (worship poems; thanksgivings; songs; complaints to God)

3. Proverbs (31 chapters of short, wise sayings or lessons)

4. Ecclesiastes (King Solomon's search for meaning amidst absolute prosperity)

5. Song of Solomon (the courtship and marriage of
   Solomon and his bride)

- Major Prophets (major in the sense that they are
  lengthier)
  1. Isaiah (Isaiah addresses the ills of Judah; numerous
     Messianic prophecies)
  2. Jeremiah (Jeremiah warns Judah of its impending fall
     to the Assyrians)
  3. Lamentations (Jeremiah weeps over the fall of
     Jerusalem and Judah)
  4. Ezekiel (Ezekiel, as an exile in Babylon, ministers to
     fallen Judah)
  5. Daniel (Daniel, as an exile in Babylon, rises to power;
     eschatology)

- Minor Prophets (shorter)
  1. Hosea (prophet of Israel; broken marriage is a symbol
     to the people)
  2. Joel (prophet of Judah; eschatological theme of the
     Day of the Lord)
  3. Amos (prophet of Israel; explores issues of corruption
     and social injustice)
  4. Obadiah (prophet of Judah; denounces the Edomites)
  5. Jonah (prophet of Israel; flees from God; challenges
     Nineveh to repent)
  6. Micah (prophet of Judah; doom; future restoration)
  7. Nahum (prophet of Judah; doom to Nineveh)
  8. Habakkuk (prophet of Judah; explores the question
     why wickedness prospers)
  9. Zephaniah (prophet of Judah; judgment on Judah and
     surrounding nations)
  10. Haggai (ministering in a post-exilic time; appeal to
     rebuild the temple)

11. Zechariah (ministering in a post-exilic time; Israel's future ultimate restoration)

12. Malachi (ministering in a post-exilic time; appeal to passion for God)

THE NEW TESTAMENT BOOKS OF THE BIBLE

The 27 New Testament books include the following classifications:

- The Gospels (addressing the life and works of Christ)
    1. Matthew (written for Jews with emphasis on Jesus the King of Israel)
    2. Mark (written for Romans with emphasis on Jesus the Servant)
    3. Luke (written for Gentiles with emphasis on Jesus the Son of Man)
    4. John (written for Believers with emphasis on Jesus the Son of God)
- History (the history of the early church)
    1. Acts (birth of the church; the rise of Paul; three missionary journeys)
- Pauline Epistles (letters written by the Apostle Paul)
    1. Romans (rich in the theological themes of sin, salvation, and sanctification)
    2. 1 Corinthians (a church riddled in division, theological, and moral conflict)
    3. 2 Corinthians (Paul's follow-up letter; autobiography on Paul)
    4. Galatians (justification by faith alone; issue of legalism is addressed)
    5. Ephesians (what we have in Christ; the church as a living body)
    6. Philippians (Paul explores selflessness, maturity, and

joy while in prison)

7. Colossians (the supremacy of Christ; practical matters)

8. 1 Thessalonians (eschatological themes; appeal to purity)

9. 2 Thessalonians (eschatological themes; appeal to work)

10. 1 Timothy (pastoral themes; warnings and cautions; leadership qualifications)

11. 2 Timothy (pastoral themes; Paul's final farewell)

12. Titus (pastoral themes; leadership qualifications)

13. Philemon (Paul appeals to a former slave-owner to show grace)

- General Epistles (by authors other than Paul)

1. Hebrews (authorship is uncertain; the superiority of Christ and Christianity)

2. James (intensely practical book on living the Christian life)

3. 1 Peter (Christians facing suffering; submission as a way of life)

4. 2 Peter (Christianity in opposition to false teachings)

5. 1 John (fellowship with God and with one another)

6. 2 John (walk in Christ's commandments)

7. 3 John (a personal letter to Gaius; a rebuke of another travelling leader)

8. Jude (beware of false teachings and heresies)

- Prophetic (dealing with the future)

1. Revelation (message to seven churches; events surrounding the return of Christ)

THE HISTORICAL FLOW AND KEY THEMES OF THE BIBLE

- God's purpose in creation is to bring glory to himself. He accomplished this chiefly by creating the cosmos, including human beings with whom he could enjoy relationship (see Psalm 19:1; 1 Corinthians 10:31; Colossians 3:17). The person, glory, and character of God are woven throughout all the books of the Bible.

- The origin of evil on earth occurred with the deception of Eve and the willing rebellion of Adam in eating of the forbidden fruit. Death and sin were now introduced to the world. The implications are universal (Genesis 3:1-24).

- God sets out to pursue human beings. He begins with a man named Abram. It is God's intention to have Abram (later Abraham) become the father of a nation who will live in relationship with God and be a light to the surrounding nations of the world. God expressed his intentions to Abraham through a covenant (Genesis 12:1-3; 13:14-16; 15:18-21; 17:1-8).

- Abraham has a son, Isaac. Isaac has a son, Jacob. Jacob has numerous children, all of whom end up in Egypt. Initially they find safety and provision there. However, in time they experience opposition and slavery. God raises up Moses to deliver the people of Israel from bondage. In their deliverance, Israel is given the law (the Ten Commandments, plus more: Exodus 14:30-31; 20:1-17).

- Israel was told that if they adhered to the law, they would experience the blessing of God, but if they disobeyed the law of God, they would find themselves under his discipline. This was recorded in the Deuteronomic Covenant (Deuteronomy 28:1-30:20).

- The people of Israel sought a king. Their first king, Saul,

proved disastrous. God then chose David to serve as king.
God made a covenant with David, which promised an
eternal king would come from the line of David. This was
a significant Messianic prophecy (2 Samuel 7:12-17).

- The remainder of the Old Testament records Israel's
  struggle with obedience. When Israel walked with God as
  a community, they experienced peace and prosperity.
  However, when they were led by godless kings, they experienced God's discipline. One of the more significant
  disciplines of God was the division of Israel into the
  Northern tribes of Israel and the Southern tribes of Judah
  (where Jerusalem was located). God continued to send
  prophets to his people, appealing to them to repent. God's
  discipline intensified to the point of having the Northern
  kingdom fall to the Assyrians (in 722 B.C.). The Southern
  Kingdom would fall to the Babylonian empire (586 B.C.).
  Most of the major and minor prophets wrote during this
  dark time.

- During this time, there was another key covenant given
  that was called the new covenant. This promise of God
  looked forward to a time of restoration with his people
  (Jeremiah 31:31-34).

- Following the writings of Malachi (the last book of the Old
  Testament), Israel entered a four hundred year period of
  silence from God, often called the "silent years." During
  this time, Alexander the Great would rise in prominence
  and then Rome would emerge as the next great world-
  power.

- In Israel, Jewish groups would divide into camps, including the Pharisees, Sadducees, the Essenes, the Scribes, and
  the Herodians. Israel was under the hand of Rome. Herod
  the Great was king, but he was under the sovereignty of

Roman rule. It is into this time that Jesus was born.

- The First Advent of the Messiah was recorded in Matthew, Mark, and Luke. John's Gospel is more theological in the description of the incarnation of Christ. All of the Gospels record how Jesus fulfilled all the Messianic prophecies of the Old Testament. Hopes were building that Jesus would usher in a new political kingdom and oust the Romans. To the surprise of all, even those closest to him, Jesus is betrayed, tried, and crucified.

- In resurrection, all becomes clear. Jesus did bring the kingdom of God. It is both now, and not yet. The "now" aspect of the kingdom of God is that faith in Christ brings us back into a relationship with God. Our sins are forgiven and we become citizens of a new world. We are now called upon to grow personally as we follow Christ, and bring the message of hope and reconciliation to a needy, lost world. This was God's will for Israel, but they failed. God's expectation is that the church now assumes this mantle.

- The task of the Great Commission and global mission will find its completion in the Second Advent of the Messiah. The world will enter a time of great darkness and judgment, followed by the ultimate return of Jesus Christ to establish his ultimate kingdom rule (Revelation 19:1-22:21).

THE THEOLOGICAL THEMES OF THE BIBLE

Theology is, broadly, "the study of God." More specifically, theology is the study of the doctrinal truths addressed in the pages of Scripture. "Biblical Theology" is the examination of the biblical themes in a given passage or section of Scripture. "Systematic Theology" is the categorizing of these themes from an examination of the Scriptures as a whole. Theologians have used these categories for centuries. While the Bible is not written thematically, packaging these themes in these categories does aid us in understanding how truth is integrated and complementary. One of the oldest creedal statements is the historic Apostles' Creed, first written in 390 A.D., and succinctly captures the essential doctrines of historic Christianity.

> *I believe in God, the Father Almighty, Creator of heaven and earth.*
>
> *I believe in Jesus Christ, his only Son, our Lord, who was conceived by the Holy Spirit, born of the virgin Mary, suffered under Pontius Pilate, was crucified, died, and was buried; he descended to the dead. On the third day he rose again; he ascended into heaven, he is seated at the right hand of the Father, and he will come to judge the living and the dead.*
>
> *I believe in the Holy Spirit, the holy catholic church, the communion of saints, the forgiveness of sins, the resurrection of the body, and the life everlasting. Amen.*

The following became the classically held headings of systematic theology (Queen of the Sciences).

- The Study of God the Father (Theology Proper)
- The Study of God the Son (Christology)
- The Study of God the Holy Spirit (Pneumatology)
- The Study of the Bible (Bibliology)
- The Study of Humanity (Anthropology)
- The Study of Sin (Hamartiology, usually linked to Anthropology)
- The Study of Salvation (Soteriology)
- The Study of the Spiritual Life (Sanctification)
- The Study of Angels (Angelology)
- The Study of Demons (Demonology, usually linked to

Angelology)

- The Study of the Church (Ecclesiology)
- The Study of End Times (Eschatology)

ASSIGNMENT: *Study the content and flow of the Bible.*

DISCUSSION: *Is this flow sufficiently clear to you? Where is the flow unclear?*

—— 30 ——

The Nature of God the Father

Earlier, we examined some selected attributes of God, and in that study we sought to enlarge our understanding and appreciation of the greatness and goodness of God. The biblical text employs numerous names and images for God. However, no image, title, or proper name communicates more tenderness than the image of a father. Jesus not only called God "Father," but he invites us to call him "Father" because we are his children.

> For you did not receive a spirit that makes you a slave again to fear, but you received the Spirit of sonship. And by him we cry, "Abba, Father." The Spirit himself testifies with our spirit that we are God's children. Now if we are children, then we are heirs— heirs of God and co-heirs with Christ, if indeed we share in his sufferings in order that we may also share in his glory. (Romans 8:15-17, NIV)

Abba is a uniquely affectionate term which communicates warmth and closeness. The term "papa" or "daddy" may give us some sense of how this word should be understood. It is a tragic reality that some of us have not had the best father figures. Some have known the sting of rejection, the pain of abandonment, the ache of neglect, or the scar of abuse. While such experiences have the power to distort our thinking, the image of a father was intended to be viewed as one of care, strength, and security. The following passages help us form a picture of the perfect father.

GOD THE FATHER LOVES SACRIFICIALLY

This is love: not that we loved God, but that he loved us and sent his Son as an atoning sacrifice for our sins. Dear friends, since God so loved us, we also ought to love one another. (1 John 4:10-11, NIV)

GOD THE FATHER IS A PROVIDER, PROTECTOR, AND DEFENDER

Command those who are rich in this present world not to be arrogant nor to put their hope in wealth, which is so uncertain, but to put their hope in God, who richly provides us with everything for our enjoyment. (1 Timothy 6:17, NIV)

Do not move an ancient boundary stone or encroach on the fields of the fatherless, for their Defender is strong; he will take up their case against you. (Proverbs 23:10-11, NIV)

GOD THE FATHER IS A LEADER AND A GUIDE

The Lord is my shepherd, I shall not be in want. He makes me lie down in green pastures, he leads me beside quiet waters, he restores my soul. He guides me in paths of righteousness for his name's sake. (Psalm 23:1-3, NIV)

GOD THE FATHER IS A COMFORTER AND CONSOLER

Even though I walk through the valley of the shadow of death, I will fear no evil, for you are withme; your rod and your staff, they comfort me. (Psalm 23:4, NIV)

> *May your unfailing love be my comfort, according to your promise to your servant.* (Psalm 119:76, NIV)

GOD THE FATHER IS AN INSTRUCTOR AND CORRECTOR

> *Teach me, O Lord, to follow your decrees; then I will keep them to the end. Give me understanding, and I will keep your law and obey it with all my heart. Direct me in the path of your commands, for there I find delight. Turn my heart toward your statutes and not toward selfish gain. Turn my eyes away from worthless things; preserve my life according to your word.* (Psalm 119:33-37, NIV)

> *And have you forgotten the exhortation that addresses you as sons?*
>
> *"My son, do not regard lightly the discipline of the Lord, nor be weary when reproved by him. For the Lord disciplines the one he loves and chastises every son whom he receives."*
>
> *It is for discipline that you have to endure. God is treating you as sons. For what son is there whom his father does not discipline? If you are left without discipline, in which all have participated, then you are illegitimate children and not sons.* (Hebrews 12:5-11, ESV)

GOD THE FATHER IS ONE WHO GIVES MEANINGFUL FREEDOM

> *The Lord God took the man and put him in the Garden of Eden to work it and take care of it. And the Lord God commanded the man, "You are free to eat from any tree in the garden; but you*

must not eat from the tree of the knowledge of good and evil, for
when you eat of it you will surely die. (Genesis 2:15-17, NIV)

GOD THE FATHER FORGIVES

For as high as the heavens are above the earth, so great is his love
for those who fear him; as far as the east is from the west, so far
has he removed our transgressions from us. As a father has com-
passion on his children, so the Lord has compassion on those who
fear him. (Psalm 103:11-13, NIV)

While God is our Almighty Sovereign Lord whom we should respect
and fear, God is also our Heavenly Father. As our Father, he can be trusted,
he should be listened to, and he should be obeyed. We can go to him as
frightened children needing support, comfort, consolation, and compassion.

ASSIGNMENT: *Describe your father and how the two of you relate or re-*
lated.

DISCUSSION: *What are the practical implications on your life when you*
view God as a Father? Consider each of the above cited characteristics.

—— 31 ——
The Nature of God the Son of God

There are those occasions when a young man and woman meet and they feel an instant sense of compatibility and understanding. They think they know each other. When they become engaged to be married, they realize that their depth of understanding has deepened. After twenty-five years, they realize just how much more there is to discover about their life partner. Knowing God is like this, only so much richer. We have been introduced to Jesus Christ, but it is significant that we understand with increasing depth who he is. In this study, we will explore three movements.

JESUS' IDENTITY AND WORK PROPHESIED

Isaiah was a prophet who lived and prophesied some seven hundred years before the coming of Christ. In these passages, we see how a coming Messiah (anointed one) would redeem God's people. He would be born of a virgin, would establish God's kingdom rule, and yet he would suffer on behalf of his people as a sacrifice.

Therefore the Lord himself will give you a sign: The virgin will be with child and will give birth to a son, and will call him Immanuel. (Isaiah 7:14, NIV)

For to us a child is born, to us a son is given, and the government will be on his shoulders. And he will be called Wonderful Counselor, Mighty God, Everlasting Father, Prince of Peace. Of the increase of his government and peace there will be no end. He will reign on David's throne and over his kingdom, establishing and upholding it with justice and righteousness from that time on and forever. The zeal of the Lord Almighty will accomplish this. (Isaiah 9:6-7, NIV)

Who has believed what he has heard from us? And to whom has the arm of the Lord been revealed? For he grew up before him like a young plant, and like a root out of dry ground; he had no form or majesty that we should look at him, and no beauty that we should desire him. He was despised and rejected by men; a man of sorrows, and acquainted with grief; and as one from whom men hide their faces he was despised, and we esteemed him not.

Surely he has borne our griefs and carried our sorrows; yet we esteemed him stricken, smitten by God, and afflicted. But he was wounded for our transgressions; he was crushed for our iniquities;

upon him was the chastisement that brought us peace, and with his stripes we are healed. All we like sheep have gone astray; we have turned—every one—to his own way; and the Lord has laid on him the iniquity of us all.

He was oppressed, and he was afflicted, yet he opened not his mouth; like a lamb that is led to the slaughter, and like a sheep that before its shearers is silent, so he opened not his mouth. By oppression and judgment he was taken away; and as for his gen-

eration, who considered that he was cut off out of the land of the living, stricken for the transgression of my people? And they made his grave with the wicked and with a rich man in his death, although he had done no violence, and there was no deceit in his mouth.

Yet it was the will of the Lord to crush him; he has put him to grief; when his soul makes an offering for guilt, he shall see his off-spring; he shall prolong his days; the will of the Lord shall prosper in his hand. Out of the anguish of his soul he shall see and be sat-isfied; by his knowledge shall the righteous one, my servant, make many to be accounted righteous, and he shall bear their iniquities. (Isaiah 53:1-12, ESV)

JESUS WAS BORN AS A MAN

The Gospel of Matthew records the birth of Jesus. Here, the prophecy of his virgin birth is realized. It is evident that he is human in that he has a physical mother, and yet divine in the sense that his conception is a super-natural act of God.

Now the birth of Jesus Christ took place in this way. When his mother Mary had been betrothed to Joseph, before they came to-gether she was found to be with child from the Holy Spirit. And her husband Joseph, being a just man and unwilling to put her to shame, resolved to divorce her quietly. But as he considered these things, behold, an angel of the Lord appeared to him in a dream, saying, "Joseph, son of David, do not fear to take Mary as your wife, for that which is conceived in her is from the Holy Spirit. She will bear a son, and you shall call his name Jesus, for he will save his people from their sins." All this took place to fulfill what the Lord had spoken by the prophet:

"Behold, the virgin shall conceive and bear a son, and they shall call his name Immanuel" (which means, God with us). When Joseph woke from sleep, he did as the angel of the Lord com-

manded him: he took his wife, but knew her not until she had given birth to a son. And he called his name Jesus. (Matthew 1:18-25, ESV)

JESUS' IDENTITY, WORK, AND REIGN ARE DECISIVE

Have this attitude in yourselves which was also in Christ Jesus, who, although He existed in the form of God, did not regard equality with God a thing to be grasped, but emptied Himself, taking the form of a bond-servant, and being made in the likeness of men. Being found in appearance as a man, He humbled Himself by becoming obedient to the point of death, even death on a cross. For this reason also, God highly exalted Him, and bestowed on Him the name which is above every name, so that at the name of Jesus EVERY KNEE WILL BOW, of those who are in heaven and on earth and under the earth, and that every tongue will confess that Jesus Christ is Lord, to the glory of God the Father. (Philippians 2:5-11, NASB)

This passage is enormously significant in that it describes the identity of Jesus as being God, and yet he humbled himself to become a man. The phrase "made himself nothing" carries the idea of "emptying himself." Jesus did not cease to be God, but he willingly emptied himself of the glory of God and of the independent use of his divine attributes. He submitted to God the Father by becoming a man. The passage further describes the work of Christ in his death on the cross and continues with the reign of Christ. One day, all of creation will bow to his authority.

ASSIGNMENT: *What does the thought of Jesus becoming human do to your reflections on God? What does the thought of Jesus being God do to your reflections on God?*

DISCUSSION: *Why does culture in general terms not have difficulty in talking about God, but finds it difficult to speak about the person of Jesus by name?*

— 32 —
The Nature of God the Holy Spirit

The Bible most often describes God as the Almighty, Lord, and Father. In the New Testament, we are introduced to the person of Jesus Christ, the Son of God. However, we are also made aware of the person and work of the Holy Spirit. The Holy Spirit is alluded to infrequently in the Old Testament, and significantly in the New Testament. However, there is often a measure of unawareness and bewilderment around the person of the Holy Spirit. The Holy Spirit is also God and is the third person of the Trinity.[36] The following passages will help us understand more fully the identity and workings of God, the Holy Spirit.

THE HOLY SPIRIT IS A PERSON (NOT A FORCE) AND HAS AN INTELLECT

But God has revealed it to us by his Spirit. The Spirit searches all things, even the deep things of God. For who among men knows the thoughts of a man except the man's spirit within him? In the same way no one knows the thoughts of God except the Spirit of God. (1 Corinthians 2:10-11, NIV)

THE HOLY SPIRIT IS A PERSON (NOT A FORCE) AND HAS EMOTIONS

And do not grieve the Holy Spirit of God, with whom you were sealed for the day of redemption. (Ephesians 4:30, NIV)

THE HOLY SPIRIT IS A PERSON (NOT A FORCE) AND HAS A WILL

All these are the work of one and the same Spirit, and he gives them to each one, just as he determines. (1 Corinthians 12:11, NIV)

THE HOLY SPIRIT SHARES THE IDENTITY AND ATTRIBUTES OF GOD

Therefore go and make disciples of all nations, baptizing them in the name of the Father and of the Son and of the Holy Spirit, and teaching them to obey everything I have commanded you. And surely I am with you always, to the very end of the age. (Matthew 28:19-20, NIV)

May the grace of the Lord Jesus Christ, and the love of God, and the fellowship of the Holy Spirit be with you all. (2 Corinthians 13:14, NIV)

Then Peter said, "Ananias, how is it that Satan has so filled your heart that you have lied to the Holy Spirit and have kept for yourself some of the money you received for the land? Didn't it belong to you before it was sold? And after it was sold, wasn't the money at your disposal? What made you think of doing such a thing? You have not lied to men but to God." (Acts. 5:3-4, NIV)

Where can I go from your Spirit? Where can I flee from your presence? (Psalm 139:7, NIV)

The Spirit of God has made me; the breath of the Almighty gives me life. (Job 33:4, NIV)

THE HOLY SPIRIT IS ACTIVE AND AT WORK IN THE LIFE OF THE BELIEVER

And I will ask the Father, and he will give you another Counselor to be with you forever—the Spirit of truth. The world cannot accept him, because it neither sees him nor knows him. But you know him, for he lives with you and will be in you. (John 14:16-17, NIV)

But you will receive power when the Holy Spirit comes on you; and you will be my witnesses in Jerusalem, and in all Judea and Samaria, and to the ends of the earth. (Acts 1:8, NIV)

But the fruit of the Spirit is love, joy, peace, patience, kindness, goodness, faithfulness, gentleness and self-control. Against such things there is no law. (Galatians 5:22-23, NIV)

Do not get drunk on wine, which leads to debauchery. Instead, be filled with the Spirit. (Ephesians 5:18, NIV)

Just as each of us has one body with many members, and these members do not all have the same function, so in Christ we who are many form one body, and each member belongs to all the others. We have different gifts, according to the grace given us. If a man's gift is prophesying, let him use it in proportion to his faith. If it is serving, let him serve; if it is teaching, let him teach; if it is encouraging, let him encourage; if it is contributing to the needs of others, let him give generously; if it is leadership, let him govern diligently; if it is showing mercy, let him do it cheerfully. (Romans 12:4-8, NIV)

This final observation is particularly practical and encouraging. The Holy Spirit is not only with us, but he indwells us. The Holy Spirit gives us supernatural power to carry out the work of God. He gifts us with unique spiritual gifts to be used strategically for ministry purposes. The Holy Spirit brings about changes in our lives and replaces old habits with new virtues such as love, joy, peace, patience, kindness, goodness, faithfulness, gentleness, and self-control. The passage in Ephesians tells us to avoid being under the influence of wine (or anything else for that matter), and to be filled—or under the influence—of the Holy Spirit.

ASSIGNMENT: *The Father is God; the Son is God; the Holy Spirit is God. The Father is not the Son; the Father is not the Holy Spirit; the Son is not the Holy Sprit. God is one in essence; God is three in person. When you think of the relational nature of God, how does God as a Triune being enhance or complement this understanding? What does this do to our view of human unity and harmony in relationships?*

DISCUSSION: *What new discovery did you make with this study?*

33

The Nature of Humanity

Understanding God gives us our anchor. However, we do need to understand ourselves. The study of anthropology, psychology, and sociology all
shed valuable insight on the human condition, but this must be interpreted
through the lens of how God understands us.

OUR ORIGINS

Exploring our origins has surfaced numerous theories and models. Atheis-
tic evolution posits that all forms of life evolved gradually by chance from a
single cell which developed from nonliving chemicals. Theistic evolution
teaches that God started and guided the development of all living forms by
means of biological evolution. Creative evolution presents the model that
nature possesses an imminent life-force which accounts for all evolutional
development and leaps from within. This is sometimes associated with
pantheistic evolution. Progressive creation seeks to take the biblical ac-

count seriously (but with some figures) and suggests that all basic life forms were created by God at different times over millions of years. Fiat creation takes the biblical text seriously and most literally, teaching that all forms of life were created directly and immediately by God within six solar days (Genesis 1:1; Colossians 1:16). The key phrase often linked to creationism is *ex nihilo*, which means "out of nothing." The key premise of *ex nihilo* creation is that the universe is not eternal; only God is.

The issue of origins is significant. One of the most noteworthy assaults that Christianity has sustained over the past two centuries is Darwinian evolution, in that it has offered a theory on the origins of humanity without the need for a divine creator. This debate is significant and ongoing. Evolution, however, does not sufficiently address numerous issues and these issues deserve research and honest discussion.[37] The following are dilemmas, logical conclusions, and questions that the evolutionary model does not sufficiently address:

- We have something. Can nothing produce something?
- We have life. Can the non-living produce the living?
- We have personality. Can the non-personal produce the personal?
- The evidence is that everything produces after its kind. Can one kind produce a new kind?
- All basic life forms began suddenly and abundantly. Can time and chance create life?
- There are great gaps in the fossil record between kinds. Where are the transitional kinds?
- The second law of thermodynamics shows things are running down and not improving. How can evolution suggest that life is evolving and improving?
- In cases of mutations, mutations are invariably weaker, not stronger. Where is the evidence that mutations are

stronger and better?

The theological implications of embracing evolution are defining. Do we come from nothing? Do we come from a divine source? Was there a real historic fall of man? The issues of soul, meaning, morality, and destiny must all be wrestled with as well.

OUR NATURE

> So God created man in his own image, in the image of God he created him; male and female he created them God blessed them and said to them, "Be fruitful and increase in number; fill the earth and subdue it. Rule over the fish of the sea and the birds of the air and over every living creature that moves on the ground."
> (Genesis 1:27-28, NIV)

The Genesis account tells us that man was made in the image of God, having mind (intellect), emotion (feelings), and will (volition). We have been given the stewardship and responsibility of choice. Furthermore, we are like God in that we are relational and social beings. God is an eternal community, reflected in his Triune essence as the Trinity. We are also creative like God. We were charged with the responsibility of naming the animals and the stewardship of ruling earth. We find creative expression through the arts, music, literature, discovery, and like pursuits.

We are also created as two genders, male and female. Both are made in God's image implying equality but distinction. Later in the Genesis account, we read:

> The man gave names to all the cattle, and to the birds of the sky, and to every beast of the field, but for Adam there was not found a helper suitable for him. So the Lord God caused a deep sleep to fall upon the man, and he slept; then He took one of his ribs and closed up the flesh at that place. The Lord God fashioned into a

*woman the rib which He had taken from the man, and brought
her to the man.*

*The man said, "This is now bone of my bones, and flesh of
my flesh; she shall be called Woman, because she was taken out of
Man."*

*For this reason a man shall leave his father and his mother,
and be joined to his wife; and they shall become one flesh.* (Genesis 2:20-24, NASB)

These two unique genders provide the basis for a complementary union called marriage. Biblical marriage was of divine design and origin, was
designed to take place between a man and a woman (heterosexual), was
designed to take place between one man and one woman (monogamous),
was designed to be permanent and enduring, was symbolically sealed
through sexual union, was a covenant (promise) before God in the presence of a community, and was a symbolic reflection of God's covenant relationship with his people (Ephesians 5).

The Bible also defines us as having a material and an immaterial part.
We are a soul-body unity.

*The Lord God formed the man from the dust of the ground
and breathed into his nostrils the breath of life, and the man became a living being.* (Genesis 2:7, NIV)

*Remember him—before the silver cord is severed, or the
golden bowl is broken; before the pitcher is shattered at the
spring, or the wheel broken at the well, and the dust returns to
the ground it came from, and the spirit returns to God who gave
it.* (Ecclesiastes 12:6-7, NIV)

We are more than what we see. We have a soul that will live on. However, we are not just a soul. We have bodies that are a part of who we are.
This is why, for example, when our soul aches it can affect our physical

body and our emotions, and vice versa. This is why we minister to the soul with the Gospel and why we build hospitals and soup kitchens to meet the practical needs of the body.

OUR TRAGIC FALL

Now the serpent was more crafty than any beast of the field which the Lord God had made. And he said to the woman, "Indeed, has God said, 'You shall not eat from any tree of the garden'?"

The woman said to the serpent, "From the fruit of the trees of the garden we may eat; but from the fruit of the tree which is in the middle of the garden, God has said, 'You shall not eat from it or touch it, or you will die.'"

The serpent said to the woman, "You surely will not die!

"For God knows that in the day you eat from it your eyes will be opened, and you will be like God, knowing good and evil."

When the woman saw that the tree was good for food, and that it was a delight to the eyes, and that the tree was desirable to make one wise, she took from its fruit and ate; and she gave also to her husband with her, and he ate. Then the eyes of both of them were opened, and they knew that they were naked; and they sewed fig leaves together and made themselves loin coverings. They heard the sound of the Lord God walking in the garden in the cool of the day, and the man and his wife hid themselves from the presence of the Lord God among the trees of the garden.

Then the Lord God called to the man, and said to him, "Where are you?"

He said, "I heard the sound of You in the garden, and I was afraid because I was naked; so I hid myself."

And He said, "Who told you that you were naked? Have you eaten from the tree of which I commanded you not to eat?"

The man said, "The woman whom You gave to be with me,

she gave me from the tree, and I ate."

Then the Lord God said to the woman, "What is this you have done?"

And the woman said, "The serpent deceived me, and I ate."

The Lord God said to the serpent, "Because you have done this, cursed are you more than all cattle, and more than every beast of the field; on your belly you will go, and dust you will eat all the days of your life; and I will put enmity between you and the woman and between your seed and her seed; He shall bruise you on the head, and you shall bruise him on the heel."

To the woman He said, "I will greatly multiply your pain in childbirth, in pain you will bring forth children; yet your desire will be for your husband, and he will rule over you."

Then to Adam He said, "Because you have listened to the voice of your wife, and have eaten from the tree about which I commanded you, saying, 'You shall not eat from it'; Cursed is the ground because of you; in toil you will eat of it all the days of your life. "Both thorns and thistles it shall grow for you; and you will eat the plants of the field; by the sweat of your face you will eat bread, till you return to the ground, because from it you were taken; for you are dust, and to dust you shall return." (Genesis 3:1-19, NASB)

This is most often referred to as the fall of humanity. While Eve was deceived, Adam wilfully, knowingly disobeyed God. This is the essence of sin: disobeying God. More specifically, sin is believing that God is somehow deficient and that we, in our decisions of self-governance, are better off. Disobedience is rooted in disbelief.

The consequences were far-reaching. We now experience pain and physical death, along with spiritual death (Ephesians 2:1) that ultimately becomes eternal death (Revelation 20:4). The totality of who we are was affected, and we became depraved (see also Genesis 6:5; Psalm 14:1-3; Mark 7:20-23). All of humanity was now ill, polluted, sick, in prison, poor, broken, and disconnected from God and from each other. Even our environment was affected (Genesis 3:16-19; Romans 8:19-21).

Paul, in Romans 3, describes humanity with dark candour as he quotes from other passages:

> *What then? Are we better than they? Not at all; for we have already charged that both Jews and Greeks are all under sin; as it is written, "THERE IS NONE RIGHTEOUS, NOT EVEN ONE; THERE IS NONE WHO UNDERSTANDS, THERE IS NONE WHO SEEKS FOR GOD; ALL HAVE TURNED ASIDE, TOGETHER THEY HAVE BECOME USELESS; THERE IS NONE WHO DOES GOOD, THERE IS NOT EVEN ONE. THEIR THROAT IS AN OPEN GRAVE, WITH THEIR TONGUES THEY KEEP DECEIVING, THE POISON OF ASPS IS UNDER THEIR LIPS; WHOSE MOUTH IS FULL OF CURSING AND BITTERNESS; THEIR FEET ARE SWIFT TO SHED BLOOD, DESTRUCTION AND MISERY ARE IN THEIR PATHS, AND THE PATH OF PEACE THEY HAVE NOT KNOWN. THERE IS NO FEAR OF GOD BEFORE THEIR EYES."*
>
> *Now we know that whatever the Law says, it speaks to those who are under the Law, so that every mouth may be closed and all the world may become accountable to God; because by the works of the Law no flesh will be justified in His sight; for through the Law comes the knowledge of sin.*
>
> *But now apart from the Law the righteousness of God has been manifested, being witnessed by the Law and the Prophets, even the righteousness of God through faith in Jesus Christ for all those who believe; for there is no distinction; for all have sinned and fall short of the glory of God, being justified as a gift by His grace through the redemption which is in Christ Jesus; whom God displayed publicly as a propitiation in His blood through faith. This was to demonstrate His righteousness, because in the*

forbearance of God He passed over the sins previously commit-
ted; for the demonstration, I say, of His righteousness at the pre-
sent time, so that He would be just and the justifier of the one
who has faith in Jesus. (Romans 3:9-26, NASB)

OUR HOPE

As dark as this description is, we are still made in God's image and are
deeply loved by God. God has chosen to pursue us in Christ and therein
lies our hope. This is what we will next examine.

ASSIGNMENT: *Explore further the issues related to the theory of evolution.*

DISCUSSION: *When you consider your own depravity and sin, what does*
this do to any attitudes of pride?

34

The Nature of Salvation

In the previous chapter, we were humbled and painfully reminded of how dark the human soul had become. Indeed, we are all capable of deep ugliness, selfishness, and sin. Thankfully, God was not dissuaded by our hard and evil hearts.

> For he has rescued us from the dominion of darkness and brought us into the kingdom of the Son he loves, in whom we have redemption, the forgiveness of sins. (Colossians 1:13-14, NIV)

A rescue was launched by God Almighty. This rescue plan involved deep sacrifice: the death of Jesus, God's Son. The language of salvation is diverse in the Bible, particularly in the Gospels. The following is a list of some of the ways salvation is discussed:

- Redemptive language: The rescuer pays our debt by offering his own life.

- Salvific language: The heavenly liberator comes to the rescue of his oppressed people.

- Sacrificial language: The shedding and sprinkling of Christ's blood atones, satisfies God.

- Messianic language: The breaking in of the age of God's promised rule.

- Mystic language: The receiving and enjoying "eternal life," being "in Christ," are all mysterious.

- Legal language: The righteous judge pronounces the unrighteous forgiven. We are justified.

- Personal language: The Father reconciles his wayward children. This is a relational element.

- Cosmic language: The universal Lord claims universal dominion over the powers of evil.[38]

Take some time to carefully interact with these passages on salvation. They are rich in meaning and implications.

GOD THE FATHER IS RESPONSIBLE FOR LEADING AND DRAWING US TO SALVATION (ELECTION) AND KEEPING US IN THE GRIP OF HIS LOVE (SECURITY)

Blessed be the God and Father of our Lord Jesus Christ, who has blessed us in Christ with every spiritual blessing in the heavenly places, even as he chose us in him before the foundation of the world, that we should be holy and blameless before him. In love he predestined us for adoption as sons through Jesus Christ, according to the purpose of his will, to the praise of his glorious grace, with which he has blessed us in the Beloved. In him we have redemption through his blood, the forgiveness of our trespasses, according to the riches of his grace, which he lavished upon us, in all wisdom and insight making known to us the mystery of his will, according to his purpose, which he set forth in

Christ as a plan for the fullness of time, to unite all things in him,
things in heaven and things on earth.

In him we have obtained an inheritance, having been predes-
tined according to the purpose of him who works all things ac-
cording to the counsel of his will, so that we who were the first to
hope in Christ might be to the praise of his glory. In him you also,
when you heard the word of truth, the Gospel of your salvation,
and believed in him, were sealed with the promised Holy Spirit,
who is the guarantee of our inheritance until we acquire posses-
sion of it, to the praise of his glory. (Ephesians. 1:3-14, ESV)

GOD THE SON IS RESPONSIBLE FOR OUR BEING MADE RIGHTEOUS (JUSTIFICATION)

That is why it depends on faith, in order that the promise may
rest on grace and be guaranteed to all his offspring—not only to
the adherent of the law but also to the one who shares the faith of
Abraham, who is the father of us all, as it is written, "I have made
you the father of many nations"—in the presence of the God in
whom he believed, who gives life to the dead and calls into exis-
tence the things that do not exist. In hope he believed against
hope, that he should become the father of many nations, as he
had been told, "So shall your offspring be." He did not weaken in
faith when he considered his own body, which was as good as
dead (since he was about a hundred years old), or when he con-
sidered the barrenness of Sarah's womb. No distrust made him
waver concerning the promise of God, but he grew strong in his
faith as he gave glory to God, fully convinced that God was able to
do what he had promised. That is why his faith was "counted to
him as righteousness." But the words "it was counted to him"
were not written for his sake alone, but for ours also. It will be
counted to us who believe in him who raised from the dead Jesus
our Lord, who was delivered up for our trespasses and raised for
our justification. (Romans 4:16-25)

Therefore, since we have been justified by faith, we have peace with God through our Lord Jesus Christ. Through him we have also obtained access by faith into this grace in which we stand, and we rejoice in hope of the glory of God. More than that, we rejoice in our sufferings, knowing that suffering produces endurance, and endurance produces character, and character produces hope, and hope does not put us to shame, because God's love has been poured into our hearts through the Holy Spirit who has been given to us.

For while we were still weak, at the right time Christ died for the ungodly. For one will scarcely die for a righteous person—though perhaps for a good person one would dare even to die—but God shows his love for us in that while we were still sinners, Christ died for us. Since, therefore, we have now been justified by his blood, much more shall we be saved by him from the wrath of God. For if while we were enemies we were reconciled to God by the death of his Son, much more, now that we are reconciled, shall we be saved by his life. More than that, we also rejoice in God through our Lord Jesus Christ, through whom we have now received reconciliation.

Therefore, just as sin came into the world through one man, and death through sin, and so death spread to all men because all sinned—for sin indeed was in the world before the law was given, but sin is not counted where there is no law. Yet death reigned from Adam to Moses, even over those whose sinning was not like the transgression of Adam, who was a type of the one who was to come.

But the free gift is not like the trespass. For if many died through one man's trespass, much more have the grace of God and the free gift by the grace of that one man Jesus Christ abounded for many. And the free gift is not like the result of that one man's sin. For the judgment following one trespass brought condemnation, but the free gift following many trespasses brought justification. For if, because of one man's trespass, death reigned through that one man, much more will those who receive the abundance of grace and the free gift of righteousness reign in life through the one man Jesus Christ.

Therefore, as one trespass led to condemnation for all men, so one act of righteousness leads to justification and life for all men. For as by the one man's disobedience the many were made sinners, so by the one man's obedience the many will be made righteous. Now the law came in to increase the trespass, but where sin increased, grace abounded all the more, so that, as sin reigned in death, grace also might reign through righteousness leading to eternal life through Jesus Christ our Lord. (Romans 5:1-21, ESV)

GOD THE HOLY SPIRIT IS RESPONSIBLE FOR MAKING US INTO NEW PEOPLE (REGENERATION)

For we ourselves were also once foolish, disobedient, deceived, serving various lusts and pleasures, living in malice and envy, hateful and hating one another. But when the kindness and the love of God our Savior toward man appeared, not by works of righteousness which we have done, but according to His mercy He saved us, through the washing of regeneration and renewing of the Holy Spirit, whom He poured out on us abundantly through Jesus Christ our Savior, that having been justified by His grace we should become heirs according to the hope of eternal life. (Titus 3:3-7, NKJV)

ASSIGNMENT: As you reflect on your depravity and God's benevolence, what is your response to God?

DISCUSSION: Do you sometimes question your salvation? What does this study do for your faith?

35

The Nature of the Spiritual Life

But now you must rid yourselves of all such things as these: anger,
rage, malice, slander, and filthy language from your lips. Do not
lie to each other, since you have taken off your old self with its
practices and have put on the new self, which is being renewed in
knowledge in the image of its Creator. (Colossians 3:8-10, NIV)

Sanctification technically means "to be set apart." Theologically, this theme explores the process by which we grow, become holy, and are conformed into the image of Christ in our lives. In our previous study, we examined God's role in delivering us from the penalty of sin. In this study, we will explore how God delivers us from the power of sin and the presence of sin.

GOD HAS DELIVERED US FROM THE ENSLAVING POWER OF SIN (BUT THE STRUGGLE CONTINUES)

Or do you not know, brethren (for I am speaking to those who
know the law), that the law has jurisdiction over a person as long

as he lives?

For the married woman is bound by law to her husband while he is living; but if her husband dies, she is released from the law concerning the husband.

So then, if while her husband is living she is joined to another man, she shall be called an adulteress; but if her husband dies, she is free from the law, so that she is not an adulteress though she is joined to another man.

Therefore, my brethren, you also were made to die to the Law through the body of Christ, so that you might be joined to another, to Him who was raised from the dead, in order that we might bear fruit for God.

For while we were in the flesh, the sinful passions, which were aroused by the Law, were at work in the members of our body to bear fruit for death.

But now we have been released from the Law, having died to that by which we were bound, so that we serve in newness of the Spirit and not in oldness of the letter.

What shall we say then? Is the Law sin? May it never be! On the contrary, I would not have come to know sin except through the Law; for I would not have known about coveting if the Law had not said, "YOU SHALL NOT COVET."

But sin, taking opportunity through the commandment, produced in me coveting of every kind; for apart from the Law sin is dead.

I was once alive apart from the Law; but when the commandment came, sin became alive and I died; and this commandment, which was to result in life, proved to result in death for me; for sin, taking an opportunity through the commandment, deceived me and through it killed me.

So then, the Law is holy, and the commandment is holy and righteous and good. Therefore did that which is good become a cause of death for me? May it never be! Rather it was sin, in order that it might be shown to be sin by effecting my death through that which is good, so that through the commandment sin would become utterly sinful.

For we know that the Law is spiritual, but I am of flesh, sold into bondage to sin. For what I am doing, I do not understand; for I am not practicing what I would like to do, but I am doing the very thing I hate. But if I do the very thing I do not want to do, I agree with the Law, confessing that the Law is good. So now, no longer am I the one doing it, but sin which dwells in me.

For I know that nothing good dwells in me, that is, in my flesh; for the willing is present in me, but the doing of the good is not.

For the good that I want, I do not do, but I practice the very evil that I do not want.

But if I am doing the very thing I do not want, I am no longer the one doing it, but sin which dwells in me.

I find then the principle that evil is present in me, the one who wants to do good.

For I joyfully concur with the law of God in the inner man, but I see a different law in the members of my body, waging war against the law of my mind and making me a prisoner of the law of sin which is in my members.

Wretched man that I am! Who will set me free from the body of this death?

Thanks be to God through Jesus Christ our Lord! So then, on the one hand I myself with my mind am serving the law of God, but on the other, with my flesh the law of sin. (Romans 7:1-25, NASB)

GOD WANTS TO DELIVER US FROM THE PRESENCE OF SIN (BUT WE MUST YIELD TO HIS WILL)

Therefore there is now no condemnation for those who are in Christ Jesus.

For the law of the Spirit of life in Christ Jesus has set you free from the law of sin and of death.

For what the Law could not do, weak as it was through the flesh, God did: sending His own Son in the likeness of sinful flesh and as an offering for sin, He condemned sin in the flesh, so that the requirement of the Law might be fulfilled in us, who do not walk according to the flesh but according to the Spirit.

For those who are according to the flesh set their minds on the things of the flesh, but those who are according to the Spirit, the things of the Spirit.

For the mind set on the flesh is death, but the mind set on the Spirit is life and peace, because the mind set on the flesh is hostile toward God; for it does not subject itself to the law of God, for it is not even able to do so, and those who are in the flesh cannot please God.

However, you are not in the flesh but in the Spirit, if indeed the Spirit of God dwells in you But if anyone does not have the Spirit of Christ, he does not belong to Him.

If Christ is in you, though the body is dead because of sin, yet the spirit is alive because of righteousness.

But if the Spirit of Him who raised Jesus from the dead dwells in you, He who raised Christ Jesus from the dead will also give life to your mortal bodies through His Spirit who dwells in you.

So then, brethren, we are under obligation, not to the flesh, to live according to the flesh—for if you are living according to the flesh, you must die; but if by the Spirit you are putting to death the deeds of the body, you will live.

For all who are being led by the Spirit of God, these are sons of God.

For you have not received a spirit of slavery leading to fear again, but you have received a spirit of adoption as sons by which we cry out, "Abba! Father!"

The Spirit Himself testifies with our spirit that we are children of God, and if children, heirs also, heirs of God and fellow heirs with Christ, if indeed we suffer with Him so that we may also be glorified with Him.

For I consider that the sufferings of this present time are not worthy to be compared with the glory that is to be revealed to us.

For the anxious longing of the creation waits eagerly for the revealing of the sons of God.

For the creation was subjected to futility, not willingly, but because of Him who subjected it, in hope that the creation itself also will be set free from its slavery to corruption into the freedom of the glory of the children of God.

For we know that the whole creation groans and suffers the pains of childbirth together until now.

And not only this, but also we ourselves, having the first fruits of the Spirit, even we ourselves groan within ourselves, waiting eagerly for our adoption as sons, the redemption of our body.

For in hope we have been saved, but hope that is seen is not hope; for who hopes for what he already sees?

But if we hope for what we do not see, with perseverance we wait eagerly for it.

In the same way the Spirit also helps our weakness; for we do not know how to pray as we should, but the Spirit Himself intercedes for us with groanings too deep for words; and He who searches the hearts knows what the mind of the Spirit is, because He intercedes for the saints according to the will of God.

And we know that God causes all things to work together for good to those who love God, to those who are called according to His purpose.

For those whom He foreknew, He also predestined to become conformed to the image of His Son, so that He would be the firstborn among many brethren; and these whom He predestined, He also called; and these whom He called, He also justified; and these whom He justified, He also glorified.

What then shall we say to these things? If God is for us, who is against us?

He who did not spare His own Son, but delivered Him over for us all, how will He not also with Him freely give us all things?

Who will bring a charge against God's elect? God is the one who justifies; who is the one who condemns? Christ Jesus is He who died, yes, rather who was raised, who is at the right hand of God, who also intercedes for us.

Who will separate us from the love of Christ? Will tribulation, or distress, or persecution, or famine, or nakedness, or peril, or sword? Just as it is written, "FOR YOUR SAKE WE ARE BEING PUT TO DEATH ALL DAY LONG; WE WERE CONSIDERED AS SHEEP TO BE SLAUGHTERED."

But in all these things we overwhelmingly conquer through Him who loved us.

For I am convinced that neither death, nor life, nor angels, nor principalities, nor things present, nor things to come, nor powers, nor height, nor depth, nor any other created thing, will be able to separate us from the love of God, which is in Christ Jesus our Lord. (Romans 8:1-39, NASB)

MAKING SANCTIFICATION PRACTICAL

The subject of change was surfaced earlier as we studied Philippians 2.

Therefore, my dear friends, as you have always obeyed—not only in my presence, but now much more in my absence—continue to work out your salvation with fear and trembling, for it is God who works in you to will and to act according to his good purpose. (Philippians 2:12-13, NIV)

We saw how change is a dynamic cooperation between the human (our choices) and the divine (God giving us supernatural strength). As we commit ourselves to God and to his purposes, he then empowers us with the strength to continue.

WE MUST PRESENT OURSELVES TO GOD

Therefore, I urge you, brothers, in view of God's mercy, to offer your bodies as living sacrifices, holy and pleasing to God—this is your spiritual act of worship. Do not conform any longer to the pattern of this world, but be transformed by the renewing of your mind. Then you will be able to test and approve what God's will is—his good, pleasing and perfect will. (Romans 12:1-2, NIV)

WE MUST TRAIN OURSELVES WITH NEW HABITS

Everyone who competes in the games goes into strict training. They do it to get a crown that will not last; but we do it to get a crown that will last forever. (1 Corinthians 9:25, NIV)

Have nothing to do with godless myths and old wives' tales; rather, train yourself to be godly. For physical training is of some value, but godliness has value for all things, holding promise for both the present life and the life to come. (1 Timothy 4:7-8, NIV)

The application of new habits is a theme that has been explored through the centuries by theologians, monastics, and pastors alike. Numerous "spiritual disciplines" have been identified over time as having significant value to the development and maintenance of our spiritual vitality. Such disciplines include more obvious ones, such as Bible reading, prayer, meditation, and worship. However, less common, additional meaningful disciplines have been suggested, such as solitude, confession, fasting, feasting, singing, journaling, exercise, and rest. Engagement in these disciplines serves to heighten our spiritual sensitivity and have also added to our character with the virtue of self-control.

AM I GROWING?

Transformation is the expected result of sanctification. Take a few minutes and ask yourself if you are making progress in these areas.

- I am jealous/envious of others, or I rejoice in the success of others.
- I feel revenge/desire to get even or I love, bless, and pray for my enemies.
- I am angry at God or I love, seek and, worship Him.
- I am bitter, resentful, and hate my enemies or I am merciful and forgiving; a peacemaker.
- I have sexual lust or I have pure thoughts.
- I lust after power and position or I am satisfied and content.
- I am proud and boastful or I am humble, gentle, and meek.
- I feel superior and/or inferior to others or I don't compare myself with others.
- I am selfish and self-seeking or I love selflessly and am ambitious for others.
- I criticize, gossip, and slander others or I respect, honour, and encourage others.
- I have self-pity, complain, and blame others or I am joyful and take personal responsibility.
- I am self-reliant or I fully depend on God; I need others.
- I am lazy, procrastinatory, and unreliable or I am disciplined, diligent, and reliable.
- I am anxious, fearful, and worried or I have peace, faith, and believe God.
- I am headstrong and need control or I am willing to yield to God and others.
- I am addicted to TV, internet, work etc. or I use self-control and am devoted to prayer.
- I hunger for worldly pleasure and things or I hunger for God's will and His Word.

- I compromise, lack integrity, justify sin or I maintain integrity, am obedient, and am faithful.

- I lie and/or exaggerate or I am honest and uphold the truth.

- I strive for pleasure above everything or I love God and put Him first in my life.

- I put my needs and desires before others or I love and care for others as myself.

- I focus on and live for this temporal life or I am preparing for heaven; eternal life.[39]

ASSIGNMENT: *What goes into athletic training? Identify how this is similar to spiritual training.*

DISCUSSION: *Which spiritual disciplines have you engaged in? Which spiritual disciplines would you like to learn more about?*

36

The Nature of the Church

Earlier, we reflected on a working definition of the church: The church is a spiritual community organized to do God's will. It is a family, a community, a people of God. In this community we find friendship and care. We share together, laugh together, cry together, and work together.

For this study, we want to expand our understanding of the origin, purpose, function, and operation of the church.

THE ORIGIN AND IDENTITY OF THE CHURCH

The church is a unique and distinct community of believers, which came into existence at Pentecost (Acts 2). The universal church is made up of all believers in Christ everywhere, both living and dead (Colossians 1:24; 1 Corinthians 1:2; Ephesians 1:22-23).

THE PURPOSE AND FUNCTIONS OF THE CHURCH

The purpose of the church is to glorify God through the fulfillment of the great commandment and the great commission (1 Corinthians 10:31; Matthew 22:37-39; Matthew 28:18-19).

God has ordained a local expression of the church as the vehicle for accomplishing his purposes of fellowship, instruction, worship, and witness (Acts 2:43-47; 1 Timothy; 2 Timothy; Titus).

THE OPERATION OF THE CHURCH

The local church has been given gifted leaders for the administration and oversight of ministries. The two leadership offices are that of elder (bishop, overseer) and deacon. While the scriptures speak of additional leadership gifts, the elders have the primary responsibility for pastoral leadership and education, while the deacons are to complement the elders in other areas of ministry need. The scriptures provide specific spiritual and character qualifications for these ministry leaders.

> For this reason I left you in Crete, that you would set in order what remains and appoint elders in every city as I directed you, namely, if any man is above reproach, the husband of one wife, having children who believe, not accused of dissipation or rebellion. For the overseer must be above reproach as God's steward, not self-willed, not quick-tempered, not addicted to wine, not pugnacious, not fond of sordid gain, but hospitable, loving what is good, sensible, just, devout, self-controlled, holding fast the faithful word which is in accordance with the teaching, so that he will be able both to exhort in sound doctrine and to refute those who contradict. (Titus 1:5-9, NASB)
>
> It is a trustworthy statement: if any man aspires to the office of overseer, it is a fine work he desires to do. An overseer, then,

must be above reproach, the husband of one wife, temperate, prudent, respectable, hospitable, able to teach, not addicted to wine or pugnacious, but gentle, peaceable, free from the love of money. He must be one who manages his own household well, keeping his children under control with all dignity (but if a man does not know how to manage his own household, how will he take care of the church of God?), and not a new convert, so that he will not become conceited and fall into the condemnation incurred by the devil. And he must have a good reputation with those outside the church, so that he will not fall into reproach and the snare of the devil.

Deacons likewise must be men of dignity, not double-tongued, or addicted to much wine or fond of sordid gain, but holding to the mystery of the faith with a clear conscience. These men must also first be tested; then let them serve as deacons if they are beyond reproach.

Women must likewise be dignified, not malicious gossips, but temperate, faithful in all things.

Deacons must be husbands of only one wife, and good managers of their children and their own households. For those who have served well as deacons obtain for themselves a high standing and great confidence in the faith that is in Christ Jesus. (1 Timothy 3:1-13, NASB)

Church leaders are to equip believers in the discovery and development of their own unique spiritual gifts. The result is that the church (body of Christ) matures, honours God, and fulfills its purpose.

But to each one of us grace was given according to the measure of Christ's gift. Therefore it says, "WHEN HE ASCENDED ON HIGH, HE LED CAPTIVE A HOST OF CAPTIVES, AND HE GAVE GIFTS TO MEN."

(Now this expression, "He ascended," what does it mean except that He also had descended into the lower parts of the earth?

He who descended is Himself also He who ascended far above all the heavens, so that He might fill all things.)

And He gave some as apostles, and some as prophets, and some as evangelists, and some as pastors and teachers, for the equipping of the saints for the work of service, to the building up of the body of Christ; until we all attain to the unity of the faith, and of the knowledge of the Son of God, to a mature man, to the measure of the stature which belongs to the fullness of Christ.

As a result, we are no longer to be children, tossed here and there by waves and carried about by every wind of doctrine, by the trickery of men, by craftiness in deceitful scheming; but speaking the truth in love, we are to grow up in all aspects into Him who is the head, even Christ, from whom the whole body, being fitted and held together by what every joint supplies, according to the proper working of each individual part, causes the growth of the body for the building up of itself in love. (Ephesians 4:7-16, NASB)

Now concerning spiritual gifts, brethren, I do not want you to be unaware. You know that when you were pagans, you were led astray to the mute idols, however you were led.

Therefore I make known to you that no one speaking by the Spirit of God says, "Jesus is accursed"; and no one can say, "Jesus is Lord," except by the Holy Spirit.

Now there are varieties of gifts, but the same Spirit. And there are varieties of ministries, and the same Lord.

There are varieties of effects, but the same God who works all things in all persons. But to each one is given the manifestation of the Spirit for the common good.

For to one is given the word of wisdom through the Spirit, and to another the word of knowledge according to the same Spirit; to another faith by the same Spirit, and to another gifts of healing by the one Spirit, and to another the effecting of miracles, and to another prophecy, and to another the distinguishing of spirits, to another various kinds of tongues, and to another the in-

terpretation of tongues.

But one and the same Spirit works all these things, distribut-ing to each one individually just as He wills. For even as the body is one and yet has many members, and all the members of the body, though they are many, are one body, so also is Christ.

For by one Spirit we were all baptized into one body, whether Jews or Greeks, whether slaves or free, and we were all made to drink of one Spirit. (1 Corinthians 12:1-13, NASB)

There are two ordinances which the local church is to practice: baptism and the Lord's Supper. Baptism is the immersion of a believer as a symbol of the believer's own resurrection to new life by faith. This symbol was observed by followers of Jesus soon after their repentance and faith. Acts records several examples of this:

The eunuch asked Philip, "Tell me, please, who is the prophet talking about, himself or someone else?" Then Philip began with that very passage of Scripture and told him the good news about Jesus.

As they traveled along the road, they came to some water and the eunuch said, "Look, here is water. Why shouldn't I be bap-tized?" And he gave orders to stop the chariot. Then both Philip and the eunuch went down into the water and Philip baptized him. (Acts 8:34-38, NIV)

Or don't you know that all of us who were baptized into Christ Jesus were baptized into his death? We were therefore buried with him through baptism into death in order that, just as Christ was raised from the dead through the glory of the Father, we too may live a new life.

If we have been united with him like this in his death, we will certainly also be united with him in his resurrection. For we know that our old self was crucified with him so that the body of sin might be done away with, that we should no longer be slaves to sin—because anyone who has died has been freed from sin. (Romans 6:3-7, NIV)

The Lord's Supper was the second ordinance and was instituted by Christ for the commemoration of his atoning death and was to prompt believers to sombre reflection, spiritual evaluation, and worship. The Lord's Supper became a key component to the worship gatherings of the early church.

> *But in the following instructions I do not commend you, because when you come together it is not for the better but for the worse. For, in the first place, when you come together as a church, I hear that there are divisions among you. And I believe it in part, for there must be factions among you in order that those who are genuine among you may be recognized. When you come together, it is not the Lord's supper that you eat. For in eating, each one goes ahead with his own meal. One goes hungry, another gets drunk. What! Do you not have houses to eat and drink in? Or do you despise the church of God and humiliate those who have nothing? What shall I say to you? Shall I commend you in this? No, I will not.*
>
> *For I received from the Lord what I also delivered to you, that the Lord Jesus on the night when he was betrayed took bread, and when he had given thanks, he broke it, and said, "This is my body which is for you. Do this in remembrance of me." In the same way also he took the cup, after supper, saying, "This cup is the new covenant in my blood. Do this, as often as you drink it, in remembrance of me." For as often as you eat this bread and drink the cup, you proclaim the Lord's death until he comes.*
>
> *Whoever, therefore, eats the bread or drinks the cup of the Lord in an unworthy manner will be guilty concerning the body and blood of the Lord. Let a person examine himself, then, and so eat of the bread and drink of the cup. For anyone who eats and drinks without discerning the body eats and drinks judgment on*

himself. That is why many of you are weak and ill, and some have died. But if we judged ourselves truly, we would not be judged. But when we are judged by the Lord, we are disciplined so that we may not be condemned along with the world.

So then, my brothers, when you come together to eat, wait for one another—if anyone is hungry, let him eat at home—so that when you come together it will not be for judgment. About the other things I will give directions when I come. (1 Corinthians 11:17-34, ESV)

ASSIGNMENT: *Discuss the significance of baptism. Have you been baptized? If not, set a date.*

DISCUSSION: *Reflect on the focus, functioning, and health of your church. What is your assessment?*

37

The Nature of Angels

Angels are God's messengers and agents. They are supernatural beings that were able to move from the heavenly realm into the earthly realm. While we may not see them at work, their existence, presence, and ministry is very real. Reflect on the nature and work of angels in our world and in your life.

THEIR ORIGIN

> *Praise him, all his angels, praise him, all his heavenly hosts. Praise him, sun and moon, praise him, all you shining stars. Praise him, you highest heavens and you waters above the skies. Let them praise the name of the Lord, for he commanded and they were created.* (Psalm 148:2-5, NIV)

> *For by him all things were created: things in heaven and on earth, visible and invisible, whether thrones or powers or rulers or au-*

thorities; all things were created by him and for him. (Colossians 1:16, NIV)

THEIR NATURE

The following shows how these spiritual beings have personality (mind, emotion, will), are powerful, immortal, and have incredible abilities.

Are not all angels ministering spirits sent to serve those who will inherit salvation? (Hebrews 1:14, NIV)

It was revealed to them that they were not serving themselves but you, when they spoke of the things that have now been told you by those who have preached the Gospel to you by the Holy Spirit sent from heaven. Even angels long to look into these things. (1 Peter 1:12, NIV)

And the angels who did not keep their positions of authority but abandoned their own home—these he has kept in darkness, bound with everlasting chains for judgment on the great Day. (Jude 6, NIV)

And he will send his angels with a loud trumpet call, and they will gather his elect from the four winds, from one end of the heavens to the other. (Matthew 24:31, NIV)

Then he will say to those on his left, "Depart from me, you who are cursed, into the eternal fire prepared for the devil and his angels." (Matthew 25:41, NIV)

After this I saw four angels standing at the four corners of the earth, holding back the four winds of the earth to prevent any wind from blowing on the land or on the sea or on any tree. Then I saw another angel coming up from the east, having the seal of the living God. He called out in a loud voice to the four angels who had been given power to harm the land and the sea: "Do not harm the land or the sea or the trees until we put a seal on the foreheads of the servants of our God." (Revelation 7:1-3, NIV)

THEIR PURPOSE

Whenever the living creatures give glory, honor and thanks to him who sits on the throne and who lives for ever and ever, the twenty-four elders fall down before him who sits on the throne, and worship him who lives for ever and ever. They lay their crowns before the throne and say:

"You are worthy, our Lord and God, to receive glory and honor and power, for you created all things, and by your will they were created and have their being." (Revelation 4:9-11, NIV)

His intent was that now, through the church, the manifold wisdom of God should be made known to the rulers and authorities in the heavenly realms. (Ephesians 3:10, NIV)

In the year that King Uzziah died, I saw the Lord seated on a throne, high and exalted, and the train of his robe filled the temple. Above him were seraphs, each with six wings: With two wings they covered their faces, with two they covered their feet, and with two they were flying. And they were calling to one another:

"Holy, holy, holy is the Lord Almighty; the whole earth is full of his glory." (Isaiah 6:1-3, NIV)

Are not all angels ministering spirits sent to serve those who will inherit salvation? (Hebrews 1:14, NIV)

THEIR HIERARCHY

The angels appear to be organized with a hierarchy. Michael is called an archangel, however we also see such terms as "chief of princes" (Daniel 10:21), cherubim (Genesis 3:24), seraphim (Isaiah 6:2-3), and ruling spirits

(Ephesians 3:10). The same appears to be true of the demonic realm (Ephesians 6).

> *But even the archangel Michael, when he was disputing with the devil about the body of Moses, did not dare to bring a slanderous accusation against him, but said, "The Lord rebuke you!"* (Jude 9, NIV)

Satan and His "Fallen Angels"

Satan, along with his demonic host, are fallen angels. Pride filled Satan's being and he was cast from the presence and purposes of God. Satan now masquerades as an angel of light (2 Corinthians 11:14). Satan has other titles, including the devil (1 Peter 5:8), the evil one (1 John 5:19), Beelzebub (Matthew 12:24), and the accuser of the brethren (Revelation 12:10). The following passages are situated in a context that addresses both historic human leaders and Satan (also called Lucifer).

> *How you have fallen from heaven, O morning star, son of the dawn! You have been cast down to the earth, you who once laid low the nations! You said in your heart, "I will ascend to heaven; I will raise my throne above the stars of God; I will sit enthroned on the mount of assembly, on the utmost heights of the sacred mountain. I will ascend above the tops of the clouds; I will make myself like the Most High."*
>
> *But you are brought down to the grave, to the depths of the pit.* (Isaiah 14:12-15, NIV)

> *Moreover, the word of the Lord came to me: "Son of man, raise a lamentation over the king of Tyre, and say to him, Thus says the Lord God:*
>
> *You were the signet of perfection, full of wisdom and perfect in beauty. You were in Eden, the garden of God; every precious stone was your covering, sardius, topaz, and diamond, beryl,*

onyx, and jasper, sapphire, emerald, and carbuncle; and crafted in gold were your settings and your engravings. On the day that you were created they were prepared. You were an anointed guardian cherub. I placed you; you were on the holy mountain of God; in the midst of the stones of fire you walked. You were blameless in your ways from the day you were created, till unrighteousness was found in you. In the abundance of your trade you were filled with violence in your midst, and you sinned; so I cast you as a profane thing from the mountain of God, and I destroyed you, O guardian cherub, from the midst of the stones of fire.

Your heart was proud because of your beauty; you corrupted your wisdom for the sake of your splendor. I cast you to the ground; I exposed you before kings, to feast their eyes on you. By the multitude of your iniquities, in the unrighteousness of your trade you profaned your sanctuaries; so I brought fire out from your midst; it consumed you, and I turned you to ashes on the earth in the sight of all who saw you.

All who know you among the peoples are appalled at you; you have come to a dreadful end and shall be no more forever." (Ezekiel 28:11-19, ESV)

THE WORK OF SATAN AND HIS DEMONS

Satan is the catalyst for all kinds of evil in our world. While it was Satan who drew Adam and Eve into initial rebellion, his activities continue for the purpose of thwarting the work of God and distracting people from trusting God. As believers, we should be alert to his continuing work in our lives. We dare not be unaware.

> *Be self-controlled and alert. Your enemy the devil prowls around like a roaring lion looking for someone to devour.* (1 Peter 5:8, NIV)

> *For this reason, when I could stand it no longer, I sent to find out*

about your faith. I was afraid that in some way the tempter might have tempted you and our efforts might have been useless. (1 Thessalonians 3:5, NIV)

For such men are false apostles, deceitful workmen, masquerading as apostles of Christ. And no wonder, for Satan himself masquerades as an angel of light. It is not surprising, then, if his servants masquerade as servants of righteousness. Their end will be what their actions deserve. (2 Corinthians 11:13-14, NIV)

And there was war in heaven. Michael and his angels fought against the dragon, and the dragon and his angels fought back. But he was not strong enough, and they lost their place in heaven. The great dragon was hurled down—that ancient serpent called the devil, or Satan, who leads the whole world astray. He was hurled to the earth, and his angels with him.

Then I heard a loud voice in heaven say: "Now have come the salvation and the power and the kingdom of our God, and the authority of his Christ. For the accuser of our brothers, who accuses them before our God day and night, has been hurled down." (Revelation 12:7-10, NIV)

OUR RESPONSE

Submit yourselves, then, to God. Resist the devil, and he will flee from you. Come near to God and he will come near to you. Wash your hands, you sinners, and purify your hearts, you double-minded. (James 4:7-8, NIV)

Finally, be strong in the Lord and in the strength of His might. Put on the full armor of God, so that you will be able to stand firm against the schemes of the devil. For our struggle is not against flesh and blood, but against the rulers, against the powers, against the world forces of this darkness, against the spiritual forces of wickedness in the heavenly places. Therefore, take up the full ar-

mor of God, so that you will be able to resist in the evil day, and having done everything, to stand firm. Stand firm therefore, HAVING GIRDED YOUR LOINS WITH TRUTH, and HAVING PUT ON THE BREASTPLATE OF RIGHTEOUSNESS, and having shod YOUR FEET WITH THE PREPARATION OF THE GOSPEL OF PEACE; in addition to all, taking up the shield of faith with which you will be able to extinguish all the flaming arrows of the evil one. And take THE HELMET OF SALVATION, and the sword of the Spirit, which is the word of God. With all prayer and petition pray at all times in the Spirit, and with this in view, be on the alert with all perseverance and petition for all the saints. (Ephesians 6:10-18, NASB)

ASSIGNMENT: *Reflect on how you think Satan is attacking you or attempting to work in your life. What will you do about it?*

DISCUSSION: *Why do you think pride is referred to as the greatest of sins?*

38

The Nature of the Future

Prophecy is another dominant theme in the Scripture, and it was always intended as a message of hope amidst trials. When life was challenging or painful, there was also hope in the future. God will break through and bring justice and peace. This began with the anticipation of the Messiah's first coming and continues with our hope in his second coming.

While some have sought to minimize the details surrounding the future, others have sought to particularize the details of prophecy with great precision. In this study, we want to draw some basic assurances related to future events through a reading of a number of biblical passages.

JESUS CHRIST WILL RETURN IMMINENTLY TO GATHER HIS PEOPLE

While Jesus warned us to live ready and to watch for signs of the times, the Scriptures also tell us that there is a "surprise factor" in Christ's return and that he could return at any moment to set in motion "the Day of the Lord," which is a whole series of events marked by judgment and leading to resto-ration.

> *But we do not want you to be uninformed, brothers, about those who are asleep, that you may not grieve as others do who have no hope. For since we believe that Jesus died and rose again, even so, through Jesus, God will bring with him those who have fallen asleep. For this we declare to you by a word from the Lord, that we who are alive, who are left until the coming of the Lord, will not precede those who have fallen asleep. For the Lord himself will descend from heaven with a cry of command, with the voice of an archangel, and with the sound of the trumpet of God. And the dead in Christ will rise first. Then we who are alive, who are left, will be caught up together with them in the clouds to meet the Lord in the air, and so we will always be with the Lord. There-fore encourage one another with these words.*
>
> *Now concerning the times and the seasons, brothers, you have no need to have anything written to you. For you yourselves are fully aware that the day of the Lord will come like a thief in the night. While people are saying, "There is peace and security," then sudden destruction will come upon them as labor pains come upon a pregnant woman, and they will not escape. But you are not in darkness, brothers, for that day to surprise you like a thief. For you are all children of light, children of the day. We are not of the night or of the darkness. So then let us not sleep, as others do, but let us keep awake and be sober. For those who sleep, sleep at night, and those who get drunk, are drunk at night. But since we belong to the day, let us be sober, having put on the breastplate of faith and love, and for a helmet the hope of salva-tion. For God has not destined us for wrath, but to obtain salva-tion through our Lord Jesus Christ, who died for us so that whether we are awake or asleep we might live with him. There-fore encourage one another and build one another up, just as you are doing.* (1 Thessalonians 4:13-5:11, ESV)

THE WORLD WILL GO THROUGH A TIME OF SUFFERING AND JUDGMENT

> *Now concerning the coming of our Lord Jesus Christ and our be-*
> *ing gathered together to him, we ask you, brothers, not to be*
> *quickly shaken in mind or alarmed, either by a spirit or a spoken*
> *word, or a letter seeming to be from us, to the effect that the day*
> *of the Lord has come. Let no one deceive you in any way. For that*
> *day will not come, unless the rebellion comes first, and the man of*
> *lawlessness is revealed, the son of destruction, who opposes and*
> *exalts himself against every so-called god or object of worship, so*
> *that he takes his seat in the temple of God, proclaiming himself to*
> *be God. Do you not remember that when I was still with you I*
> *told you these things? And you know what is restraining him now*
> *so that he may be revealed in his time. For the mystery of lawless-*
> *ness is already at work. Only he who now restrains it will do so*
> *until he is out of the way. And then the lawless one will be re-*
> *vealed, whom the Lord Jesus will kill with the breath of his mouth*
> *and bring to nothing by the appearance of his coming. The com-*
> *ing of the lawless one is by the activity of Satan with all power and*
> *false signs and wonders, and with all wicked deception for those*
> *who are perishing, because they refused to love the truth and so*
> *be saved. Therefore God sends them a strong delusion, so that*
> *they may believe what is false, in order that all may be con-*
> *demned who did not believe the truth but had pleasure in un-*
> *righteousness.* (2 Thessalonians 2:1-12, ESV)

JESUS CHRIST WILL ESTABLISH HIS REIGN ON THE EARTH

When Jesus was on earth he proclaimed that the Kingdom of God was at hand. The Kingdom of God has often been understood as a "now, not yet" concept. When a person trusts Christ, that person becomes a part of God's Kingdom. There is a present nature to the Kingdom of God. There

is, however, a sense in which we still await the final culmination and realization of the Kingdom reign of Christ. Thus, it is "not yet," but it one day
"will be," The last book of the Bible, Revelation speaks to this:

> Then I saw heaven opened, and behold, a white horse! The one
> sitting on it is called Faithful and True, and in righteousness he
> judges and makes war. His eyes are like a flame of fire, and on his
> head are many diadems, and he has a name written that no one
> knows but himself. He is clothed in a robe dipped in blood, and
> the name by which he is called is The Word of God. And the ar-
> mies of heaven, arrayed in fine linen, white and pure, were follow-
> ing him on white horses. From his mouth comes a sharp sword
> with which to strike down the nations, and he will rule them with
> a rod of iron. He will tread the winepress of the fury of the wrath
> of God the Almighty. On his robe and on his thigh he has a name
> written, King of kings and Lord of lords.
>
> Then I saw an angel standing in the sun, and with a loud
> voice he called to all the birds that fly directly overhead, "Come,
> gather for the great supper of God, to eat the flesh of kings, the
> flesh of captains, the flesh of mighty men, the flesh of horses and
> their riders, and the flesh of all men, both free and slave, both
> small and great." And I saw the beast and the kings of the earth
> with their armies gathered to make war against him who was sit-
> ting on the horse and against his army. And the beast was cap-
> tured, and with it the false prophet who in its presence had done
> the signs by which he deceived those who had received the mark
> of the beast and those who worshiped its image. These two were
> thrown alive into the lake of fire that burns with sulfur. And the
> rest were slain by the sword that came from the mouth of him
> who was sitting on the horse, and all the birds were gorged with
> their flesh. (Revelation 19:11-21, ESV)
>
> Then I saw an angel coming down from heaven, holding in his
> hand the key to the bottomless pit and a great chain. And he

seized the dragon, that ancient serpent, who is the devil and Sa-
tan, and bound him for a thousand years, and threw him into the
pit, and shut it and sealed it over him, so that he might not de-
ceive the nations any longer, until the thousand years were ended.
After that he must be released for a little while.

Then I saw thrones, and seated on them were those to whom
the authority to judge was committed. Also I saw the souls of
those who had been beheaded for the testimony of Jesus and for
the word of God, and those who had not worshiped the beast or
its image and had not received its mark on their foreheads or
their hands. They came to life and reigned with Christ for a thou-
sand years. The rest of the dead did not come to life until the
thousand years were ended. This is the first resurrection. Blessed
and holy is the one who shares in the first resurrection! Over such
the second death has no power, but they will be priests of God
and of Christ, and they will reign with him for a thousand years.

And when the thousand years are ended, Satan will be re-
leased from his prison and will come out to deceive the nations
that are at the four corners of the earth, Gog and Magog, to
gather them for battle; their number is like the sand of the sea.
And they marched up over the broad plain of the earth and sur-
rounded the camp of the saints and the beloved city, but fire came
down from heaven and consumed them. (Revelation 20:1-9, ESV)

JESUS CHRIST WILL JUDGE SATAN AND THOSE WHO HAVE REJECTED GOD

The Bible teaches that those who reject God's offer of forgiveness and life
in Christ will suffer forever without God in a place of torment, absent of
God. This is profoundly sobering.

And the devil who had deceived them was thrown into the lake of
fire and sulfur where the beast and the false prophet were, and
they will be tormented day and night forever and ever.
Then I saw a great white throne and him who was seated on

it. From his presence earth and sky fled away, and no place was found for them. And I saw the dead, great and small, standing before the throne, and books were opened. Then another book was opened, which is the book of life. And the dead were judged by what was written in the books, according to what they had done. And the sea gave up the dead who were in it, Death and Hades gave up the dead who were in them, and they were judged, each one of them, according to what they had done. Then Death and Hades were thrown into the lake of fire. This is the second death, the lake of fire. And if anyone's name was not found written in the book of life, he was thrown into the lake of fire. (Revelation 20:10-15, ESV)

JESUS CHRIST WILL ESTABLISH A NEW HEAVEN AND A NEW EARTH FOR THE PEOPLE OF GOD

Then I saw a new heaven and a new earth, for the first heaven and the first earth had passed away, and the sea was no more. And I saw the holy city, new Jerusalem, coming down out of heaven from God, prepared as a bride adorned for her husband. And I heard a loud voice from the throne saying, "Behold, the dwelling place of God is with man. He will dwell with them, and they will be his people, and God himself will be with them as their God. He will wipe away every tear from their eyes, and death shall be no more, neither shall there be mourning, nor crying, nor pain anymore, for the former things have passed away."

And he who was seated on the throne said, "Behold, I am making all things new." Also he said, "Write this down, for these words are trustworthy and true." And he said to me, "It is done! I am the Alpha and the Omega, the beginning and the end. To the thirsty I will give from the spring of the water of life without payment. The one who conquers will have this heritage, and I will be his God and he will be my son. But as for the cowardly, the faithless, the detestable, as for murderers, the sexually immoral,

sorcerers, idolaters, and all liars, their portion will be in the lake
that burns with fire and sulfur, which is the second death."

Then came one of the seven angels who had the seven bowls
full of the seven last plagues and spoke to me, saying, "Come, I
will show you the Bride, the wife of the Lamb." And he carried me
away in the Spirit to a great, high mountain, and showed me the
holy city Jerusalem coming down out of heaven from God, having
the glory of God, its radiance like a most rare jewel, like a jasper,
clear as crystal. It had a great, high wall, with twelve gates, and at
the gates twelve angels, and on the gates the names of the twelve
tribes of the sons of Israel were inscribed—on the east three gates,
on the north three gates, on the south three gates, and on the
west three gates. And the wall of the city had twelve foundations,
and on them were the twelve names of the twelve apostles of the
Lamb. (Revelation 21:1-14, ESV)

Then the angel showed me the river of the water of life, bright as
crystal, flowing from the throne of God and of the Lamb through
the middle of the street of the city; also, on either side of the river,
the tree of life with its twelve kinds of fruit, yielding its fruit each
month. The leaves of the tree were for the healing of the nations.
No longer will there be anything accursed, but the throne of God
and of the Lamb will be in it, and his servants will worship him.
They will see his face, and his name will be on their foreheads.
And night will be no more. They will need no light of lamp or
sun, for the Lord God will be their light, and they will reign for-
ever and ever. (Revelation 22:1-5, ESV)

OUR RESPONSE

The return of Jesus Christ to fulfill his promises and purposes is not an abstraction. The realization that Jesus will come back and establish his reign
should cause every believer to be motivated to share their faith and live
expectantly and godly. Peter challenges us:

Since all these things are thus to be dissolved, what sort of people ought you to be in lives of holiness and godliness, waiting for and hastening the coming of the day of God, because of which the heavens will be set on fire and dissolved, and the heavenly bodies will melt as they burn! But according to his promise we are waiting for new heavens and a new earth in which righteousness dwells.

Therefore, beloved, since you are waiting for these, be diligent to be found by him without spot or blemish, and at peace. And count the patience of our Lord as salvation, just as our beloved brother Paul also wrote to you according to the wisdom given him, as he does in all his letters when he speaks in them of these matters. There are some things in them that are hard to understand, which the ignorant and unstable twist to their own destruction, as they do the other Scriptures. You therefore, beloved, knowing this beforehand, take care that you are not carried away with the error of lawless people and lose your own stability. But grow in the grace and knowledge of our Lord and Savior Jesus Christ. To him be the glory both now and to the day of eternity. Amen. (2 Peter 3:11-18, ESV)

ASSIGNMENT: *For further study, read the entire book of Revelation.*

DISCUSSION: *What kinds of activities are you motivated to be involved in because of this reality?*

— 39 —
The Cultivation of Christian Character

Character is who we are on the inside. Character is who we are when we are alone. Character is not the same as our heart, but it is the quality, measurement, or moral assessment of our heart. Our heart is the core of who we are. Our heart is not just the centre of our emotions; it is the very centre of who we are. It is out of this core that everything emanates.

There are numerous Hebrew and Greek words which have been translated into the English word "character." These words vary in meaning including "reputation," "standing," or "inner qualities." While there is no single defining word (from which we could do an etymological study) that thoroughly enlightens us, context appears to be our most helpful aid. Consider the following ways in which the word translated "character" is used.

> *And now, my daughter, don't be afraid. I will do for you all you ask. All my fellow townsmen know that you are a woman of noble character.* (Ruth 3:11, NIV)

A wife of noble character is her husband's crown, but a disgraceful wife is like decay in his bones. (Proverbs 12:4, NIV)

A wife of noble character who can find? She is worth far more than rubies. (Proverbs 31:10, NIV)

Now the Bereans were of more noble character than the Thessalonians, for they received the message with great eagerness and examined the Scriptures every day to see if what Paul said was true. (Acts 17:11, NIV)

Not only so, but we also rejoice in our sufferings, because we know that suffering produces perseverance; perseverance, character; and character, hope. (Romans 5:3-4, NIV)

Do not be misled: "Bad company corrupts good character." (1 Corinthians 15:33, NIV)

The theme that the "inner life" is the foundation of the outer life is a frequent message that Jesus highlighted. Again, consider:

So He said to them, "Are you thus without understanding also? Do you not perceive that whatever enters a man from outside cannot defile him, because it does not enter his heart but his stomach, and is eliminated, thus purifying all foods?" And He said, "What comes out of a man, that defiles a man. For from within, out of the heart of men, proceed evil thoughts, adulteries, fornications, murders, thefts, covetousness, wickedness, deceit, lewdness, an evil eye, blasphemy, pride, foolishness. All these evil things come from within and defile a man." (Mark 7:18-23, NKJV)

"Woe to you, scribes and Pharisees, hypocrites! For you cleanse the outside of the cup and dish, but inside they are full of extortion and self-indulgence. Blind Pharisee, first cleanse the inside of the cup and dish, that the outside of them may be clean also.

"Woe to you, scribes and Pharisees, hypocrites! For you are

like whitewashed tombs which indeed appear beautiful outwardly, but inside are full of dead men's bones and all uncleanness. Even so you also outwardly appear righteous to men, but inside you are full of hypocrisy and lawlessness. (Matthew 23:25-28, NKJV).

Another word or theme which sheds light on this study is the Bible's use of "heart." In our current cultural context, "heart" is usually used to describe one's emotions. Perhaps the most notable exception (or qualifier) to this is the classic Disney/Hollywood appeal to "just follow your heart!" The meaning of this is essentially that we should follow our gut hunches or drives. Biblically, however, "heart" appears to be a description of the core of one's very being. It is the mysterious and complex centre of our longings, thinking, motivation, and values. Out of our "heart" proceed our choices, behaviours, and emotions. Our heart has been damaged by the fall, but can be changed by God.

Consider the transformative work of God and the biblical character qualities that we should emulate.

And you, my son Solomon, acknowledge the God of your father, and serve him with wholehearted devotion and with a willing mind, for the Lord searches every heart and understands every motive behind the thoughts. If you seek him, he will be found by you; but if you forsake him, he will reject you forever. (1 Chronicles 28:9, NIV)

He also rebelled against King Nebuchadnezzar, who had made him take an oath in God's name. He became stiff-necked and hardened his heart and would not turn to the Lord, the God of Israel. (2 Chronicles 36:13, NIV)

And David shepherded them with integrity of heart; with skillful hands he led them. (Psalm 78:72, NIV)

Teach me your way, O Lord, and I will walk in your truth; give me an undivided heart, that I may fear your name. (Psalm 86:11, NIV)

Above all else, guard your heart, for it is the wellspring of life.
(Psalm 4:23, NIV)

*Hope deferred makes the heart sick, but a longing fulfilled is a
tree of life.* (Proverbs 13:12, NIV)

*The heart is deceitful above all things and beyond cure. Who can
understand it "I the Lord search the heart and examine the mind,
to reward a man according to his conduct, according to what his
deeds deserve."* (Jeremiah 17:9-10, NIV)

*"I will give them an undivided heart and put a new spirit in them;
I will remove from them their heart of stone and give them a
heart of flesh."* (Ezekiel 11:19, NIV)

FAITH, HOPE, AND LOVE

The New Testament frequently highlights the supreme value of faith, hope,
and love as indispensible virtues to the believer. Paul writes:

*Though I speak with the tongues of men and of angels, but have
not love, I have become sounding brass or a clanging cymbal. And
though I have the gift of prophecy, and understand all mysteries
and all knowledge, and though I have all faith, so that I could remove mountains, but have not love, I am nothing. And though I
bestow all my goods to feed the poor, and though I give my body
to be burned, but have not love, it profits me nothing.*

*Love suffers long and is kind; love does not envy; love does
not parade itself, is not puffed up; does not behave rudely, does
not seek its own, is not provoked, thinks no evil; does not rejoice
in iniquity, but rejoices in the truth; bears all things, believes all
things, hopes all things, endures all things. Love never fails. But
whether there are prophecies, they will fail; whether there are
tongues, they will cease; whether there is knowledge, it will vanish*

away. For we know in part and we prophesy in part. But when that which is perfect has come, then that which is in part will be done away. When I was a child, I spoke as a child, I understood as a child, I thought as a child; but when I became a man, I put away childish things. For now we see in a mirror, dimly, but then face to face. Now I know in part, but then I shall know just as I also am known.

And now abide faith, hope, love, these three; but the greatest of these is love. (1 Corinthians 13:1-13, NKJV)

We always thank God, the Father of our Lord Jesus Christ, when we pray for you, because we have heard of your faith in Christ Jesus and of the love you have for all the saints—the faith and love that spring from the hope that is stored up for you in heaven and that you have already heard about in the word of truth, the Gospel that has come to you. All over the world this Gospel is bearing fruit and growing, just as it has been doing among you since the day you heard it and understood God's grace in all its truth. (1 Colossians 1:3-6, NIV)

But by faith we eagerly await through the Spirit the righteousness for which we hope. For in Christ Jesus neither circumcision nor uncircumcision has any value. The only thing that counts is faith expressing itself through love. (Galatians 5:5-6, NIV)

We always thank God for all of you, mentioning you in our prayers. We continually remember before our God and Father your work produced by faith, your labor prompted by love, and your endurance inspired by hope in our Lord Jesus Christ. (1 Thessalonians 1:2-3, NIV)

THE FRUIT OF THE SPIRIT

Christ-like character is demonstrated outwardly in the virtues known as the fruit of the Spirit.

But the fruit of the Spirit is love, joy, peace, patience, kindness, goodness, faithfulness, gentleness and self-control. Against such things there is no law. Those who belong to Christ Jesus have crucified the sinful nature with its passions and desires. Since we live by the Spirit, let us keep in step with the Spirit. (Galatians 5:22-25, NIV)

THE ROLE OF OBEDIENCE AND SUBMISSION

"Why do you call me, 'Lord, Lord,' and do not do what I say?" (Luke 6:46, NIV)

Wives, submit to your own husbands, as is fitting in the Lord. Husbands, love your wives and do not be bitter toward them. Children, obey your parents in all things, for this is well pleasing to the Lord. Fathers, do not provoke your children, lest they become discouraged. Bondservants, obey in all things your masters according to the flesh, not with eyeservice, as men-pleasers, but in sincerity of heart, fearing God. And whatever you do, do it heartily, as to the Lord and not to men, knowing that from the Lord you will receive the reward of the inheritance; for you serve the Lord Christ. But he who does wrong will be repaid for what he has done, and there is no partiality.

Masters, give your bondservants what is just and fair, knowing that you also have a Master in heaven. (Colossians 3:18-4:1, NKJV)

Beloved, I urge you as aliens and strangers to abstain from fleshly lusts which wage war against the soul. Keep your behavior excellent among the Gentiles, so that in the thing in which they slander you as evildoers, they may because of your good deeds, as they observe them, glorify God in the day of visitation.

Submit yourselves for the Lord's sake to every human institution, whether to a king as the one in authority, or to governors as sent by him for the punishment of evildoers and the praise of those who do right.

For such is the will of God that by doing right you may silence the ignorance of foolish men. Act as free men, and do not use your freedom as a covering for evil, but use it as bondslaves of God. Honor all people, love the brotherhood, fear God, honor the king.

Servants, be submissive to your masters with all respect, not only to those who are good and gentle, but also to those who are unreasonable. For this finds favor, if for the sake of conscience toward God a person bears up under sorrows when suffering unjustly. For what credit is there if, when you sin and are harshly treated, you endure it with patience? But if when you do what is right and suffer for it you patiently endure it, this finds favor with God.

For you have been called for this purpose, since Christ also suffered for you, leaving you an example for you to follow in His steps, WHO COMMITTED NO SIN, NOR WAS ANY DECEIT FOUND IN HIS MOUTH; and while being reviled, He did not revile in return; while suffering, He uttered no threats, but kept entrusting Himself to Him who judges righteously; and He Himself bore our sins in His body on the cross, so that we might die to sin and live to righteousness; for by His wounds you were healed. For you were continually straying like sheep, but now you have returned to the Shepherd and Guardian of your souls.

In the same way, you wives, be submissive to your own husbands so that even if any of them are disobedient to the word, they may be won without a word by the behavior of their wives, as they observe your chaste and respectful behavior.

Your adornment must not be merely external—braiding the hair, and wearing gold jewelry, or putting on dresses; but let it be the hidden person of the heart, with the imperishable quality of a gentle and quiet spirit, which is precious in the sight of God. For in this way in former times the holy women also, who hoped in

God, used to adorn themselves, being submissive to their own husbands; just as Sarah obeyed Abraham, calling him lord, and you have become her children if you do what is right without being frightened by any fear.

You husbands in the same way, live with your wives in an understanding way, as with someone weaker, since she is a woman; and show her honor as a fellow heir of the grace of life, so that your prayers will not be hindered. (1 Peter 2:11-3:7, NASB)

Remember your leaders, who spoke the word of God to you. Consider the outcome of their way of life and imitate their faith. Jesus Christ is the same yesterday and today and forever... Obey your leaders and submit to their authority. They keep watch over you as men who must give an account. Obey them so that their work will be a joy, not a burden, for that would be of no advantage to you. (Hebrews 13:7, 17, NIV)

THE ROLE OF PURITY

God has created us as sexual beings. Our identity is gender anchored, and our sexuality seeks for expression. Sexual intimacy is often misunderstood and misappropriated, however it was created as a pleasurable expression to be enjoyed. The Bible deals with the theme of sexuality in a rich and robust way. God has not only created the expression of sex, but he gave us the desire for sexual pleasure. There need not be any guilt for having sexual desire, but it is an appetite that must be directed appropriately. Sexual desire is to be expressed in the context of a monogamous, heterosexual marriage. Anything beyond this is a distortion of God's intended ideal.

But since there is so much immorality, each man should have his own wife, and each woman her own husband. The husband should fulfill his marital duty to his wife, and likewise the wife to her husband. The wife's body does not belong to her alone but also to her husband. In the same way, the husband's body does not belong to him alone but also to his wife. Do not deprive each other except by mutual consent and for a time, so that you may devote yourselves to prayer. Then come together again so that Satan will not tempt you because of your lack of self-control. (1 Corinthians 7:2-5, NIV)

Sexual intimacy is to be enjoyed legitimately in marriage in order to safeguard illegitimate expressions outside of marriage. This is why the Scriptures speak repeatedly of the danger and damage of lust and impure sexual expressions

It is God's will that you should be sanctified: that you should avoid sexual immorality; that each of you should learn to control his own body in a way that is holy and honorable, not in passionate lust like the heathen, who do not know God; and that in this matter no one should wrong his brother or take advantage of him. The Lord will punish men for all such sins, as we have already told you and warned you." (1 Thessalonians 4:3-6, NIV)

You have heard that it was said, "Do not commit adultery." But I tell you that anyone who looks at a woman lustfully has already committed adultery with her in his heart. If your right eye causes you to sin, gouge it out and throw it away. It is better for you to lose one part of your body than for your whole body to be thrown into hell. And if your right hand causes you to sin, cut it off and throw it away. It is better for you to lose one part of your body than for your whole body to go into hell." (Matthew 5:27-30, NIV)

THE ROLE OF KINDNESS, COMPASSION, AND FORGIVENESS

Be kind and compassionate to one another, forgiving each other, just as in Christ God forgave you. (Ephesians 4:32, NIV)

Put on then, as God's chosen ones, holy and beloved, compas-

sionate hearts, kindness, humility, meekness, and patience, bearing with one another and, if one has a complaint against another forgiving each other; as the Lord has forgiven you, so you also must forgive. And above all these put on love, which binds everything together in perfect harmony. And let the peace of Christ rule in your hearts, to which indeed you were called in one body. And be thankful. Let the word of Christ dwell in you richly, teaching and admonishing one another in all wisdom, singing psalms and hymns and spiritual songs, with thankfulness in your hearts to God. And whatever you do, in word or deed, do everything in the name of the Lord Jesus, giving thanks to God the Father through him. (Colossians 3:12-17, ESV)

ASSIGNMENT: *Identify three character issues that you are prompted to address. What needs to be done to tackle these character weaknesses?*

DISCUSSION: *Our culture is obsessed with image. Religion is often obsessed with outward behaviour. How is the Gospel truly radical and transformative?*

40

The Attitude of Humility

We know that pride was the downfall of Satan. By contrast, Jesus is the ultimate humble servant. The following passages are counterintuitive, countercultural, and yet inspiring.

> *James and John, the two sons of Zebedee, came up to Jesus, saying, "Teacher, we want You to do for us whatever we ask of You."*
>
> *And He said to them, "What do you want Me to do for you?"*
>
> *They said to Him, "Grant that we may sit, one on Your right and one on Your left, in Your glory."*
>
> *But Jesus said to them, "You do not know what you are asking. Are you able to drink the cup that I drink, or to be baptized with the baptism with which I am baptized?"*
>
> *They said to Him, "We are able."*
>
> *And Jesus said to them, "The cup that I drink you shall drink; and you shall be baptized with the baptism with which I am baptized. But to sit on My right or on My left, this is not Mine to give;*

but it is for those for whom it has been prepared."

Hearing this, the ten began to feel indignant with James and John.

Calling them to Himself, Jesus said to them, "You know that those who are recognized as rulers of the Gentiles lord it over them; and their great men exercise authority over them. But it is not this way among you, but whoever wishes to become great among you shall be your servant; and whoever wishes to be first among you shall be slave of all. For even the Son of Man did not come to be served, but to serve, and to give His life a ransom for many." (Mark 10:35-45, NASB)

The proud are selfish. The proud want to be served. The humble are selfless. The humble serve.

Therefore if there is any encouragement in Christ, if there is any consolation of love, if there is any fellowship of the Spirit, if any affection and compassion, make my joy complete by being of the same mind, maintaining the same love, united in spirit, intent on one purpose. Do nothing from selfishness or empty conceit, but with humility of mind regard one another as more important than yourselves; do not merely look out for your own personal interests, but also for the interests of others.

Have this attitude in yourselves which was also in Christ Jesus, who, although He existed in the form of God, did not regard equality with God a thing to be grasped, but emptied Himself, taking the form of a bond-servant, and being made in the likeness of men. Being found in appearance as a man, He humbled Himself by becoming obedient to the point of death, even death on a cross. (Philippians 2:1-8, NASB)

Pride expressed in selfishness was a problem in Philippi just as it is a problem today. Selfishness and self-love is seen everywhere in such extreme examples as affairs, divorce, the betrayal of friendships, breakdowns with work colleagues, abortions, and in virtually every crime or violation of a commandment. Pride and selfishness evidence themselves in everyday activities as well. Evil grows out of placing the interests, desires, and wants of self ahead of everything and everyone else.

Pride, self-centeredness, and selfishness are all interwoven and constitute the greatest of sins. Selfishness leads to division and isolation. Selfishness is placing self first. Selfishness divides us and separates us from relationship. Selfishness, in the end, leaves us alone and wanting. Jesus offers us something very different: selfless humility. Selflessness is not about putting yourself down. The virtue of selflessness is the priority of placing the needs of others ahead of the desires of self.

Leonard Bernstein was asked which was the hardest instrument to play. His reply: "Second fiddle." The issue has nothing to do with difficulty of instrument, skill, or technique of the musician, but everything to do with attitude. No one naturally wants to be second—not in marriage, not as siblings, not in competitions, not in work. This is a mystery. This is radical. This is counterintuitive. But this is the way of the Lord Jesus. And this is the virtue he calls us to.

ASSIGNMENT: *Do something selfless for another, something that costs you.*

DISCUSSION: *What things are you most proud of? How does your attitude need to change?*

—— 41 ——

The Place of Pain

Earlier in our study, we looked at why there is pain and suffering in the world. We saw how some pain and suffering was for the purpose of shaping and developing our character. The Apostle Paul reflected upon a time of seeking God for deliverance from chronic pain. The answer he received back may not have initially been welcoming, but there was a purpose for it.

SEEKING GOD FOR ANSWERS

Because of the surpassing greatness of the revelations, for this reason, to keep me from exalting myself, there was given me a thorn in the flesh, a messenger of Satan to torment me—to keep me from exalting myself! Concerning this I implored the Lord three times that it might leave me. And He has said to me, "My grace is sufficient for you, for power is perfected in weakness." Most gladly, therefore, I will rather boast about my weaknesses, so that the power of Christ may dwell in me. Therefore I am well content with weaknesses, with insults, with distresses, with persecutions, with difficulties, for Christ's sake; for when I am weak, then I am strong. I have become foolish; you your-selves compelled me. Actually I should have been commended by you, for in no respect was I inferior to the most eminent apostles, even though I am a nobody. (2 Corinthians 12:7-11, NASB)

While the Scripture is full of stories of miraculous healings, Paul's pursuit of healing and deliverance from pain was met with the answer that he would have to continue to live with this unwelcome ache. God determined that the pain in Paul's life would do more good than if he were free from it. In Paul's case, the pain was to keep him humble and dependent on God. This dependence actually became the ongoing source of Paul's spiritual strength and resilience.

SEEKING GOD FOR WISDOM

When we find ourselves reeling in the dilemma of pain, confused over its purpose and why God does not deliver us from it, James invites us to ask God for wisdom. He declares:

> *Count it all joy, my brothers, when you meet trials of various kinds, for you know that the testing of your faith produces stead-fastness. And let steadfastness have its full effect, that you may be perfect and complete, lacking in nothing.*
>
> *If any of you lacks wisdom, let him ask God, who gives gen-erously to all without reproach, and it will be given him.* (James 1:2-5, ESV)

James invites us to reflect with joy on the presence of pain. Implied is that pain has a role to play in our lives. Pain can teach us truths about our-selves or God. Further, pain has the capacity to make us strong and perse-vering. Pain, in many people's lives, only serves to make them weaker or cynical. The difference between whether or not pain serves us is our response to the hurt, disappointment, or tragedy.

Talking about pain can be abstract when we find ourselves in a healthy, prosperous, harmonious place in life. However, pain will come. Loss will visit us. Disappointment will become a cloud over us. Illness and aging will ultimately overtake all of us, if we are given the years. While pain and physical decay are the final residual consequences of the dramatic fall of man, God in his grace still uses pain to help us learn, grow, and trust him.

ASSIGNMENT: *Take some time and write out the major painful experiences through which you have gone. How have these impacted you? What have you learned, or can you learn, from these experiences?*

DISCUSSION: *As it relates to the theme of pain, discuss this statement: "The question is not 'Why.' The question is, 'What can I learn from it?'"*

42

Maturing Through Theological Paradoxes

God has revealed truth so that we may know things accurately and truly. As we mature as disciples, we develop a deepening sense of conviction over things that matter. Such examples may be: the authority and sufficiency of the Christ, the nature of God, the authority and sufficiency of the Scriptures, an uncompromising belief in moral truth, or the responsibility to love. However, mystery and paradox sometimes enter our faith alongside these deeply held convictions. These perplexities sometimes defy simple explanation, but they must be acknowledged.

A paradox is an apparent contradiction. Some prefer the word antinomy. The nuance differs little. Antinomies are two apparently contradictory truths. They seem to be mutually incompatible. These are tensions or opposites, and yet each on its own is defendable and reasonable. While we are sometimes given to simple answers and prospective extremes, the mature disciple will navigate complexity, mystery, ambiguity, and paradox with grace and integrity. Consider these theological paradoxes:

GOD IS ONE; GOD IS THREE

> *Hear, O Israel: The Lord our God, the Lord is one.* (Deuteronomy 6:4, NIV)

The unity of God is a central attribute of God. However, we also have significant biblical data to explain God as a triune being, usually referred to as the Trinity. There is biblical support that God the Father, God the Son, and God the Holy Spirit all share the same qualities of divinity: infinity, eternity, immutability, omnipresence, omnipotence, omniscience, sovereignty, holiness, righteousness, justice, grace, mercy, love, truth, and personality. God is one. God is three. While this is infinitely perplexing, it is who God is.

JESUS IS GOD; JESUS IS MAN

> *In the beginning was the Word, and the Word was with God, and the Word was God. He was with God in the beginning. Through him all things were made; without him nothing was made that has been made... The Word became flesh and made his dwelling among us. We have seen his glory, the glory of the One and Only, who came from the Father, full of grace and truth.* (John 1:1-3, 14, NIV)

Jesus was God. In him resided all the attributes of divinity. And yet, at his incarnation, Jesus became a man in the fullest sense of what it meant to be human, except without sin (1 Peter 2:22). This is a mystery that theologians have wrestled with. To emphasize one over the other is to create an imbalance in truth, and thus a heresy. Church history has borne this out.

GOD IS SOVEREIGN; MAN DETERMINES HIS DESTINY

That God calls us and chooses us has already been explored (Ephesians 1). Nothing that takes place surprises God. God is sovereign over the affairs of time, humanity, and the cosmos. However, human beings are called upon to make real choices for which they will be held accountable. This may be the choice to follow God or not. Somehow, these two truths exist together in a mysterious harmony. To emphasize one over the other would be to dilute their truth. We must embrace both that God is sovereign and man determines his destiny.

> *Now fear the Lord and serve him with all faithfulness. Throw away the gods your forefathers worshiped beyond the River and in Egypt, and serve the Lord. But if serving the Lord seems undesirable to you, then choose for yourselves this day whom you will serve, whether the gods your forefathers served beyond the River, or the gods of the Amorites, in whose land you are living. But as for me and my household, we will serve the Lord.* (Joshua 24:14-15, NIV)

I COME TO JESUS MY SAVIOUR WITH NOTHING; I OFFER JESUS MY LORD EVERYTHING

> *For it is by grace you have been saved, through faith—and this not from yourselves, it is the gift of God—not by works, so that no one can boast.* (Ephesians 2:8-9, NIV)

> *Then he said to them all: "If anyone would come after me, he must deny himself and take up his cross daily and follow me."* (Luke 9:23, NIV)

Our salvation is a complete gift of God, inspired by God and provided by God. We are broken, depraved, spiritually blind, and enslaved to sin. We come to God in order to receive, because we have nothing of merit to give.

However, in coming to Christ and receiving forgiveness and relationship, we then offer God our all.

Jesus is our Lord. Jesus is our master. We will spend the rest of our lives learning as disciples to live in submission to his Lordship. Some within theological circles want to emphasize the grace of God's provision. Others want to emphasize the gravity of our commitment. Both are true. We need God's grace, but we also must commit ourselves to his Lordship. Our failures do not necessarily indicate illegitimacy in our faith. Recall how Peter denied Christ three times (Mark 14:66-72). Recall the rebuking of the immoral Christian (1 Corinthians 5:1-12). Christians should be committed, but Christians do fail. Thankfully, the same grace of God that redeemed us continues to hold us in his secure grip.

PRAYER CHANGES THINGS; PRAYER CHANGES US

Someone once said, "Prayer moves the hand that moves the world."[40] Jesus invited us to believe in the impossible:

> Jesus replied, "I tell you the truth, if you have faith and do not doubt, not only can you do what was done to the fig tree, but also you can say to this mountain, 'Go, throw yourself into the sea,' and it will be done. If you believe, you will receive whatever you ask for in prayer." (Matthew 21:21-22, NIV)

And yet, in prayer, I establish alignment to the will and purpose of God. While Jesus was in prayer, he brought himself under the will of his Father.

> Jesus went out as usual to the Mount of Olives, and his disciples followed him. On reaching the place, he said to them, "Pray that you will not fall into temptation." He withdrew about a stone's throw beyond them, knelt down and prayed, "Father, if you are willing, take this cup from me; yet not my will, but yours be

done." An angel from heaven appeared to him and strengthened him. And being in anguish, he prayed more earnestly, and his sweat was like drops of blood falling to the ground. (Luke 22:39-44, NIV)

God Does Not Need Us; God Chooses to Use Us

God does not need the assistance of human beings, and yet, in his divine purposes, he has chosen to use us, to involve us in his kingdom agenda. This is a theological conclusion. However, it is deeply personal and practical. We dare not think too highly of ourselves (Romans 12:3), and yet we dare not think of ourselves too lowly or insignificantly. God has called us and he has gifted us with a purpose (Ephesians 2:10).

I Am a Selfish Sinner; I Am Made in the Image of God and in Christ Become a Saint

The blood of Adam continues to flow through our veins. Our study of Romans 3 made this abundantly clear. We are all capable of tremendous darkness and should never think ourselves above temptation. Paul further reminds us that as we walk with Christ we gradually take on the image of God himself. Indeed, this is a paradox. We are capable of exceeding sin and exceeding nobility.

> *Do not lie to each other, since you have taken off your old self with its practices and have put on the new self, which is being renewed in knowledge in the image of its Creator.* (Colossians 3:9-10, NIV)

I Must Choose to Change; God Changes Me

Grappling with our pull to sin is a lifelong struggle. While in Christ, we are freed from the natural bondage to sin. We continue to wrestle with the routine temptations of life. Paul identifies with us soberly in Romans 7.

> *For we know that the Law is spiritual, but I am of flesh, sold into bondage to sin.*
>
> *For what I am doing, I do not understand; for I am not practicing what I would like to do, but I am doing the very thing I hate. But if I do the very thing I do not want to do, I agree with the Law, confessing that the Law is good.*
>
> *So now, no longer am I the one doing it, but sin which dwells in me. For I know that nothing good dwells in me, that is, in my flesh; for the willing is present in me, but the doing of the good is not. For the good that I want, I do not do, but I practice the very evil that I do not want. But if I am doing the very thing I do not want, I am no longer the one doing it, but sin which dwells in me.*
>
> *I find then the principle that evil is present in me, the one who wants to do good.* (Romans 7:14-25, NASB)

Sometimes we get become exasperated with ourselves. After enough berating of self, we often give up and just tell ourselves, "Well, this is just the way I am." Then, every once in a while, we meet someone who has changed, really changed. They authentically seem more gracious, more patient, more kind. Perhaps they have dropped a twenty-year habit and truly seem to be free. And we wonder, how? How did this happen? How did they change? This introduces us to yet another theological paradox. However, this one too has a pointed application to how we live. The essential principle seems to be this: I can't change without God's help, and yet I can't change unless I want to. This tension is best illustrated with a study of two biblical stories.

God used Moses to lead the Hebrew people out of oppression and slavery in Egypt. Because of their unresponsive hearts, they wandered in the wilderness of the Middle East for forty years while a whole generation of sceptics and doubters died. Finally, they reach the edge of the Jordon

River. Moses has died, and Joshua is their new Prime Minister. God says, "It's time to enter your new home; it's just across the river." Joshua 3 records the preparations of two million people who are about to cross the Jordon River, which was now at flood levels, possibly up to a mile wide and likely moving with a strong and dangerous current. The priests are commanded to lead the people in crossing the Jordon while carrying the Ark of the Covenant. As the priests step into the water, the miracle takes place:

> *So it was, when the people set out from their camp to cross over the Jordan, with the priests bearing the ark of the covenant before the people, and as those who bore the ark came to the Jordan, and the feet of the priests who bore the ark dipped in the edge of the water (for the Jordan overflows all its banks during the whole time of harvest), that the waters which came down from upstream stood still, and rose in a heap very far away at Adam, the city that is beside Zaretan. So the waters that went down into the Sea of the Arabah, the Salt Sea, failed, and were cut off; and the people crossed over opposite Jericho. Then the priests who bore the ark of the covenant of the Lord stood firm on dry ground in the midst of the Jordan; and all Israel crossed over on dry ground, until all the people had crossed completely over the Jordan. (Joshua 3:14-17, NKJV)*

There was a clear cooperation at work here. The people were to obey, but it was God who did the work. This is illustrated in a New Testament story as well, where Jesus heals ten lepers.

> *Now it happened as He went to Jerusalem that He passed through the midst of Samaria and Galilee. Then as He entered a certain village, there met Him ten men who were lepers, who stood afar off. And they lifted up their voices and said, "Jesus, Master, have mercy on us!"*
>
> *So when He saw them, He said to them, "Go, show your-*

selves to the priests." And so it was that as they went, they were
cleansed. (Luke 17:11-14, NKJV)

The priests had to certify that the lepers were now clean and could
therefore re-enter community life and worship. The key to this paradox is
in the phrase: "And as they went, they were cleansed." The lepers had to
want to change; they had to want the miracle; they had to do something.
However, it was God who did the miracle. The message is this: When we
step out, God steps in. God told the people of Israel, "Step into the water."
They did and the waters dried up. Jesus told the lepers, "Go to the priests."
They went and were cleansed along the way. The principle of the cooperation of the human and the divine in our changing is taught repeatedly.

> *Therefore, my dear friends, as you have always obeyed—not only*
> *in my presence, but now much more in my absence—continue to*
> *work out your salvation with fear and trembling, for it is God who*
> *works in you to will and to act according to his good purpose.*
> (Philippians 2:12-13, NIV)

> *To this end I labor, struggling with all his energy, which so pow-*
> *erfully works in me.* (Colossians 1:29, NIV)

When we step out, God steps in. Thus, we must choose to change, but
it is God who changes us.

ASSIGNMENT: *Think of an area in your life that needs to change. What*
steps can you take now?

DISCUSSION: *Discuss each of the tensions highlighted in this chapter. Does*
the concept of paradox help or confuse further?

43

Maturing Through Life and Ministry Paradoxes

Paradox is found in biblical doctrines, but they also surface in life and ministry. Reflecting on these will only equip us better as we navigate maturity as disciples.

PEOPLE ARE WEAKER THAN WE THINK; PEOPLE ARE STRONGER THAN WE THINK

We all know of people who are strong-willed, with moral fibre of iron and resolve. They appear tough, resilient, tenacious, and determined. We marvel at their strength and fortitude. We can also quickly think of people who are emotional china dolls, people who find it taxing to cope with the most routine stress. Such people are easily set off, often anxious and fretful. Such frailty can be found in both men and women. Similarly, we can think of people who seem to be temptation dominoes. They seem to fall all the time. And then there are those temptation-resistant people, like prophets of old: focused, determined, relentless, and uncompromising.

The Apostle Paul seems so focused and so strong, and yet we then think of Peter's denial or King David's fall into sin. We can be so strong and yet we can be so weak. This is yet another tension, a paradox, if you will— two seemingly contradictory truths

> *So, if you think you are standing firm, be careful that you don't fall! No temptation has seized you except what is common to man. And God is faithful; he will not let you be tempted beyond what you can bear. But when you are tempted, he will also provide a way out so that you can stand up under it.* (1 Corinthians 10:12-13, NIV)

Paul challenged us not to overestimate our strength or to underestimate the power of temptation. Yet he also assures us that we always have a way of escape. Paul reminds the Corinthians that yes, we are fragile. Do not underestimate the power of sin. However, we are also capable of great strength. Do not underestimate the power of God to which we have access to. Paul returns to this theme in his second letter.

> *And lest I should be exalted above measure by the abundance of the revelations, a thorn in the flesh was given to me, a messenger of Satan to buffet me, lest I be exalted above measure. Concerning this thing I pleaded with the Lord three times that it might depart from me. And He said to me, "My grace is sufficient for you, for My strength is made perfect in weakness." Therefore most gladly I will rather boast in my infirmities, that the power of Christ may rest upon me. Therefore I take pleasure in infirmities, in reproaches, in needs, in persecutions, in distresses, for Christ's sake. For when I am weak, then I am strong.* (2 Corinthians 12:7-10, NKJV)

Paul serves us a principle: When you admit human weakness, you access divine strength.

PAIN MAKES US WEAK; PAIN MAKES US STRONG

We have all experienced losses and painful experiences that have drained us of strength and energy. We know that the accumulation of stressful episodes in our lives within a short period of time can have damaging consequences. This is the reality of our human fragility. Yet, we take inspiration and insight from James:

> Count it all joy, my brothers, when you meet trials of various kinds, for you know that the testing of your faith produces steadfastness. And let steadfastness have its full effect, that you may be perfect and complete, lacking in nothing.
>
> If any of you lacks wisdom, let him ask God, who gives generously to all without reproach, and it will be given him. (James 1:2-5, ESV)

I WANT LIFE TO BE EASY; I NEED LIFE TO BE CHALLENGING

I pray regularly for peace and prosperity, for good health and happiness, for relational harmony and ministry success. But I also find that I pray the most when I am in the midst of challenges and trials. I don't like to admit it, but it is true. I pray the most when I have needs.

Remember the wealthy man who had amassed great surpluses of resources, who said:

> "And I'll say to myself, 'You have plenty of good things laid up for many years. Take life easy; eat, drink and be merry.'" (Luke 12:19, NIV)

However, challenges make us resilient, and resilience makes us strong.

James 1 taught us this. It taught us to stick with a task when the opposition is severe, to endure fatigue, ridicule, failure, and attack when you believe you are doing what you should. The trials and challenges are the very things that make us strong. James asks us to cultivate a joy amidst trials.

Rather than asking "Why?" in the midst of our trials, we should ask, "What can I learn from this experience, however painful?" Sometimes when asking this question, we need wisdom. James 1:5 invites us to ask for wisdom. Wisdom here is *sophia*. This is the application of knowledge to life. James here speaks of wisdom, not in broad generalities, but of the wisdom that we need to navigate this particular paradox.

So when you lose your job, when your health evaporates and you've got to spend a small mint on medication, when your car dies before it's even paid for, when you fail to make the grade, make the cut, or realize your long-aspired-to dream, and when you face trials of many kinds, not consequences of poor choices, but real trials or challenges that you truly didn't deserve, and nothing makes sense, that is the time we need to ask for wisdom as we wrestle with this paradox.

I MUST WORK HARD; I NEED TO REST

The Scriptures give us a natural rhythm of work and rest. We are to work for six days and rest on the seventh. Because work is difficult, we are tempted to think that work is a result of the curse. Work was a pre-fall responsibility. However, Genesis 3 does tell us that work would became more difficult. Work is not part of the curse; it is part of God's will. Yet we look forward to rest in our routine. We need both.

THE PAST ANCHORS ME; THE FUTURE INSPIRES ME

> *Being confident of this, that he who began a good work in you will carry it on to completion until the day of Christ Jesus.* (Phi-

lippians 1:6, NIV)

God started something in our past and will complete it in the future. The Old Testament is full of similar emphases on the past and the future. Over and over again, the prophets call on the people of God to remember the works of God, to remember his promise to Abraham, Isaac, and Jacob. Israel was to remember his deliverance of Israel from their enslavement in Egypt. Israel was to remember how he provided for the people in the wilderness. The Scriptures always motivate us by looking to the future. Israel was to look forward to the time when the Messiah would come. As Christians, we look forward to the ultimate return of Jesus. Here is the paradox at work: the past anchors us, and the future inspires us. Both are needed. We need history. We need hope. We need a past. We need a future.

THE PROCESS IS IMPORTANT; THE PRODUCT IS IMPORTANT

We learn in process. We discover through experiences. We mature in relationship. We grow over time. The process matters. The process imprints our minds and experiences with lessons which will be remembered. However, we do want to see results. Nothing motivates like results. Thus, the product matters as well.

I LIVE FOR TODAY WITH JOY; I ANTICIPATE ETERNITY WITH HOPE

> *For to me, to live is Christ and to die is gain. But if I am to live on in the flesh, this will mean fruitful labor for me; and I do not know which to choose. But I am hard-pressed from both directions, having the desire to depart and be with Christ, for that is very much better; yet to remain on in the flesh is more necessary for your sake.* (Philippians 1:21-24, NASB)

Eternal life begins the moment we believe. The abundant life spoken of in

John 10:10 is for the present. We are called to bring kingdom qualities to the earth through our acts of righteousness and good deeds. We should work at changing our world's conditions. Yet we all do get ill, fatigued, old, and slowly out of touch and heaven begins to look very attractive. Paul lived with this tension. He wanted to live on in order to minister, but he was quite excited about the prospect of life with Christ in heaven.

I DEMONSTRATE MY AUTHENTICITY WHEN I ADMIT MY HUMANITY AND MY FAILINGS; I DEMONSTRATE DISCIPLINE AND DECORUM WHEN I CONTROL MY EMOTIONS AND MY EXPRESSIONS

Yes, we are human and should be vulnerable about this. There is a time and a place when we should be open, transparent, and honest with each other. We are even commanded to confess our sins to each other (James 5:16). However, unlimited and unrestrained transparency is not always the wisest of expressions. As a leader and teacher, when I come to a leadership meeting or a worship gathering, I need to be ready. I am expected to be ready. If I am tired or if I have had a bad week or if my children were acting up, there may be occasions to share this, but these occasions should be carefully determined. Transparency has become a cultural value in certain contexts; however, we should be discreet in our communications.

I LOVE THIS PERSON; I AM ANGRY WITH THIS PERSON

Love is a commitment proved in action. But it is also an emotion. We feel love, and we like that feeling. We tend to think that anger is in contradiction with love. Popular culture tells us, "If we argue, we must not be right for each other." One of the tests of maturity is our ability to live with emotional ambiguity or paradox. I love my wife, and yet I can be angry with her. We can love our children and yet find ourselves exasperated with them. We can love our church and yet be frustrated from time to time. Such conflicting emotions should not force us to side with one or the other. Rather, we must learn to live with and process these ambiguous emotions when they occur.

I Must Say Hard Things; I Must Say Kind Things

This is true of parents, marriages, pastors, employers, governmental leaders, and leaders of all kinds. There are times when fathers say exceedingly kind things.

> *For you know that we dealt with each of you as a father deals with his own children, encouraging, comforting and urging you to live lives worthy of God, who calls you into his kingdom and glory.* (1 Thessalonians 2:11-12, NIV)

Here Paul is talking about how he as a pastor treated the flock at Thessalonica. He treated them like a caring and tender father who spoke kind and encouraging words. However, we also know that fathers must say hard things from time to time.

> *And you have forgotten the exhortation which speaks to you as to sons: "My son, do not despise the chastening of the Lord, Nor be discouraged when you are rebuked by Him; For whom the Lord loves He chastens, And scourges every son whom He receives."*
>
> *If you endure chastening, God deals with you as with sons; for what son is there whom a father does not chasten? But if you are without chastening, of which all have become partakers, then you are illegitimate and not sons. Furthermore, we have had human fathers who corrected us, and we paid them respect. Shall we not much more readily be in subjection to the Father of spirits and live? For they indeed for a few days chastened us as seemed best to them, but He for our profit, that we may be partakers of His holiness. Now no chastening seems to be joyful for the pre-*

sent, but painful; nevertheless, afterward it yields the peaceable
fruit of righteousness to those who have been trained by it. (Hebrews 12:5-11, NKJV)

I HATE CONFLICT; CONFLICT RESOLUTION BRINGS US CLOSER

Most people do not welcome conflict, although some actually quite thrive
on creating it. Most people work at avoiding conflict. While a gracious
countenance can reduce conflict, we all face conflict and must navigate it
when it arises. As much as we dislike it, conflict resolution invariably brings
us closer to one another. This is true in family relationships, friendships,
and professional relationships.

I NEED TO BE ALONE; I NEED TO BE WITH PEOPLE

We are all wired differently. Some of us are introverts and some of us are
extroverts. Whatever our personality type, we should all be aware of just
how much we need both alone time and relating time. We do grow when
we ponder, reflect, and mediate on our own. However, we also grow in
community.

I HAVE FREEDOM IN CHRIST; I CHOOSE NOT TO USE MY FREEDOM

This paradox must be humbly reflected upon and wisely applied. The danger is to quickly slip into either a zone of excessive license or oppressive
legalism. Paul addresses this theme extensively in 1 Corinthians 8 and 9.
Paul cautions,

> *But take care that this right of yours does not somehow become a*
> *stumbling block to the weak. For if anyone sees you who have*
> *knowledge eating in an idol's temple, will he not be encouraged, if*
> *his conscience is weak, to eat food offered to idols? And so by*

your knowledge this weak person is destroyed, the brother for whom Christ died. Thus, sinning against your brothers and wounding their conscience when it is weak, you sin against Christ. Therefore, if food makes my brother stumble, I will never eat meat, lest I make my brother stumble. (1 Corinthians 8:9-13, ESV)

Paul then explains:

For though I am free from all, I have made myself a servant to all, that I might win more of them. To the Jews I became as a Jew, in order to win Jews. To those under the law I became as one under the law (though not being myself under the law) that I might win those under the law. To those outside the law I became as one outside the law (not being outside the law of God but under the law of Christ) that I might win those outside the law. To the weak I became weak, that I might win the weak. I have become all things to all people, that by all means I might save some. I do it all for the sake of the Gospel, that I may share with them in its blessings. (1 Corinthians 9:19-23, ESV)

Paul here reminds us of our freedom and also that we do not need to use our freedom. When Paul uses the phrase "to stumble," he is referring to a falling back into sin. While he may enjoy a personal freedom, he chooses not to use it if it might cause another believer to fall back into old habits.

ORGANIZATIONAL SUCCESS: IT ALL DEPENDS ON LEADERS; IT ALL DEPENDS ON FOLLOWERS

Moses was a leader who followed the purposes of God in his life with faith and endurance. Sometimes he was passionately excited, while at other times he was reluctant and discouraged. In all, he was faithful to the discipline of following God's vision for his life. Examining Moses as a leader surfaces some valuable insights. The people of Israel had initially moved to

Egypt due to a famine in their own land. For many years, they were tolerated and even accepted because of the leadership influence of Joseph. However, with time the people of Israel prospered and increased in population, causing concern within the circles of power in Egypt. Something would have to be done. So God raises up a leader, Moses.

While Moses starts off arguing with God, he submits and in time emerges as Israel's deliverer. Even though Moses demonstrated consistent leadership and from a human perspective was a model leader, he nevertheless faced tremendous opposition and resistance from the people of Israel. While leadership was pivotal, so was followership.

The story of Moses (particularly in Exodus and Numbers) demonstrates the following:

First, God uses leaders. Leaders are imperfect and they blow it. Moses blew it. David blew it. Peter blew it. No leader bats a thousand in good judgment... but God still uses them. Same with parents... parents lead families. None are perfect, but they have a God-ordained role. Hopefully, the children or followers will follow respectfully and in the process learn to respect and bow the knee under the ultimate leadership and lordship of Jesus Christ.

Second, leaders are to lead. Leaders take real initiative to move an organization or community forward in the fulfillment of a purpose or objective. Now, this looks a little different from culture to culture, from generation to generation, from family to family, from church to church. Consider what has gone on during the last fifty to sixty years.

World War II created strong sentiments against dictators. Hitler, Stalin, and Mussolini all left the world with great concerns over how power corrupts and how absolute control must be prevented. Obviously this is a good thing; however, what it did was cause the pendulum to swing. After this, leaders were patterned after an enabler model. Enablers facilitate, but they don't provide strong direction or guidance. This mentality moved through business, and certainly the church.

Naturally there were exceptions, but we did move into a season of enabler leaders. This movement hit its peak in the late 60s and has been finding balance since that time. Yes, we want to enable people, but moreover, we want to equip people. That is, leaders (Christian leaders) are called to keep the mission of Christ before the people and train them to do the work of the ministry. We have a job! We have a mission. We have a calling. We have a responsibility… and leaders call us to that task and serve us by training us to do that task. Leaders are more than just laissez-faire facilitators. They initiate. They influence. They call us to action.

Third, followers are to follow. While followers need to be brought on board and followers need information, followers will buy in when they understand the vision, and when they own the vision. Yes, followers will ask questions; that's a good thing. But followers can make life easy by complying with grace, or they can make life hard by fighting, challenging, or worse, undermining.

Fourth, leaders and followers together advance the will and purposes of God. Here is an observation on ministry effectiveness. Where the congregation leads and the "leaders" do the ministry, growth potential is limited. Where the "leaders" lead (including leading by example), and the congregation does the work of the ministry, the growth potential accelerates. Leadership depends on leaders—leadership depends on followers.

I AM CONTENT; I AM AMBITIOUS

As Christians, we must learn to cultivate core contentment with the provisions and circumstances of life. Paul said:

> *I know what it is to be in need, and I know what it is to have plenty. I have learned the secret of being content in any and every*

situation, whether well fed or hungry, whether living in plenty or
in want. I can do everything through him who gives me strength.
(Philippians 4:12-13, NIV)

Paul also knew what it meant to be ambitions.

It has always been my ambition to preach the Gospel where
Christ was not known, so that I would not be building on some-
one else's foundation. (Romans 15:20, NIV)

SMALL IS GOOD; BIG IS GOOD

Cultures differ, as do eras. For example, small gatherings have value; however, large ones also have their place and role. In the New Testament, we
see house churches and home gatherings. These settings provided opportunities for the "one another's" of life to be fleshed out. However, we also
see the value of large gatherings, as in the case of celebrations. The temple
in Jerusalem was frequently the hub of religious celebrations, as well as for
the worship of the early church.

I MUST GIVE ATTENTION TO THE DETAILS; I MUST FOCUS ON THE BIG PICTURE

Details matter in life. Parents, leaders, and artisans all give careful attention
to the details. And yet there are times when we must fly at thirty thousand
feet in our perspective.

BALANCE LEADS TO HEALTH; FOCUS LEADS TO GREATER IMPACT

This is a curious paradox. Health is the result of proper diet, exercise, and
rest. Generally speaking, people who lead balanced lives (emotionally, socially, physically, and spiritually) live full and healthy lives. However, there
are all kinds of examples of people who live extremely focused lives which

are imbalanced. Olympic athletes, pioneer missionaries, and extremely bright academics are just a few of the many examples of people who limited their lives dramatically in order to accomplish something impacting. Which is right and which is wrong? Again, we have another paradox.

ASSIGNMENT: *Take some time to write out reflections on each of these apparent tensions.*

DISCUSSION: *Which paradoxes create significant dissonance or tension in your thinking?*

PART FOUR

The Path of Multiplying

INTRODUCTION

Along this journey, we have travelled the path of seeking and inquiry, the path of making new faith discoveries, the path of spiritual growth and maturity, and now we find ourselves beginning the path of stewarding our resources, our influence, our leadership, and our responsibility to reproduce and multiply.

The purpose of *Disciple* is to shape our thinking and our behaviour in ways that cause us to view the word disciple as a noun (what we are: learners and followers), and as a verb (what we do: reproduce the quality of a disciple in another). Every believer is given the awesome mandate of becoming a reproducing, multiplying disciple-maker. This, by definition, implies leadership. Leadership is a spiritual gift that some possess. However, leadership is also a spiritual responsibility for all of us. In one way or another, every one of us will assume a leadership role in some capacity. As parents, we lead our children; as disciple-makers, we lead others in their faith; as gifted members within the body of Christ, we are called to mentor and help equip others in the development of their spiritual gifting.

Whether you believe you have the spiritual gifting of leadership or not, you have a responsibility to cultivate the character and skills that will allow you to be a mature, multiplying disciple of Jesus Christ.

At the end of this time of study and collaboration, we should: (1) feel a sense of responsibility to act as a steward of influence and leadership, (2) understand and be able to employ basic biblical leadership skills in our home, church, community, and world, and (3) be committed to the process of multiplication.

44

The Disciple's Mindset as a Steward

A PARABLE

For it will be like a man going on a journey, who called his servants and entrusted to them his property. To one he gave five talents, to another two, to another one, to each according to his ability. Then he went away. He who had received the five talents went at once and traded with them, and he made five talents more. So also he who had the two talents made two talents more. But he who had received the one talent went and dug in the ground and hid his master's money.

Now after a long time the master of those servants came and settled accounts with them. And he who had received the five talents came forward, bringing five talents more, saying, "Master, you delivered to me five talents; here I have made five talents more."

His master said to him, "Well done, good and faithful servant. You have been faithful over a little; I will set you over much. Enter into the joy of your master."

And he also who had the two talents came forward, saying, "Master, you delivered to me two talents; here I have made two talents more."

His master said to him, "Well done, good and faithful servant. You have been faithful over a little; I will set you over much. Enter into the joy of your master."

He also who had received the one talent came forward, saying, "Master, I knew you to be a hard man, reaping where you did not sow, and gathering where you scattered no seed, so I was afraid, and I went and hid your talent in the ground. Here you have what is yours."

But his master answered him, "You wicked and slothful servant! You knew that I reap where I have not sown and gather where I scattered no seed? Then you ought to have invested my money with the bankers, and at my coming I should have received what was my own with interest. So take the talent from him and give it to him who has the ten talents. For to everyone who has will more be given, and he will have an abundance. But from the one who has not, even what he has will be taken away. And cast the worthless servant into the outer darkness. In that place there will be weeping and gnashing of teeth." (Matthew 25:14-30, ESV)

A talent was a specific amount of silver which was used as currency. A talent could weigh anywhere from 58-80 pounds and represented anywhere from several months' to a year's worth of wages. Here, a wealthy man entrusts his property to three individuals and leaves. These three individuals were called stewards. A steward was a hired manager, and administrator of another's affairs. Often wealthy individuals would obtain the services of a steward to oversee all the financial and investment matters of the owner. A modern day equivalent could be a financial planner or advisor, or a personal accountant, or as some might have, a personal business manager.

Your wealth is still your wealth, however you entrust the control and oversight of your possessions to another. Of course, this is a risk for the owner, and it a huge responsibility for the manager. It was a risk in biblical times, and remains a risk today.

The owner in this story takes the risk. One steward is given five talents, another is given two, while the last is given one. Note that each receives an amount based on what the owner assesses the manager's abilities and expertise to be. Two of these individuals prove to be faithful, and for their faithfulness, wisdom, and responsibility they are commended, given more responsibility, and enjoy a reward. Their reward is based on their faithfulness and dependability, not on the actual amount of the increase. The third is judged as wicked and lazy. He is unfaithful and unreliable. It is implied that he would not even risk putting the sum of money in the bank in order to receive interest because the monies would have to be registered in the name of the owner. This manager was hoping to simply keep the money for himself.

Why do we have two different kinds of managers or stewards? Why were two of them faithful? Why was one unfaithful? What made the difference? At the heart of the contrast is one's view of God. A correct concept of God is foundational.

Two of the stewards saw that God is good, God is gracious, God is generous, God is our Creator, Lord, Master, and Father. God is seen as our ruler, general, boss, and Lord. This concept is hard for us because most people do not like to take orders from anyone.

Furthermore, these two faithful stewards believed that God had given them everything that they had; their life, breath, abilities, and resources. God was their ultimate provider. Growing out of this correct view of God was a right concept of stewardship. They believed that everything belonged to God. They had the attitude: "What's mine is God's!"

It would appear that the third individual had a wrong view of God. Perhaps he thought God was like an angry boss—looking for an opportunity to humble him. Perhaps he thought God really didn't care or wasn't really all that involved or on top of it. Perhaps he simply chose not to think about God at all.

It also appears evident that he had a wrong view of stewardship. He thought, "The money is in my hands now; it belongs to me." He likely mused, "What's God's is mine to do with as I please."

The parallels of this story are clear: Christ entrusts us with responsibility and leaves us to carry out this responsibility. God calls us stewards and has entrusted us similarly with responsibilities. This principle finds multiple applications. I have a knowledge of truth… it is not mine, it is God's. But I must tell it. I have talents, abilities, and spiritual gifts. These gifts are not mine; they are God's. But I must use them. I have resources, possessions, and treasures. These resources are not mine; they are God's. But I must give them. I must share them. I have time, I have today, twenty-four hours, the same as everyone else. This time is not mine; it belongs to God. But I must use it wisely.

We will give account to God for this stewardship! "To whom much is given much is required," the Scriptures tell us. Have we spoken the truth? The more truth we know, the more accountable we become. Have we used our talents for worthy purposes? The more gifted we are, the more responsibility we have. Have we used our wealth to invest in kingdom purposes? Have we shared? The more we have, the more God expects of us. Have we used our time wisely?

What we have is God's truth, God's talents, God's treasure, God's time. It's all God's! This concept of stewardship is foundational for the leadership and influence of the growing, committed, serving disciple of Christ.

ASSIGNMENT: *What impacts you most about this story told by Jesus?*

DISCUSSION: *Discuss the expectations that Christ places on us.*

45

The Disciple as a Servant Leader

Jesus was a leader. Jesus taught leadership and modeled leadership. He brought some very distinctive and sobering perspectives to the matter of leadership. He also sought to dispel common misconceptions held by his own disciples.

Perhaps the best example of Christ in the role of the servant leader is the account where he washes the feet of his disciples.

> *During supper, when the devil had already put it into the heart of Judas Iscariot, Simon's son, to betray him, Jesus, knowing that the Father had given all things into his hands, and that he had come from God and was going back to God, rose from supper. He laid aside his outer garments, and taking a towel, tied it around his waist. Then he poured water into a basin and began to wash the disciples' feet and to wipe them with the towel that was wrapped around him. He came to Simon Peter, who said to him, "Lord, do you wash my feet?"*

Jesus answered him, "What I am doing you do not understand now, but afterward you will understand."

Peter said to him, "You shall never wash my feet."

Jesus answered him, "If I do not wash you, you have no share with me."

Simon Peter said to him, "Lord, not my feet only but also my hands and my head!"

Jesus said to him, "The one who has bathed does not need to wash, except for his feet, but is completely clean. And you are clean, but not every one of you." For he knew who was to betray him; that was why he said, "Not all of you are clean."

When he had washed their feet and put on his outer garments and resumed his place, he said to them, "Do you understand what I have done to you? You call me Teacher and Lord, and you are right, for so I am. If I then, your Lord and Teacher, have washed your feet, you also ought to wash one another's feet. For I have given you an example, that you also should do just as I have done to you. Truly, truly, I say to you, a servant is not greater than his master, nor is a messenger greater than the one who sent him. If you know these things, blessed are you if you do them." (John 13:2-17, ESV)

"A new command I give you: Love one another. As I have loved you, so you must love one another. By this all men will know that you are my disciples, if you love one another." (John 13:34-35, NIV)

At this time, Jesus was preparing to share the Passover feast with his friends. As they gathered for this special ceremonial celebration, it was customary to have one's feet washed. Sandals only covered the bottoms of the feet and thus feet were usually dirty from the dusty roads of Palestine. To wash the feet of the guests at a feast was the office of a slave. The rabbi's disciples were supposed to render their masters personal service, but a service like this, performed by a rabbi to his disciples, would never have been dreamed of.

SERVANT LEADERS IDENTIFY NEEDS

The key concept here is perception. No one among the disciples was willing to assume the role of hosting, of humbly performing the customary washing of the guests' feet, since these were rented quarters. Jesus saw the need. Jesus constantly modeled this. He was always identifying and meeting needs. Whether it was the need of touch, forgiveness, healing, encouragement, release from bondage, offering hope, extending grace, or giving strength, Jesus saw the need and then offered to meet it. He knows our real needs. He also knows our wants, but offers no promise to meet all our wants.

In the Gospels, we see Jesus meeting surface needs as a means of getting to deeper spiritual needs. This is what servants do. They see needs. They perceive needs. They recognize problems. What needs do you see? There are needs all around us: micro-needs, personal needs; macro-needs, societal needs. Leaders see these.

SERVANT LEADERS TAKE INITIATIVE

Here, the key concept of initiative is applied. Jesus not only saw needs, but he responded to them. In this case, Jesus simply took up a basin and did the job no one else was willing to do. Jesus took strategic, purposeful, proactive, appropriate action. Note the kind of action that Jesus takes. It is a serving action.

Consider this cross reference to Mark 10:42-45:

> But Jesus called them to Himself and said to them, "You know
> that those who are considered rulers over the Gentiles lord it over
> them, and their great ones exercise authority over them. Yet it

> *shall not be so among you; but whoever desires to become great among you shall be your servant. And whoever of you desires to be first shall be slave of all. For even the Son of Man did not come to be served, but to serve, and to give His life a ransom for many."*
> (Mark 10:42-45, NKJV)

While the disciples remained passive, Jesus took action. Jesus challenged the popular perceptions and standards of the role and image of leadership. In Jesus' culture, most notable leaders were found in military circles. Kings, generals, and warriors were held high as enviable influencers and shapers. Wealth would also play a role. Thus, the sending away of the "rich, young ruler" by Jesus would have no doubt perplexed the disciples (Luke 18:18-30). The disciples likely would have viewed such a man as a "real catch" in the establishment of a new kingdom agenda.

Jesus, however, presents a radically new way of looking at leadership. To Jesus, the leader was not the commander. The leader was ultimately a servant. Leadership, then, was all about servanthood, rather than giving orders and "lording it over" others. The word translated "lord it over" is *katakurieuo*. It speaks of "gaining dominion over," "gaining power over someone," or "subduing." Jesus' next negative descriptor is "exercising authority." This word is *katexousiazo* and is appropriately translated "exercise authority," but can further mean "tyrannize." Jesus effectively dismissed the military model of leadership and offered a radically new paradigm.

Serving is the act of meeting the needs of the moment. Servants do what needs to be done. Servants offer care where care is needed, assistance where assistance is needed, correction where correction is needed, training where training is needed, empowerment where empowerment is needed, and love where love is needed. Leaders may not do what everyone wants them to do, but the real needs will be met. As leaders humbly serve, influence is gained and leadership takes place. Such is the method of Christ.

Jesus taught that the greatest leader is the greatest servant and he modeled it through his life. The Gospels record many examples of this value being lived out, thus displaying Jesus as not only the Saviour of humanity, but also as the ultimate model leader and permanent head of the church (see Ephesians 5:23).

SERVANT LEADERS ARE HUMBLE

The key concept to observe here is selflessness. Jesus was the mentor. Jesus was the Rabbi, yet he was humble and selfless enough to take on the role of the lowest position in the room. Jesus was humble. Jesus was selfless. Character always precedes skill, and character clothes our skill.

Sometimes we feel that we are too distinguished to do the humble things; we feel we are too important to have to do some menial task. Jesus was not so. Remember, too, in Luke's account of the Passover celebration, when the disciples were arguing, yet again over who was the most significant. Luke 22:24 describes this night, the night of the last supper and states, "A dispute arose among them as to which of them was considered to be greatest." The disciples had been arguing over precedence and prestige. They had all walked past the large waterpots at the door used for foot cleansing. Yet because of their competitive spirit, not one of them could even imagine taking on the role of foot washing.

SERVANT LEADERS ARE EXAMPLES

Here the key concept is modeling. Jesus instructs his disciples that they are to emulate his example (John 13:12-17). 1 Peter 5:2-3 adds to Jesus teaching:

> "Be shepherds of God's flock that is under your care, serving as overseers—not because you must, but because you are willing, as God wants you to be; not greedy for money, but eager to serve; not lording it over those entrusted to you, but being examples to

the flock." (1 Peter 5:2-3, NIV)

SERVANT LEADERS LOVE SACRIFICIALLY

Jesus calls this commandment to love "a new commandment." This was new in the sense that this commandment was a superior, better, higher commandment. While there had been a command to love before, now we are to love as Christ loves. Christ loves us selflessly, always with our interests and needs in view. Christ loves us sacrificially, willing to die for us. Love costs. Christ loves us understandingly, even though he knows us with all of our weaknesses. Love is not blind. It is wide-eyed. Christ also loves us forgivingly, knowing that we will falter even to the point of denying our knowledge of him. This love is to be the most powerful witness to a suspicious, sceptical world. Love is to be our distinguishing mark.

Love may involve emotions... but it is immensely more than a mere emotion. Love may make us feel good inside, but love is a verb; it is a decision, demonstrated in action. Love, it is said, can happen at first sight, but love moves beyond sight to substance. Jesus modeled selfless, sacrificial love. Jesus commanded us to love like he loves, selflessly, sacrificially, understandingly, forgivingly. When we love like Christ loves and not with fickleness, vacillation, or hesitancy, but consistently, resolutely, and without wavering, the world will notice and want what we have.

This kind of love will be grander than the savviest marketing scheme, more influential than the most powerful governments, more gripping than the greatest of blockbuster movies, more convincing than the most reasoned philosophical argument, and more persuasive than scientific evidence for intelligent design. This kind of love will become the ultimate apologetic.

ASSIGNMENT: *List three areas where you are presently an influencer or* *leader. What can you do specifically to serve in these settings?*

DISCUSSION: *Contrast our culture's focus on confident (often arrogant) and directive leadership with that of biblical servant leadership.*

46

The Disciple's Character
Based Leadership

This is a faithful saying: If a man desires the position of a bishop, he desires a good work. A bishop then must be blameless, the husband of one wife, temperate, sober-minded, of good behavior, hospitable, able to teach; not given to wine, not violent, not greedy for money, but gentle, not quarrelsome, not covetous; one who rules his own house well, having his children in submission with all reverence (for if a man does not know how to rule his own house, how will he take care of the church of God?); not a novice, lest being puffed up with pride he fall into the same condemnation as the devil. Moreover he must have a good testimony among those who are outside, lest he fall into reproach and the snare of the devil. (1 Timothy 3:1-7, NKJV)

For this reason I left you in Crete, that you should set in order the things that are lacking, and appoint elders in every city as I com-

*manded you—if a man is blameless, the husband of one wife, hav-
ing faithful children not accused of dissipation or insubordina-
tion. For a bishop must be blameless, as a steward of God, not
self-willed, not quick-tempered, not given to wine, not violent,
not greedy for money, but hospitable, a lover of what is good, sober-minded, just, holy, self-controlled, holding fast the faithful
word as he has been taught, that he may be able, by sound doctrine, both to exhort and convict those who contradict.* (Titus 1:5-
9, NKJV)

Image can actually carry us for a while, even in ministry, it appears. However, sooner or later our character will surface and declare who we really
are. As Paul gave Titus and Timothy (see also 1 Timothy 3) a list of qualifications for spiritual leadership, it is significant to note how many are skill-
based and how many are character-based. The contrast in percentages is
stark between skills and character qualifications. While we have already
been introduced to the role of character, we want to reinforce this value by
noting how character absolutely defines our leadership influence.

CHARACTER IS THE QUALITY OF YOUR HEART

Above all else, guard your heart, for it is the wellspring of life.
(Proverbs 4:23, NIV)

Character is not the same as your heart, but it is the quality, measurement,
or moral assessment of your heart. Your heart is the core of who you are.
Your heart determines everything, your core longings, your inner motives.
We feel the way we do because of choices, thoughts, and core longings. We
cannot just change our feelings. We must move backwards, to the core.

Character is the quality of our heart, the quality of that core. Character
is why we do what we do. It is the foundation of our life's efforts. Character
is the groundwork, the underpinning of the leader's depth and breadth of

influence. Character extends our leadership platform. Character also affects the nature and quality of decisions. Everything emanates from the core, from the heart!

If that core is dysfunctional, rotten, jaded, self-seeking, or vengeful, that will soon be evident. But if character is worthy, if it holds integrity, if it holds high the quality of virtue, it produces a very different kind of fruit and that fruit produces trust in the heart of a follower.

If a follower trusts the heart of his leader, you have a priceless connection, glue, and a chain link that will not be easily threatened. The character of the leader and the quality of the leader's heart has given him or her credibility.

God is looking for a heart of quality, virtue, obedience, and love.

CHARACTER IS THE CORNERSTONE OF CREDIBILITY

Credibility is a commodity. Credibility is a currency. Credibility leads to influence. Managers can put pressure on employees. Military leaders can give orders. Positional leaders have leverage. They have the proverbial "big stick." But in a volunteer organization, and most notably in the church, we don't have a "big stick." We don't have outside "leverage." But if we are trusted, we have credibility, and people will go so much further than minimal expectations if they trust the credibility of the leader. People give their time, energy, and even lives for leaders they trust.

Credibility is the building-block for leadership. This is an absolute must for leaders. Think of the qualifications of an elder that we saw in Titus 1 or 1 Timothy 3. There are some fifteen qualifications here. Only two are skill-related. These are "apt to teach" and "able to manage his family." The remaining qualities are internal qualities, which build trust and shout, "This person is a credible person! This person is the real thing! This person can be trusted!"

This is why our best leadership usually begins following several years of service. People have seen the fruit of our heart. They now know us and trust us. They will now follow us because they know that we really love God, that we really love them, and that we are truly and relentlessly committed to the purposes of God and the call of God on our lives. Do not expect someone to follow you into battle who does not yet know you and who does not yet trust the integrity of your heart. Conversely, this is why some of us are not seeing our leadership influence expand. When we do not return phone calls, do not say thank you, do not demonstrate real authentic care for underdogs, or are prone to being curt with people or losing our temper, we hurt our credibility.

Thus, when we read in Proverbs 4:23, "Above all else, guard your heart, for it is the wellspring of life" (NIV), the application is clear. Everything is an outflow of our heart. Character is the quality of that heart. Character is the cornerstone of credibility. You must guard your heart. You must protect your character.

CHARACTER IS SHAPED BY OUR RESPONSE TO LIFE'S INPUTS

Character is shaped, and it continues to be shaped. We are impacted by our family of origin, by pain, by our environment, by our education, and by various additional kinds of input, both good and bad. While we cannot control many of life's inputs, we can control our response to those inputs and learn from them.

A model may prove helpful. Life development can be seen as somewhat of a progressive, unfolding continuum from the state of *Being* to *Becoming* to *Doing*.

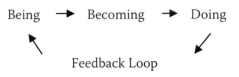

We see ourselves in a certain light (being), we then grow with inner changes (becoming), and we act on the basis of our self-perception and growth (doing). Significant and impacting experiences in our *Doing* phase creates a *Feedback Loop* which takes us from *Doing* back to *Being*. Change and maturity is not a single, linear progression. Rather, it is a series of ongoing cycles of responses and feedback.

If I increasingly view myself as a child of God (*being*), continue to pursue hard after developing the characteristics of Christlikeness (*becoming*) and I work diligently as a servant leader fulfilling my vision (*doing*), but in the process I am criticized, the criticism hurts deeply and thrusts me back to my core identity (*feedback loop* back to *being*). I may be tempted to view myself (*being*) poorly, inadequately, and somehow as less valuable because I or my ideas have been rejected. However, I can look at the situation very differently. By reminding myself that I am not inadequate or less valuable because of this response, I can grow to a leadership initiative. I am nevertheless God's child (*being*) who is growing (*becoming*) and serving (*doing*) him.

I can now seek to learn and grow as I objectively evaluate the nature of the criticism. Perhaps I could have done something differently, or perhaps I am simply being disagreed with as so many leaders have experienced before me. At any rate, the *feedback loop* has made me stronger. I have learned, and my self-concept (*being*) matures further and becomes more resolved. This then impacts my ongoing *becoming* and *doing,* creating an ongoing cycle toward maturity.

CHARACTER IS DEFECTIVE AND DECEIVING

Motive is a Pandora's Box. We often prefer not to even ask what our motivation is for fear of what we might discover. James Thurber has observed that "all men should strive to learn before they die, what they are running from, and to, and why."[41] This is an exceedingly penetrating question.

What drives you? What motivates you? What are you fleeing from? What are you running toward? What are you passionate about? How might you keep your passion alive for God?

All a man's ways seem innocent to him, but motives are weighed by the Lord. (Proverbs 16:2, NIV)

> *Therefore judge nothing before the appointed time; wait till the Lord comes. He will bring to light what is hidden in darkness and will expose the motives of men's hearts. At that time each will receive his praise from God.* (1 Corinthians 4:5, NIV)

I am not suggesting that God cannot use us unless we have completely pure motives. In fact, just the opposite is true and this reality is concerning. Consider,

> *But what does it matter? The important thing is that in every way, whether from false motives or true, Christ is preached.* (Philippians 1:18, NIV)

God does use people with ill motives. However, how much better will he use us if we serve well and with honourable motives? Some people are pleasers and others are ambitious for mixed reasons. Oftentimes, the very thing that we are most praised for and most effective at is an initiative that is done with mixed motives. What is the answer to this dilemma? Understanding and acknowledging this reality is essential.

CHARACTER IS FORGIVABLE AND REDEEMABLE

For this last statement, a case study is in order. King David is the unquestionable golden boy of Israel's royal line. To this day, his reign remains the standard by which all subsequent leaders have been measured. The stellar reputation of David is multifaceted.

First, David had fearless courage. Whether it was lions, bears, giants, well-armed armies, or maniacal kings, David's boldness and confidence in God propelled him forward (1 Samuel 17).

Second, David had unwavering loyalty. David and Jonathan's friendship stands as a role model in loyalty, comradery, and friendship (1 Samuel 18-20). His loyalty was also applied to his army, which were his mighty men of valour (1 Samuel 22-23). David remained resolute in his loyalty to King Saul, even while the king was seeking to take his life (1 Samuel 24-26).

Third, David had a magnetic and inspiring leadership style. The ultimate litmus test of leadership is: "Is anyone following?" David never walked for long before people started to follow him (1 Samuel 16-2 Samuel 24).

Fourth, David had missional focus. David modeled this; however, it is the New Testament that comments thus:

> For when David had served God's purposes in his own generation, he fell asleep. (Acts 13:36, NIV)

David had a vision for a united nation, as he brought together these factious twelve tribes. He had a vision for a safe nation as he defended his people from marauders, predators, and evil oppressors. His vision was that this nation be led with authentic, spiritual leadership, under the ultimate reign of God himself. He did what God wanted him to do, appropriate to his generation and to his cultural context. When David was finished, he died.

Fifth, David reflected a tender compassion. Following the death of Saul and much of his family, David demonstrates a rare kind of compassion when he takes Mephibosheth into his home. Mephibosheth was a son of Saul who was disabled, and therefore unable to care for himself (2 Samuel 9).

Sixth, David had a resilient spirituality. I love the story where David finds himself in the desert, living in Ziklag, on the run from Saul. His family and the families of his men have been kidnapped by the Amalekites. David's men were grumbling and anxious and David feels the weight of leadership closing in on him. Rather than lose perspective, he found strength and correct perspective in turning to God (1 Samuel 30:6).

However, here is a deeply significant question: Is this why David is so highly revered and honoured when his life reflected several abysmal failures? These include: adultery with Bathsheba (2 Samuel 11); the murder of Uriah (2 Samuel 11); his passivity with internal family conflict; his son Amnon raping his daughter Tamar; his other son, Absalom, murdering Amnon; Absalom initiating a revolt and being finally killed (2 Samuel 13-18); and his pride-inspired census (2 Samuel 24; 1 Chronicles 21). Surely, these horrible behaviours take away from the glow and leave David as tarnished as the rest of us, do they not?

I want to suggest that the reason for David's larger-than-life reputation has less to do with his leadership in good days, and more to do with his response in difficult and dark days. David's response after his sin was one of absolute brokenness.

> *O Lord, do not rebuke me in Your anger, Nor chasten me in Your hot displeasure.*
> *Have mercy on me, O Lord, for I am weak; O Lord, heal me, for my bones are troubled.*
> *My soul also is greatly troubled; But You, O Lord—how long?*
> *Return, O Lord, deliver me! Oh, save me for Your mercies' sake!*
> *For in death there is no remembrance of You; In the grave who*

will give You thanks?

I am weary with my groaning; All night I make my bed swim; I
drench my couch with my tears.

My eye wastes away because of grief; It grows old because of all
my enemies (Psalm 6:1-7, NKJV).

Blessed is he whose transgression is forgiven, Whose sin is
covered.

Blessed is the man to whom the Lord does not impute iniquity,
And in whose spirit there is no deceit.

When I kept silent, my bones grew old Through my groaning all
the day long.

For day and night Your hand was heavy upon me; My vitality was
turned into the drought of summer. Selah.

I acknowledged my sin to You, And my iniquity I have not
hidden. I said, "I will confess my transgressions to the Lord,"
And You forgave the iniquity of my sin. Selah. (Psalm 32:1-5,
NKJV)

Have mercy upon me, O God, According to Your lovingkindness;
According to the multitude of Your tender mercies, Blot out
my transgressions.

Wash me thoroughly from my iniquity, And cleanse me from my
sin.

For I acknowledge my transgressions, And my sin is always
before me.

Against You, You only, have I sinned, And done this evil in Your
sight—That You may be found just when You speak, And
blameless when You judge. (Psalm 51:1-4, NKJV)

When Nathan confronted David with his sin, David was instantly broken. When David witnessed the fallout in his family, his heart ached with
an unimaginable degree of regret and pain. When David awoke to his pride
at the census, he was again grief-stricken and he confessed his sin. He

agreed with God that his actions were sinful.

David was said to be a man after God's own heart. This was because David had a sensitive heart that was humble before God. This is what distinguished David before God, before the leaders of old, and before many of the leaders of today. Today, when we are confronted with our wrongdoings, we excuse, we blame, we explain, or we defend. David agreed. He humbly confessed. He grieved regretfully, and corrected his behaviour. Our character is defective and deceiving. Know this. Own this. But, thank God, your character is forgivable and redeemable. So, whatever sinful things that may be driving you, confess them. Understand them. Bring them under the control of the Lordship of Christ.

ASSIGNMENT: *As objectively as possible, assess your own character.*

DISCUSSION: *Discuss the various motives that may be at work in your life.*

47

The Disciple's Commitment
to Reproduction

And the things you have heard me say in the presence of many witnesses entrust to reliable men who will also be qualified to teach others. (2 Timothy 2:2, NIV)

It has often been stated that "Christianity is just one generation from extinction." It is the responsibility of one generation to pass on their faith and wisdom to the next. The genius of multiplication is its potential for rapid growth. If one person disciples two people a year, and each of those people in turn disciple two people a year, the law of multiplication would quickly reach exponential proportions. This book is dedicated to the theme of discipleship. Discipleship is often viewed as mentoring; however, mentoring may be viewed as a more personal transfer of knowledge, skills, and values. Whether occasional or intensive, mentoring is more often understood as the investment of a more mature or experienced person (the mentor) into the life of another less mature or less-experienced person (the protégé). While mentoring may be broader than discipleship, in that a mentor may focus on a particular set of skills or abilities, discipleship is mentoring that has biblical truth as its anchor.

The language of mentoring has its roots in Greek mythology. Homer's *Odyssey* describes how the goddess Athena takes on the appearance of an old man named "Mentor" in order to guide a young man named "Telemachus" through challenges. History records numerous mentor-protégé relationships, and the Bible records mentoring relationships between Jethro and Moses, Moses and Joshua, Ezra and Nehemiah, Elijah and Elisha, Barnabas and John Mark, and Paul and Timothy. However, the ultimate mentoring investment was the one Jesus made with his twelve disciples.

Jesus carefully, prayerfully selected those into whom he would pour particular time and energy, and we are wise to follow his example. We may not be able to invest as heavily in as many, but we should make it a point of reproducing ourselves at a deeper level with someone every few years. The themes of this entire discipleship resource are foundational; however, the following principles will help us to drill deeper into our mentoring practices with better structure.

MENTORING PRACTICES

- Share your story. Share your history, your family of origin, your pain, and your joys with your protégé. Relationships of trust are built on openness and vulnerability. We cannot mentor someone while aloof and distant. Protégés are hungry to learn from an older, wiser individual.
- Share your beliefs. Share your faith, your values, and your convictions. Protégés are interested in knowing how we got to where we are, what shaped our beliefs and values.

They are interested in knowing what is central and foundational to our personal worldview. They want to know about our walk with God.

- Share your behaviours. Share your practices, your personal disciplines, your physical exercise habits, your marriage practices, your parenting practices, your work practices, your neighbourhood practices, your citizenship practices, your ministerial practices, and any other life skills that may help. We should never assume that these are intuited or always understood by others.

- Challenge your protégé. Challenge them to set goals for their own growth. These goals may be personal, spiritual, relational, ministry, or professional. Help them to think critically, biblically, and strategically. The ultimate objective of a mentor is to see real change in the thinking and living of the protégé.

MENTORING SUGGESTIONS[42]

- Establish the mentoring expectations and goals.
- Jointly agree on the purpose of the relationship.
- Determine the regularity of interaction.
- Determine the type of accountability.
- Set up communication mechanisms.
- Clarify the level of confidentiality.
- Set the life cycle of the relationship.
- Evaluate the relationship from time to time.
- Modify expectations to fit the real-life mentoring situation.
- Bring closure to the mentoring relationship.

ASSIGNMENT: *Pray and seek to identify someone you could mentor.*

DISCUSSION: *Discuss the people who deeply shaped you. How did they do this?*

48

The Single Disciple

While marriage is the longing of most people, it is not necessarily the preferred or expected status of the disciple. While we do not know what Paul's marital status was before his conversion, we do know what his marital status was as a follower of Christ. Paul believed that singleness provided a strategic advantage to the disciple of Christ and to his or her ability to focus. Paul addresses this in his first epistle to the Corinthian believers:

> Now, getting down to the questions you asked in your letter to me. First, Is it a good thing to have sexual relations? Certainly—but only within a certain context. It's good for a man to have a wife, and for a woman to have a husband. Sexual drives are strong, but marriage is strong enough to contain them and provide for a balanced and fulfilling sexual life in a world of sexual disorder. The marriage bed must be a place of mutuality—the husband seeking to satisfy his wife, the wife seeking to satisfy her husband. Marriage is not a place to "stand up for your rights."

Marriage is a decision to serve the other, whether in bed or out. Abstaining from sex is permissible for a period of time if you both agree to it, and if it's for the purposes of prayer and fasting—but only for such times. Then come back together again. Satan has an ingenious way of tempting us when we least expect it. I'm not, understand, commanding these periods of abstinence—only providing my best counsel if you should choose them. Sometimes I wish everyone were single like me—a simpler life in many ways! But celibacy is not for everyone any more than marriage is. God gives the gift of the single life to some, the gift of the married life to others.

I do, though, tell the unmarried and widows that singleness might well be the best thing for them, as it has been for me. But if they can't manage their desires and emotions, they should by all means go ahead and get married. The difficulties of marriage are preferable by far to a sexually tortured life as a single.

And if you are married, stay married. This is the Master's command, not mine. If a wife should leave her husband, she must either remain single or else come back and make things right with him. And a husband has no right to get rid of his wife.

For the rest of you who are in mixed marriages—Christian married to non-Christian—we have no explicit command from the Master. So this is what you must do. If you are a man with a wife who is not a believer but who still wants to live with you, hold on to her. If you are a woman with a husband who is not a believer but he wants to live with you, hold on to him. The unbelieving husband shares to an extent in the holiness of his wife, and the unbelieving wife is likewise touched by the holiness of her husband. Otherwise, your children would be left out; as it is, they also are included in the spiritual purposes of God.

On the other hand, if the unbelieving spouse walks out, you've got to let him or her go. You don't have to hold on desperately. God has called us to make the best of it, as peacefully as we can. You never know, wife: The way you handle this might bring your husband not only back to you but to God. You never know, husband: The way you handle this might bring your wife not only back to you but to God.

And don't be wishing you were someplace else or with someone else. Where you are right now is God's place for you. Live and obey and love and believe right there. God, not your marital status, defines your life. Don't think I'm being harder on you than on the others. I give this same counsel in all the churches.

Were you Jewish at the time God called you? Don't try to remove the evidence. Were you non-Jewish at the time of your call? Don't become a Jew. Being Jewish isn't the point. The really important thing is obeying God's call, following his commands.

Stay where you were when God called your name. Were you a slave? Slavery is no roadblock to obeying and believing. I don't mean you're stuck and can't leave. If you have a chance at freedom, go ahead and take it. I'm simply trying to point out that under your new Master you're going to experience a marvelous freedom you would never have dreamed of. On the other hand, if you were free when Christ called you, you'll experience a delightful "enslavement to God" you would never have dreamed of.

All of you, slave and free both, were once held hostage in a sinful society. Then a huge sum was paid out for your ransom. So please don't, out of old habit, slip back into being or doing what everyone else tells you. Friends, stay where you were called to be. God is there. Hold the high ground with him at your side.

The Master did not give explicit direction regarding virgins, but as one much experienced in the mercy of the Master and loyal to him all the way, you can trust my counsel. Because of the current pressures on us from all sides, I think it would probably be best to stay just as you are. Are you married? Stay married. Are you unmarried? Don't get married. But there's certainly no sin in getting married, whether you're a virgin or not. All I am saying is that when you marry, you take on additional stress in an already stressful time, and I want to spare you if possible.

I do want to point out, friends, that time is of the essence. There is no time to waste, so don't complicate your lives unnecessarily. Keep it simple—in marriage, grief, joy, whatever. Even in ordinary things—your daily routines of shopping, and so on. Deal as sparingly as possible with the things the world thrusts on you. This world as you see it is on its way out.

I want you to live as free of complications as possible. When you're unmarried, you're free to concentrate on simply pleasing the Master. Marriage involves you in all the nuts and bolts of domestic life and in wanting to please your spouse, leading to so many more demands on your attention. The time and energy that married people spend on caring for and nurturing each other, the unmarried can spend in becoming whole and holy instruments of God. I'm trying to be helpful and make it as easy as possible for you, not make things harder. All I want is for you to be able to develop a way of life in which you can spend plenty of time together with the Master without a lot of distractions.

If a man has a woman friend to whom he is loyal but never intended to marry, having decided to serve God as a "single," and then changes his mind, deciding he should marry her, he should go ahead and marry. It's no sin; it's not even a "step down" from celibacy, as some say. On the other hand, if a man is comfortable in his decision for a single life in service to God and it's entirely his own conviction and not imposed on him by others, he ought to stick with it. Marriage is spiritually and morally right and not inferior to singleness in any way, although as I indicated earlier, because of the times we live in, I do have pastoral reasons for encouraging singleness.

A wife must stay with her husband as long as he lives. If he dies, she is free to marry anyone she chooses. She will, of course, want to marry a believer and have the blessing of the Master. By now you know that I think she'll be better off staying single. The Master, in my opinion, thinks so, too. (1 Corinthians 7:1-40, MSG)

While this passage explores the themes of marriage, desertion, and divorce, it presses the value of singleness as an attractive option for the disciple of Christ. Singleness is not to be seen as a curse, or even a disadvantage. Rather, singleness is to be seen as a gift that can strategically advance Great Commission ministry. Paul observes the following benefits to single living:

- Singleness means less distress from a hostile world (verse 26).
- Singleness means less distress in personal matters (verses 27-28).
- Singleness means more time to do ministry (verses 29-30).
- Singleness means more time to enjoy a spiritual relationship with God (verses 32-35).

ASSIGNMENT: *Identify the various implications (positive and negative) of living as a single disciple. List specific benefits and drawbacks based on what Paul has observed in 1 Corinthians 7.*

DISCUSSION: *Discuss how single people are often perceived. How can we change this impression?*

—— 49 ——
The Married Disciple

Leadership in the home is a profoundly significant responsibility. Parents are supposed to disciple their children, and in so doing prepare the next generation to carry on the mission of the church. Marriage and parenting is entered into by so many without a clear sense of the magnitude of influence and significance of these relationships. We must think rightly about marriage and parenting from a biblical perspective.

UNDERSTANDING COVENANT

The word *covenant* does not translate well into many languages. The word *promise* comes close, but covenant represents so much more. The people of the Bible understood covenants well. In fact, they made all kinds of covenants to define and describe their relationships with each other. The patriarch, Abraham, made a covenant with the Philistine king, Abimelech, to resolve their conflict over a water source (Genesis 21:22-34). David and

Jonathan made a covenant of everlasting friendship that also affirmed David's right to the throne of Israel (1 Samuel 18:23). The fundamental difference between covenants and other agreements is the relationship established between the covenant makers. Such covenant relationships went far beyond legal concepts.

Covenant parties viewed each other as friends who were bound together permanently. Though our biblical translations refer to people "making" a covenant, the Hebrews described the establishment of this type of relationship as "cutting" a covenant. The cutting, symbolized by the slaughter and sacrifice of an animal (Exodus 24:5, 8) indicated that each party promised to give his or her own life to keep the terms. To break a covenant was to invite one's own death as a penalty.

The most notable and celebrated covenant ever made in the Bible is the covenant that God makes with his people. First, there is the covenant with Abraham.

> *Now the Lord said to Abram, "Go forth from your country, and from your relatives and from your father's house, to the land which I will show you;*
>
> *And I will make you a great nation, and I will bless you, and make your name great; and so you shall be a blessing;*
>
> *And I will bless those who bless you, and the one who curses you I will curse and in you all the families of the earth will be blessed."* (Genesis 12:1-3, NASB)

Abraham was excited, but there was something that made this offer impossible. He and Sarah were childless. Genesis 15:2-10 and 17-18 describes the covenant that God made with Abraham. By passing between the two pieces of sacrificed animals, God swore fidelity to His promises and placed obligation for their fulfillment on Himself alone.

Remember how the story unfolds? God created human beings with the ability, and furthermore the deep need, to be in relationship with him. When Adam and Eve sinned, they severed that friendship. But God pursued humanity. To help them understand the depth and endurance of his love and his commitment, God chose to seal the relationship with the familiar expression, the covenant.

God was telling us that he wanted to bond eternally with the very creatures that rejected him. It further shows that God was willing to demonstrate his devotion to the relationship by offering his own life. Still further, this shows that God not only was willing to offer his own life to keep the covenant, but he also was willing to pay the price for any covenant failure on the part of the human beings with whom he was in relationship. This by far exceeded the limits of human covenants.

A covenant was an unbreakable relationship. This is how they were viewed. They were far more than legal contracts, mutual agreements, or even promises. These were relationships for life.

HOW COVENANTS WERE EXPRESSED

We can see how the relationship within the covenant is expressed. This unbreakable relationship—God as Father with us, husband and wife, parent and child, friend with friend—all were modeled by what the Bible refers to as God's *hesed* love, which is God's covenantal love, or loyal love. This too is an ancient Hebrew concept. Let's look at an example of this:

> For as high as the heavens are above the earth, so great is his steadfast love toward those who fear him; as far as the east is from the west, so far does he remove our transgressions from us. As a father shows compassion to his children, so the Lord shows compassion to those who fear him. For he knows our frame; he remembers that we are dust.
>
> As for man, his days are like grass; he flourishes like a flower

of the field; for the wind passes over it, and it is gone, and its place knows it no more. But the steadfast love of the Lord is from everlasting to everlasting on those who fear him, and his righteousness to children's children, to those who keep his covenant and remember to do his commandments. (Psalm 103:11-18, ESV)

In the New Testament, the Greek word *agape* emerges as the dominant word, meaning unconditional love. The meanings of *hesed* and *agape* are complementary. The original concept of covenant has been rapidly eroded and is nearly lost. It has been replaced with contractual terms and understandings. These are more contractual relationships whereby they only work if both parties fulfill their end of the arrangement.

Early or immature covenants begin as unilateral covenants (one-way), such as in a parent-infant relationship or even some marriages. The goal is that they mature and become bilateral or mutual covenant relationships. Growth in relationships can be blocked or retarded when one person in the relationship is unable or unwilling to reciprocate. Marriage is intended to be a covenant, an unbreakable relationship. Parenting is intended to be a covenant, an unbreakable relationship. Family is intended to be a covenant, an unbreakable relationship.

THE MARRIAGE COVENANT

Some Pharisees came to Jesus, testing Him and asking, "Is it lawful for a man to divorce his wife for any reason at all?"

And He answered and said, "Have you not read that He who created them from the beginning MADE THEM MALE AND FEMALE, and said, 'FOR THIS REASON A MAN SHALL LEAVE HIS FATHER AND MOTHER AND BE JOINED TO HIS WIFE, AND THE TWO SHALL BECOME ONE FLESH'? So they are no longer two, but one flesh. What therefore God has joined together, let no man separate."

> They said to Him, "Why then did Moses command to GIVE
> HER A CERTIFICATE OF DIVORCE AND SEND her AWAY?"
>
> He said to them, "Because of your hardness of heart Moses
> permitted you to divorce your wives; but from the beginning it
> has not been this way. And I say to you, whoever divorces his
> wife, except for immorality, and marries another woman commits
> adultery." (Matthew 19:3-9, NASB)

Many Jewish men were using a passage from the Law of Moses (Deuteronomy 24:1-4) to justify their divorce initiatives. Jesus scolds them and corrects them. Yes, he acknowledges that divorce does happen, but he reminds them that divorce is always less than ideal (life is full of less than ideals). Jesus wants to once again raise the bar concerning the value of marriage. To do so, Jesus goes back to the first book in the Bible (Genesis 2). Jesus' point was that the Genesis account described the way it is supposed to be.

Here is what God's idea of marriage looks like:

THE ESSENCE OF MARRIAGE

- Marriage is of divine design and origin. Marriage was God's idea and God's plan. Ideas that begin with the creator work. God made us as relational beings, and we long to connect at a deeper level. Marriage provides for this.
- Marriage is designed to take place between a man and a woman. Marriage was heterosexual in nature. The two genders complement each other physiologically, emotionally, spiritually, and mentally.
- Marriage is designed to take place between one man and one woman. God's plan was that marriage be monogamous. While the Bible records stories of polygamy, it does not do so with the purpose of establishing a model; the Bible simply records that this happened.

- Marriage is designed to be permanent and enduring. While divorce does happen, divorce always hurts and always leaves scars. God's design is that when we get married, we stay married, and thus enjoy the security of permanence and trust.

- Marriage is symbolically sealed through sexual union. Marriage involves commitment, but with it, romance, chemistry, attraction and passion. This is what makes marriage different from all other relationships. This is why sexual intimacy is to be enjoyed exclusively in the marriage relationship. Marriage is now a "one-flesh" relationship.

- Marriage is a covenant before God and in the presence of the community. It is helpful to compare the concept of covenant with that of a contract. A "contract" involves a relationship of obligation between individuals and, sometimes, involves privileges as well. The relationship is conceived, however, in linear or horizontal terms between two parties. In contrast, a covenant is not a linear relationship; it is a triangular one. It adds a third party to the arrangement, and the third party is God. He is the witness to the covenant commitment at its inauguration. As a covenant, the intention is that it be unconditional. It is not a commitment or contract that says, "I will stay married as long as you satisfy these requirements or expectations." It is a covenant that says, "I promise to be your husband or wife... period." Marriage is also publically recognized.

- Marriage is a symbolic reflection of God's covenant relationship with his people. This concept is not initially introduced in Genesis, but it is a theme that surfaces quickly in the Biblical text. Israel is often compared to being a faithful wife, and tragically, more often an unfaithful wife.

In the New Testament (Ephesians 5), marriage is called a
mystery that reflects God's enduring love for the church,
his bride.

ASSIGNMENT: *What do you expect to get from marriage? What do you expect to put into marriage? Make a list of these expectations. Be specific.*

DISCUSSION: *Why do people so quickly resort to divorce?*

───── 50 ─────

The Disciple's Intimacy in Marriage

As human beings we have very strong sexual desires. As a culture we are very unsatisfied, so we keep seeking, keep searching, keep pursuing, keep experimenting, keep looking for sexual fulfillment. Does it exist? Can it be found? If sexual fulfillment is found, can it be maintained? Are those who have discovered it willing to share who they are, and how they found it?

Western culture seems to suggest that sexual pleasure is found any and everywhere but in the marriage relationship. It is found when we abandon our inhibitions and freely pursue our wildest sexual interests. Whatever you do, don't weigh yourself down with a "ball-and-chain" in a restrictive relationship called marriage. Marriage is often portrayed as a wet blanket that is thrown over one's sexual life. Is this true? Does marriage sentence us to a life of sexual self-denial or does a monogamous marriage make sexual intimacy better?

Linda Waite and Maggie Gallagher are two research specialists who have engaged in extensive survey work examining sexual fulfillment in people. Their research is secular and religiously unmotivated. Nevertheless, their findings are revealing:

> Married people have both more and better sex than singles do. They not only have sex more often, but they enjoy it more, both physically and emotionally, than do their unmarried counterparts. Only cohabitors have more sex than married couples, but they don't enjoy it as much. Marriage, it turns out, is not only good for you, it is good for your libido too.[43]

These studies tell us that married people enjoy intimacy more frequently, but quantity isn't everything. These surveys showed that husbands and wives were more satisfied with sex than the sexually active singles. The reason, both theory and evidence suggest, is that the secret ingredient that marriage adds is commitment. For women, the idea that committed sex is better sex proves virtually a truism; however, men, too, derive great satisfaction from the security of a committed relationship. Waite and Gallagher observe:

> Emotional commitment improves one's sex life in other ways as well. For example, sex with someone you love literally doubles your sexual pleasure: You get satisfaction not only from your own sexual response but from your partner's as well. Emotional commitment to a partner makes satisfying him or her important in and of itself. Demanding a loving relationship before having sex, using sex to express love, and striving to meet the sexual needs of one's partner all increase satisfaction with sex. Love and a concern for one's partner shifts the focus away from the self in a sexual relationship and toward the other person. This selfless approach to sex, paradoxically, is far more likely to bring sexual satisfaction to both men and women.[44]

These results should not surprise us. People want powerful sexual feelings to have a meaning. And the meaning that is most satisfying appears to be, "I love you. Our lives are joined as our bodies."[45] This is what the Bible calls becoming "one flesh." The Bible explains how healthy sexuality grows out of a healthy and clear theology of marriage. Once we understand what marriage is, we can then explore more fully the purposes behind sexual union.

SEXUAL INTIMACY IS A SYMBOL AND SEAL OF THE MARRIAGE UNION

For this reason a man will leave his father and mother and be united to his wife, and they will become one flesh. (Genesis 2:24, NIV)

Do you not know that your bodies are members of Christ himself? Shall I then take the members of Christ and unite them with a prostitute? Never! Do you not know that he who unites himself with a prostitute is one with her in body? For it is said, "The two will become one flesh." (1 Corinthians 6:15-16, NIV)

SEXUAL INTIMACY PROVIDES FOR REPRODUCTION AND PARENTHOOD

So God created man in his own image, in the image of God he created him; male and female he created them. God blessed them and said to them, "Be fruitful and increase in number; fill the earth and subdue it. Rule over the fish of the sea and the birds of the air and over every living creature that moves on the ground." (Genesis 1:27-28, NIV)

SEXUAL INTIMACY IS A PLEASURABLE EXPRESSION OF LOVE TO BE ENJOYED

Abraham's wife, Sarah, perceived the sexual relationship to be a "pleasure."

He said, "I will surely return to you at this time next year; and be-

hold, Sarah your wife will have a son." And Sarah was listening at
the tent door, which was behind him.

Now Abraham and Sarah were old, advanced in age; Sarah
was past childbearing.

Sarah laughed to herself, saying, "After I have become old,
shall I have pleasure, my lord being old also?"

And the Lord said to Abraham, "Why did Sarah laugh, say-
ing, 'Shall I indeed bear a child, when I am so old?' Is anything too
difficult for the Lord? At the appointed time I will return to you,
at this time next year, and Sarah will have a son."

Sarah denied it however, saying, "I did not laugh"; for she was
afraid. And He said, "No, but you did laugh."

Then the men rose up from there, and looked down toward
Sodom; and Abraham was walking with them to send them off.

The Lord said, "Shall I hide from Abraham what I am about
to do, since Abraham will surely become a great and mighty na-
tion, and in him all the nations of the earth will be blessed?"
(Genesis 18:10-18, NASB)

Isaac sought to bring sexual pleasure to his wife by "caressing" her.

When the men of that place asked him about his wife, he said,
"She is my sister," because he was afraid to say, "She is my wife."
He thought, "The men of this place might kill me on account of
Rebekah, because she is beautiful."

When Isaac had been there a long time, Abimelech king of
the Philistines looked down from a window and saw Isaac caress-
ing his wife Rebekah. So Abimelech summoned Isaac and said,
"She is really your wife! Why did you say, 'She is my sister'?"

Isaac answered him, "Because I thought I might lose my life
on account of her." (Genesis 26:7-9, NIV)

The Law required that newly married soldiers stay with their new
brides for a period of one year in order to bring "happiness" or sexual

pleasure to their wives.

> *If a man has recently married, he must not be sent to war or have any other duty laid on him. For one year he is to be free to stay at home and bring happiness to the wife he has married.* (Deuteronomy 25:5, NIV)

The Proverbs speak of the joy of sexual intimacy.

> *Let your fountain be blessed, and rejoice in the wife of your youth, a lovely deer, a graceful doe. Let her breasts fill you at all times with delight; be intoxicated always in her love. Why should you be intoxicated, my son, with a forbidden woman and embrace the bosom of an adulteress?*(Proverbs 5:18-20, ESV)

SEXUAL INTIMACY IS TO BE ENJOYED LEGITIMATELY IN MARRIAGE IN ORDER TO SAFEGUARD ILLEGITIMATE EXPRESSIONS OUTSIDE OF MARRIAGE

> *But because of the temptation to sexual immorality, each man should have his own wife and each woman her own husband. The husband should give to his wife her conjugal rights, and likewise the wife to her husband. For the wife does not have authority over her own body, but the husband does. Likewise the husband does not have authority over his own body, but the wife does. Do not deprive one another, except perhaps by agreement for a limited time, that you may devote yourselves to prayer; but then come together again, so that Satan may not tempt you because of your lack of self-control.* (1 Corinthians 7:2-5, ESV)

FAN THE FLAMES OF MARRIAGE

If you are married, do not be looking for greener grass. Cherish your marriage. Protect it. Nourish it! Remember your vows. *The Book of Common Prayer* of 1552 has given us a classic set of vows which are often spoken at marriage ceremonies to this day.

> I take thee to have and to hold, from this day forward, for better
> for worse, for richer for poorer, in sickness and in health, to love
> and to cherish, till death do us part, according to God's holy ordi-
> nance and thereto I give thee my troth. With this ring, I thee wed,
> with my body I thee worship, and with my worldly goods I thee
> endow.[46]

A wise man named Agur observed:

> *There are three things that are too amazing for me, four that I do
> not understand: the way of an eagle in the sky, the way of a snake
> on a rock, the way of a ship on the high seas, and the way of a
> man with a maiden.* (Proverbs 30:18-19, NIV)

Romance is a breathtaking mystery. Marriage is a magnificent covenant. Intimacy is a beautiful gift. Revel in these wonders to the glory of
God.

ASSIGNMENT: *Given a biblical view of sexuality, what are the moral implications on current social trends such as homosexuality, pornography, and
any kind of sexual expression outside of marriage?*

DISCUSSION: *If you are married, discuss this chapter with your spouse.*

—— 51 ——
The Disciple's Conflict Resolution in Marriage

We long to find ourselves in a healthy, intimate, caring, and loving marriage. While this is our aspiration, life lobs many disappointments and challenges our way. Marriage has many predators. Here are a few that lurk in the dark:

TIME PRESSURE

We have too many commitments and not enough time, energy, and focus. The danger here is that we have so many voices calling to us that we eventually neglect that which matters the most: our faith, our family, our health, and our marriage.

MONEY PRESSURE

Money issues are the subject matters most frequently argued about. Curiously, so many cultural contexts are marked by prosperity, and yet we find ourselves in such debt.

BLAME AND SHAME

We are prone to blame each other for our failures and disappointments. This is the failure to look in the mirror and have the courage and humility to admit that we may have something to do with the problems we are facing. Stop blaming and take some responsibility here.

FICKLENESS

Yesterday, we "fell in love." Today, we are not so sure. We have become very adept, very proficient at deconstructionism, at redefining history, and at redefining words. We are working very hard at redefining words like: honesty, truth, loyalty, sex, fairness, equity, and of course, love. Love used to be a powerful word implying strength of will and commitment, fortitude, dedication, and sacrifice. Now, love is essentially perceived as an emotion that just comes and goes. "I felt it yesterday, but it appears to have vanished today." Then, we give to this fleeting emotion the authority to govern our lives. "Because I don't feel love for my wife or husband, I am getting out!"

This mindset, though pervasive, is contrary to everything the Bible teaches about love. There are times when I do not feel like going to work. I do not always feel like cleaning up after myself. I do not always feel like controlling my comments. I do not always feel like driving the speed limit. But if we lived our lives based on passing, fleeting, fickle emotions, life would be nothing short of disastrous. I am not suggesting that emotions and feelings are immaterial or meaningless—far from it—but we dare not make life decisions based on how we feel at the moment.

Marital love involves commitment, resolve, perseverance, endurance, stick-to-itiveness, and determination. Don't quit!

DOUBT

I must find my soul mate. And so, when the emotion runs dry, we doubt. Somewhere we heard about this idea of a "soul mate." Choose your spouse wisely. Seek out counsel from people you trust. Do not be in a rush to dive into marriage. This is an enormously significant decision. But once you decide, and once you say your vows to that person, that person is your soul mate. Don't doubt otherwise.

EXPECTATIONS

We all enter marriage with expectations. "You should be like me. You should meet my needs. I shouldn't have to change. Marriage is 50-50," and the like. These may be common expectations, but are they realistic? Or are we just setting ourselves up for major disappointment? The gap between how we think life should work and what it actually delivers is what can disappoint. Many of us experience huge disappointments in marriage, not because our marriages are bad, but because we had excessive or unrealistic expectations.

Who said that husband and wife should be clones? Who said that marriage will meet every possible need you have in life? Who said that you can stay the same and your spouse should do all the adjusting? Life is full of change, and if I am not changing, I am likely dead and decomposing. Who said marriage is 50-50? Marriage is "for better for worse, for richer for poorer, in sickness and in health." It should be 100-100, but sometimes it is

60-40, and sometimes it is 90-10, because sometimes one in the partnership gets ill, gets discouraged, gets fatigued, and the other must carry a larger load.

LAZINESS

Sometimes this crazy thought enters our mind: "If it takes hard work, we must not be right for each other." All relationships require effort. Marriage, parenting, business partnerships, customer relations, they all take effort. Good marriages do not happen by accident. A good marriage is not the result of genetics. Good marriages are not the result of astrological compatibility. Good marriages take effort!

RESENTMENT

Anger, bitterness, pride, and a lack of conflict resolution skills can all lead to enormous resentment, and this will create a gigantic wall between marriage partners. You must learn to forgive and request forgiveness. Here are nine powerful words: "I am sorry, I was wrong, please forgive me!"

TEMPTATION

This usually takes the form of the myth of greener pastures. Our temptations may be of a covetous, sexual nature; however, temptations of all kinds can lead to addictions and compulsions which can destroy us. Gambling, workaholism, alcoholism, and substance abuse of all kinds can offer us temporary relief, but when the relief evaporates, the shame comes, the emptiness returns, and then we drink at the same dirty trough of our idol yet again. Build protective measures into your relationship.

SELFISHNESS

We demand, "Me first; my way!" If there is anything that will surely annihilate your marriage, it is selfishness. Genesis 3 records for us the catastrophic consequences of humanity's fall from grace. God had created a paradise, a world of wonder, beauty, and discovery. Into this masterpiece of nature, God placed animal life of all kinds, but as a crowning climax, God created a being called man with two genders, male and female. They would communicate, interact, create, love, worship, and relate with each other and with God. Then they were deceived by a real enemy. We can blame the cunning serpent, the devil, but in the end, we chose our way over God's. We thought we knew better, and then everything changed. We were cursed. It was self-initiated, and self-induced, but it was a curse.

> To the woman he said, "I will surely multiply your pain in childbearing; in pain you shall bring forth children. Your desire shall be for your husband, and he shall rule over you."
>
> And to Adam he said, "Because you have listened to the voice of your wife and have eaten of the tree of which I commanded you, 'You shall not eat of it,' cursed is the ground because of you; in pain you shall eat of it all the days of your life; thorns and thistles it shall bring forth for you; and you shall eat the plants of the field. By the sweat of your face you shall eat bread, till you return to the ground, for out of it you were taken; for you are dust, and to dust you shall return."
>
> The man called his wife's name Eve, because she was the mother of all living. And the Lord God made for Adam and for his wife garments of skins and clothed them.
>
> Then the Lord God said, "Behold, the man has become like one of us in knowing good and evil. Now, lest he reach out his hand and take also of the tree of life and eat, and live forever—" therefore the Lord God sent him out from the garden of Eden to work the ground from which he was taken. (Genesis 3:16-23,

ESV)

> *Now Adam knew Eve his wife, and she conceived and bore Cain,*
> *saying, "I have gotten a man with the help of the Lord." And*
> *again, she bore his brother Abel. Now Abel was a keeper of sheep,*
> *and Cain a worker of the ground. In the course of time Cain*
> *brought to the Lord an offering of the fruit of the ground, and*
> *Abel also brought of the firstborn of his flock and of their fat por-*
> *tions. And the Lord had regard for Abel and his offering, but for*
> *Cain and his offering he had no regard. So Cain was very angry,*
> *and his face fell. The Lord said to Cain, "Why are you angry, and*
> *why has your face fallen? If you do well, will you not be accepted?*
> *And if you do not do well, sin is crouching at the door. Its desire*
> *is for you, but you must rule over it."* (Genesis 4:1-7, ESV)

In Genesis 3, we read about how women would thereafter have pain in childbearing and men would sweat through difficult labour. There would be physical suffering and the introduction of mortality. We would now experience death. However, there is a curious phrase when God says to Eve, "Your desire will be for your husband." Was this part of the curse? The answer lies in the next chapter. The context is that Cain is jealous of his brother Abel and is allowing bitterness and rage to grow inside of him. Cain then murders Abel. However, before he does, God warns him (4:7). What is key here is the word desire. It is the same Hebrew word used in 3:16. The point is that "desire" here has a sense of mastering, control, and domination. If we go back to the consequences on Adam and Eve, God is saying, "Eve, you will want to control your husband and yet he will seek to control you." Selfishness was a consequence of the fall.

These predators and challenges visit all marriages. The most critical skill to develop in navigating these challenges is communication and conflict resolution. Consider the following.

EXPECT CONFLICT

Conflict is a reality of life that cannot be avoided. You may be able to reduce some, but it will come.

COMMIT YOURSELF TO THE GOAL OF UNITY AND TO THE CONFLICT RESOLUTION PROCESS

> *If you have any encouragement from being united with Christ, if
> any comfort from his love, if any fellowship with the Spirit, if any
> tenderness and compassion, then make my joy complete by being
> like-minded, having the same love, being one in spirit and pur-
> pose.* (Philippians 2:1-2, NIV)

Remember that diversity and unity can coexist. Two people do not have to
be identical to experience harmony. The goal is unity, not victory.

Scott Peck has used the following model to illustrate how to best resolve conflict.[47] His thesis is that many couples live in a visibly pleasant
world called "pseudo community." In this world things look good, but often
real issues go unresolved. The only way to achieve "true community" (unconditional acceptance, resolution, and harmony) is by navigating the path
of "chaos." "Chaos" is the path of conflict resolution. It is not an easy path,
but it is an absolutely necessary path.

Pseudo Community ⟶ Chaos ⟶ True Community

ADDRESS CONFLICT AS SOON AS POSSIBLE.

> *In your anger do not sin: Do not let the sun go down while you
> are still angry, and do not give the devil a foothold.* (Ephesians
> 4:26-27, NIV)

Schedule a time to talk if the present is not a good time. However, if possible, deal with conflict to completion at the time of conflict. When we fail to

address issues and we "let the sun go down" while we are still in tension, we give bitterness a foothold. Over time, these unresolved issues can create a wall of resentment. Should you reach an impasse, involve wise counsel.

DEAL APPROPRIATELY WITH YOUR EMOTIONS

> *What is the source of quarrels and conflicts among you? Is not the source your pleasures that wage war in your members? You lust and do not have; so you commit murder. You are envious and cannot obtain; so you fight and quarrel. You do not have because you do not ask. You ask and do not receive, because you ask with wrong motives, so that you may spend it on your pleasures.* (James 4:1-3, NASB)

> *Let all bitterness and wrath and anger and clamor and slander be put away from you, along with all malice. Be kind to one another, tender-hearted, forgiving each other, just as God in Christ also has forgiven you.* (Ephesians 4:31-32, NASB)

Acknowledge your emotions. Express your feelings. Talk about your emotions. Don't just display them through body language. Analyze and evaluate them to see if your anger is rooted in selfishness or hurt. Anger is not a wrong or sinful emotion. However, if it goes unaddressed, it can become bitterness, which is wrong and sinful. The goal, however, is to work our way through to forgiveness.

PACKAGING MATTERS

What you say matters. Do say: "I feel..." "Do you mean?" "Did I understand you correctly?" "What do you think?" "What do you feel?" "I am sorry. I was wrong. Will you please forgive me for..." Do not say: "You never..." "You always..." "You're just like..."

While what we say matters, so does how we say it. Cultivate love, kindness, and humility in how you speak. Packaging matters.

ASSIGNMENT: *Review your last few conflicts. What were they about? Did you navigate "chaos" well, or are there still some unresolved issues that require addressing?*

DISCUSSION: *Review the communication and conflict resolution principles. Are these applicable to other contexts (parent-child, work associates, neighbours, etc.)?*

—— 52 ——

The Disciple as Parent:
Parenting Is a Relationship

There is an old Chinese proverb that says, "It is easier to lead a nation than a family." If you are a parent, you know this is true. If you are not yet a parent, you likely have all the confidence in the world (confidence is what you have when you don't understand the situation). Parents begin the parenting process with energy, excitement, and love. However, sometimes what is lacking is a plan. Many parents parent without intentionality. The next three chapters are focused on biblical parenting and on how we can disciple our own children.

GOD AS FATHER

In the same way that marriage is God's idea, so is parenting and family life. Thus, consulting the engineer's guide will provide tremendous guidance. A critical foundation which should be observed is that in the same way that marriage is a picture of God's unconditional relationship with us, parenting is also a picture. God himself is called our Father. Thus, God himself is the ultimate example of a parent.

- God as a parent loves and cares for his children.
- God as a parent provides, protects, and defends his children.
- God as a parent leads and guides his children.
- God as a parent comforts and consoles his children.
- God as a parent instructs and corrects his children.
- God as a parent gives meaningful freedoms to his children.
- God as a parent forgives his children.
- God as a parent blesses his children with all kinds of lavish gifts.

Whenever we look at a verse or a principle on parenting, we can picture God and his approach as the ultimate role model.

RELATIONSHIP

The story of the prodigal son paints a full and tender picture of the enduring, loyal love of a parent. The following biblical texts add to our understanding of parenting as a relationship.

> *Or what man is there among you who, when his son asks for a loaf, will give him a stone? Or if he asks for a fish, he will not give him a snake, will he? If you then, being evil, know how to give good gifts to your children, how much more will your Father who is in heaven give what is good to those who ask Him!* (Matthew 7:9-11, NASB)

> *We proved to be gentle among you, as a nursing mother tenderly*

cares for her own children. Having so fond an affection for you,
we were well-pleased to impart to you not only the Gospel of God
but also our own lives, because you had become very dear to us...
just as you know how we were exhorting and encouraging and
imploring each one of you as a father would his own children, so
that you would walk in a manner worthy of the God who calls you
into His own kingdom and glory. (1 Thessalonians 2:7-8, 11-12,
NASB)

Relationships involve acceptance, respect, caring, involvement, and nurturing. Children need to know you care. They need you there. They need your involvement, but it needs to be a healthy kind of relationship. Relationships can be too distant and detached. Authors Balswick and Balswick call this relational disengagement. However, at the other end of the continuum is relational enmeshment, where families are too involved in the details of each other's lives. An appropriate balance is relational unity, but individual differentiation.[48] This means that there is unity in the family relationship, but individuality and differentiation of each person.

Love gives children security, an environment for healthy growth, environment for healthy communication (conflict), builds self-esteem, and a context for disciplining. But it is also a relationship that allows children to blossom into individuals. Relationship is foundational to everything. For example, you cannot discipline effectively without a relationship. Much of a young child's misbehaviour is begging the question, "Do you still love me?" Loving relationships are fed with eye contact, physical contact (tickle, wrestle, sitting on lap, hugs), focused attention (bedtime reading, listening, quality and quantity of time), affirmation (encouragement, building-up, complimenting skills, character, appearance).[49]

THE ROLE OF ENVIRONMENT

The environment or context into which these tools are applied is one of unconditional and unbreakable relationships. Within this relationship is *hesed*, loyal love and *agape*, unconditional love. There are times when parents have, without thinking, sent a terrible message: "Don't do that or mommy and daddy won't love you anymore." We must send the message that we love them regardless of their looks, academic ability, athletic skills, or chosen career. The message needs to be: "I love you, period!"

Parental love is characterized by respect. We ought not cut our children off, speak sarcastically to them, or treat them like a household pet. Parental love lives out the golden rule, Children have a very strong sense of fairness. Treat them the very same way you would have wanted to be treated at that age.

PARENTING PHASES

The parenting relationship goes through different phases.[50] Throughout each phase, parents should be adjusting their parenting style and how they relate to their kids.

- Modeling phase: This is the parenting phase for children from infancy to approximately age five. In this phase, children mimic and imitate their parents. Trust is developed in this phase as well, and most of a child's personality is shaped in this period.
- Instructing phase: This phase occurs for children between the ages of six and twelve. Here, children are taught, and they follow instructions because they are told to.
- Internalization phase: This phase encompasses the age of children from twelve to eighteen. In this time period, children are thinking things through on their own. They are

internalizing the principles that they have been taught and
they are choosing to own them. In this phase, they do
what they do because they choose to do so.

- Release phase: This can be a difficult phase for some parents. Somewhere around eighteen to twenty, children
must be released. Parents must "let go" and allow their
children to relate to them as adults.

ASSIGNMENT: *What stages are your children at? What relational initiatives will you make to deepen your relationship?*

DISCUSSION: *Discuss the difference between being disengaged and en-meshed with our children. If you do not have children, or are unable to have children, discuss how this reality sits with you. Can you still be content?*

──── 53 ────

The Disciple as Parent:
Parenting Is Instruction

While parenting is fundamentally a relationship, it is also a responsibility. One of the more significant functional responsibilities that parents have is to instruct their children.

THE ROLE OF INSTRUCTION

> Now this is the commandment, the statutes and the judgments which the Lord your God has commanded me to teach you, that you might do them in the land where you are going over to possess it, so that you and your son and your grandson might fear the Lord your God, to keep all His statutes and His commandments which I command you, all the days of your life, and that your days may be prolonged. O Israel, you should listen and be careful to do it, that it may be well with you and that you may multiply greatly,

just as the Lord, the God of your fathers, has promised you, in a
land flowing with milk and honey. Hear, O Israel! The Lord is our
God, the Lord is one! You shall love the Lord your God with all
your heart and with all your soul and with all your might. These
words, which I am commanding you today, shall be on your heart.
You shall teach them diligently to your sons and shall talk of them
when you sit in your house and when you walk by the way and
when you lie down and when you rise up. (Deuteronomy 6:1-7,
NASB)

This passage explains that moral and religious education is a parental responsibility, not primarily a governmental, ecclesiastical, or societal responsibility. Such agencies may support and complement the home, but
they should never replace the home. Furthermore, education is to be
rooted in God and God's truth. In the New Testament, Ephesians reinforces the responsibility.

Fathers, do not exasperate your children; instead, bring them up
in the training and instruction of the Lord. (Ephesians 6:4, NIV)

Do not exasperate your children. Do not provoke them. Do not set the
bar so high that they simply will never achieve your expectations. Rather,
"bring them up" or "nurture" them in God's ways. We certainly do this with
overt, demonstrative, intentional instruction whereby we teach skills like:

- Character skills: morality, ethics, gratitude, honesty, and
  integrity.
- Social skills: manners, making eye contact with people,
  taking initiative, kindness, conflict resolution, how to treat
  members of the opposite gender, marriage principles.
- Life skills: work ethic, money management, decision-
  making principles, distinguishing the good from the best,
  making wise purchases, politics, and the value of ongoing

education.

As we are teaching these things, we are being watched. The old adage is a true one: "More is caught than is taught." Children learn about money by watching how we save or spend. They learn about grace and forgiveness when they see how we respond to unfair treatment. They learn about sexuality when they see how parents love each other. They learn about faith when they see us pray in times of hardship and make the hard choices because they are the right choices. Instruction is intentionally verbalized, but always modeled.

All education has an instructive element (do this because it is the right and beneficial thing to do) but education also has a corrective element (the negative consequences warn us that what we did hurts us or others and we should not repeat it). Take a look at Proverbs 22.

> *Folly is bound up in the heart of a child, but the rod of discipline will drive it far from him.* (Proverbs 22:15, NIV)

This verse speaks to the role of correction or discipline. It tells us that children are not born with a blank slate. Rather, it tells us that children are born with an inclination to rebel. In the Proverbs, it is called "foolishness." Foolishness is being unteachable and demanding one's own way and is reflected in different ways at different ages. The three-year-old who throws a temper tantrum because he did not get his way is acting foolish. The thirteen-year old who slams the door because she was corrected is acting foolish. However, an adult may also express his own folly.

Parents need to help children see that life does not always go their way, that they will hear the word "no," and that the world is not waiting to serve them. We do our children a disservice if we never say no, if we never correct them, if we do not help them to see that things do not always go their way. We may want to be their friend, but we have to be their parent. Our children may get angry with us, but we have to win some battles, especially when children are young. We have to address folly.

Discipline is education (discipline relates to discipleship). Discipline is not punishment. It is not retribution. We do not discipline our children so that we can feel good. We discipline our children to help them learn. In the implementation of discipline, we need to be aware of the temptation to be either too soft or too harsh. Both of these extremes lead to unintended consequences. Balance and wisdom are needed.

Discipline is both preventative and corrective. The book of Proverbs offers great insight here. Its themes frequently focus on driving out the foolish propensities in our lives and replacing them with wisdom.

ASSIGNMENT: *What lessons, truths, and values do you want to instill into your children? How will you seek to realize this? How did your parents instill values in you?*

DISCUSSION: *Discuss ways of disciplining and correcting children which help them learn. What techniques did your parents employ that worked? What techniques did not work?*

54

The Disciple as Parent:
Parenting Is Empowerment

Parenting is a relationship. Parenting is instructing. Parenting is also empowerment. Empowering our children effectively requires thoughtful intentionality. Let's explore two rich passages.

PARENTAL GUIDANCE

> *Train a child in the way he should go, and when he is old he will not turn from it.* (Proverbs 22:6, NIV)

The word "train" is used of "dedicating" on an altar, and "to narrow one's path from folly to wisdom."[51] The etymology of this Hebrew word comes from the palate or roof of the mouth. An infant would have date juice placed on his or her mouth and this tartness would cause the infant to create the sucking action. This in turn would help ready him or her for breast-

feeding. Essentially, the parent was "whetting the appetite" for that which
was good.

The phrase "the way he should go" does not mean "in the right way,"
but rather it means "according to his bent" or "according to his temperament or abilities." In other words, our job is not to make them go our way.
Rather, our job is to figure out what they are good at and encourage them
along those paths. We do not select our children's career, but if we see
strong people skills, we should encourage that. If we see a strong science
aptitude, we should encourage that. If we see incredible artistic skills, we
should encourage that.

PARENTAL GOAL

What is the goal of parenting? What's the plan? When we start a business,
we have a goal and a plan. When we set out on a trip, we have a destination
and a route. Schools have an objective, rigorous, and stimulating curriculum for their students. However, when it comes to parenting, too many of
us are just reacting our way through the process. What is our goal? What is
our plan?

> My son, if your heart is wise, my own heart also will be glad; and
> my inmost being will rejoice when your lips speak what is right.
> Do not let your heart envy sinners, but live in the fear of the Lord
> always. Surely there is a future, and your hope will not be cut off.
> Listen, my son, and be wise, and direct your heart in the way. Do
> not be with heavy drinkers of wine, or with gluttonous eaters of
> meat; for the heavy drinker and the glutton will come to poverty,
> and drowsiness will clothe one with rags. Listen to your father
> who begot you, and do not despise your mother when she is old.
> Buy truth, and do not sell it, get wisdom and instruction and understanding. The father of the righteous will greatly rejoice, and
> he who sires a wise son will be glad in him. Let your father and

your mother be glad, and let her rejoice who gave birth to you.
Give me your heart, my son, and let your eyes delight in my ways.
(Proverbs 23:15-26, NASB)

When children mature and reflect good judgment and they have the skill of making good decisions, then everything else falls into place. They will make good spousal choices, they will choose careers in keeping with their strengths and aptitudes, they will work hard, they will make good moral and ethical conclusions, and they will follow Christ. This is what really matters, and this makes glad parents.

What then is the goal of parenting? The goal is empowerment. Empowerment means entrusting children with the life skills of maturity and self-leadership. Empowerment is rooted in the biblical word to equip. Equipping carries the concept of putting in order, restoring, mending, or healing. Training and discipline is also in view. William Barclay explains how this word may be applied in diverse contexts when he states in his commentary, "This word's military usage speaks of fully furnishing an army. Its civic usage speaks of pacifying a city, which is torn by factions. Its medical usage speaks of setting a broken bone or putting a joint back into place. The basic idea of the word is that of putting a thing into the condition in which it ought to be."[52]

We examined how parenting is a relationship and observed that we must adjust our relating style according to the age of the child. Similarly, empowerment and equipping is a sliding responsibility. When children are young, parents have high control. They direct and tell, they discipline, and they treat children as dependents. However, as children mature parents move to low control where they empower, trust, and create interdependency. When children are young they have few responsibilities. However, when they are released as adults they will have many responsibilities.

Another way to look at this process is to view the empowerment process as a series of phases as well.[53] The first phase is telling. In this phase, children are simply told what to do. Reasons may be given, but usually these reasons are not fully understood. The next phase is teaching. In this phase, we explain more fully the "whys" of our instruction. The third phase is participating, where parents are still involved, but they are increasingly passing on responsibility and skills to their children. The last phase is delegating. Here, parents simply entrust the responsibility or task completely to their mature child.

Parenting will thus require intentionality, strategy, and focus. Empowerment is training, equipping, and discipling. Discipling is what we are seeking to learn in this book.

WISDOM

We need wisdom. Wisdom is the application of truth. We must know truth and then cultivate the wisdom to apply it. The Proverbs talk a lot about wisdom. Wisdom is not a formula. It is an art form. Different styles are needed for different personalities. While we want to teach our children common truths, because of their different personalities we may need to employ differing techniques. Such is the application of wisdom.

ASSIGNMENT: *Leaders are constantly mapping out strategic plans. Parents are leaders, but we often parent reactively and not proactively. Map out a strategic plan for your parenting.*

DISCUSSION: *Describe a time when you made a quality choice. How did you come to this decision? How did you feel?*

55

Stewarding Our Money

A tool is an aid. It is an object, device, or resource that helps us accomplish a particular task, function, or objective. A tool helps achieve an end goal. The tool is never the end goal itself. Tools help us live efficiently. Tools help make life a little easier. Tools help us realize goals, objectives, and projects. But tools will never make us happy. Tools will never breathe joy into our attitudes. Tools will never fully satisfy a discontented soul. Tools were not made to do that. By definition, a tool helps us do something that may lead to happiness, joy, contentment, or accomplishment.

Curiously, a lot of people choose to pursue money. It is their end. In this study, we are going to see how money is a means. Money is just a tool.

> Jesus said to his disciples, "There was once a rich man who had a manager. He got reports that the manager had been taking advantage of his position by running up huge personal expenses. So he called him in and said, 'What's this I hear about you? You're fired.

And I want a complete audit of your books.'

"The manager said to himself, 'What am I going to do? I've lost my job as manager. I'm not strong enough for a laboring job, and I'm too proud to beg... Ah, I've got a plan. Here's what I'll do... then when I'm turned out into the street, people will take me into their houses.'

"Then he went at it. One after another, he called in the people who were in debt to his master. He said to the first, 'How much do you owe my master?'

"He replied, 'A hundred jugs of olive oil.'

"The manager said, 'Here, take your bill, sit down here—quick now—write fifty.'

"To the next he said, 'And you, what do you owe?'

"He answered, 'A hundred sacks of wheat.'

"He said, 'Take your bill, write in eighty.'

"Now here's a surprise: The master praised the crooked manager! And why? Because he knew how to look after himself. Streetwise people are smarter in this regard than law-abiding citizens. They are on constant alert, looking for angles, surviving by their wits. I want you to be smart in the same way—but for what is right—using every adversity to stimulate you to creative survival, to concentrate your attention on the bare essentials, so you'll live, really live, and not complacently just get by on good behavior."

Jesus went on to make these comments: If you're honest in small things, you'll be honest in big things; if you're a crook in small things, you'll be a crook in big things. If you're not honest in small jobs, who will put you in charge of the store? No worker can serve two bosses: He'll either hate the first and love the second or adore the first and despise the second. You can't serve both God and the Bank.

When the Pharisees, a money-obsessed bunch, heard him say these things, they rolled their eyes, dismissing him as hopelessly out of touch. So Jesus spoke to them: "You are masters at making *yourselves look good in front of others, but God knows what's behind the appearance."* (Luke 16:1-15, MSG)

Managers were a lot like financial planners today, except that they had complete control over their client's assets. It appears that this particular manager was not doing very well. He was either lazy, foolish, unethical, or perhaps all three. When the owner of the businesses confronted him about it, the manager knew he was in trouble and he did not relish the thought of a prolonged jail term. The manager came up with a plan to secure his own future and also placate the business owner. The manager went to each of the individuals to whom he had loaned money, and asked them to pay a lesser amount back (in one case 80%, in another 50%). We do not know enough about the economic climate of this situation, but commentary is made that the manager was acting shrewdly (perhaps not completely ethically, but shrewdly). It appears that the old saying "a bird in the hand is worth two in the bush" was being illustrated.

The owner, in this story, thought that it was better to get at least some money back rather than risk losing it all. Because the owner at least had some of his money returned, he commended his financial manager.

These are the lessons that Jesus is making:

MONEY IS A TOOL

Money is to be used. As a measurement of currency, it has value. But in the end, it is only a tool that can be used wisely or foolishly.

MONEY IS A TOOL TO TIN PEOPLE FOR THE KINGDOM OF GOD

When Jesus talks about gaining friends, the point is not to buy friendship. Rather, his point is this: Use your money and your possessions in generous and strategic ways to help people discover God.

The Apostle Paul says the same thing in 2 Corinthians.

> *For the ministry of this service is not only fully supplying the needs of the saints, but is also overflowing through many thanksgivings to God. Because of the proof given by this ministry, they will glorify God for your obedience to your confession of the Gospel of Christ and for the liberality of your contribution to them and to all.* (2 Corinthians 9:12-13, NASB)

MONEY, AS A TOOL, IS ALSO A TEST

Jesus teaches that if you use this tool wisely, responsibly, and as a good steward (manager), it becomes apparent that you can be trusted with more. Jesus then leaves us with a sting. He says, "No servant can serve two masters. Either he will hate the one and love the other, or he will be devoted to the one and despise the other. You cannot serve both God and Money." Jesus knew that the Pharisees, although they loved to look pious and devoted to God, actually loved money. It was controlling their motives. It was fuelling their passion. It was effectively ruling their lives.

In order to deal with this theme more comprehensively, allow me to identify four more purposes for the use of money that move beyond Jesus' story.

MONEY CAN BE A TOOL TO ALLEVIATE HUMAN SUFFERING

> *Now, brethren, we wish to make known to you the grace of God which has been given in the churches of Macedonia, that in a great ordeal of affliction their abundance of joy and their deep poverty overflowed in the wealth of their liberality. For I testify that according to their ability, and beyond their ability, they gave of their own accord, begging us with much urging for the favor of participation in the support of the saints.* (2 Corinthians 8:1-4, NASB)

What Paul then essentially says is, "Now that you are doing fairly well economically, you should help out with some of people in Judea who are going through a tough time." Specifically, Paul says:

> For I do not mean that others should be eased and you burdened; but by an equality, that now at this time your abundance may supply their lack, that their abundance also may supply your lack—that there may be equality. As it is written, "He who gathered much had nothing left over, and he who gathered little had no lack."(2 Corinthians 8:13-15, NKJV)

Paul reminds the believers at Corinth to share with others, because one day the church at Corinth may need help from the church at Jerusalem.

MONEY IS A TOOL TO PROVIDE FOR THE DAILY NECESSITIES OF LIFE

Most of us have been raised with a value system that says, "I want to be able to live responsibly in this cultural setting. I don't want to be a burden to anyone else. I want to be able to provide food for my family, a roof over our heads. I want to make my fair and appropriate contribution to my community and country by paying my taxes."

> Lazy hands make a man poor, but diligent hands bring wealth. (Proverbs 10:4, NIV)

Money is something we work for. We earn it and then we use it. With diligent work we advance ourselves.

> For even when we were with you, we gave you this rule: "If a man will not work, he shall not eat."(2 Thessalonians 3:10, NIV)

Scripture is quite straightforward here. If we do not work, we will have no money and no food. I know there may be short seasons of unemployment or transition, and we should support and encourage each other

through such challenging times. However, as a general rule, we should provide for our own needs and for those of our family.

> *If anyone does not provide for his relatives, and especially for his*
> *immediate family, he has denied the faith and is worse than an*
> *unbeliever.* (1 Timothy 5:8, NIV)

Earning money is a means for us to care for our family members, be
they a part of our nuclear family or in a broader sense. This is a responsibility we have and when we meet it, we extend our Christian reputation.
When we fail to do so, we defame our reputation. If we are not handling
our money wisely and our family is suffering as a result of it, this is a very
dark commentary on the authenticity of our faith.

MONEY IS A TOOL TO PREPARE FOR YOUR FUTURE

> *In the house of the wise are stores of choice food and oil, but a*
> *foolish man devours all he has.* (Proverbs 21:20, NIV)

The wise man plans and saves for the future, but the foolish squanders
what he has. Money is a tool to help prepare for the days when we either
can no longer work, or perhaps have extenuating needs. Good money management involves saving and delaying gratification.

> *Dishonest money dwindles away, but he who gathers money little*
> *by little makes it grow.* (Proverbs 13:11, NIV)

This speaks to the power of saving and hints at the pitfalls of sudden
large gains.

MONEY IS A TOOL TO BRING AN ADDED MEASURE OF ENJOYMENT TO LIFE

> *He who loves silver will not be satisfied with silver; nor he who*
> *loves abundance, with increase. This also is vanity. When goods*

increase, they increase who eat them; so what profit have the owners except to see them with their eyes? The sleep of a laboring man is sweet, whether he eats little or much; but the abundance of the rich will not permit him to sleep. There is a severe evil which I have seen under the sun: riches kept for their owner to his hurt. But those riches perish through misfortune; when he begets a son, there is nothing in his hand. As he came from his mother's womb, naked shall he return, to go as he came; and he shall take nothing from his labor which he may carry away in his hand. And this also is a severe evil—just exactly as he came, so shall he go. And what profit has he who has labored for the wind? All his days he also eats in darkness, and he has much sorrow and sickness and anger.

Here is what I have seen: It is good and fitting for one to eat and drink, and to enjoy the good of all his labor in which he toils under the sun all the days of his life which God gives him; for it is his heritage. As for every man to whom God has given riches and wealth, and given him power to eat of it, to receive his heritage and rejoice in his labor—this is the gift of God. For he will not dwell unduly on the days of his life, because God keeps him busy with the joy of his heart. (Ecclesiastes 5:10-20, NKJV)

This is honest. Solomon delivers here a strong warning. He cries, "Do not love money. Enjoy some of its benefits, but do not allow it to become the object of your affections." If it is not a tool, it will rule. Money can become a god, an obsession. You cannot take it with you. But then he instructs us to enjoy it. In other words, if money is seen properly as a tool and only a tool, and we use it wisely, and it is not a god to us, and it is not ruling us, money can be used to add a little enjoyment to life.

The conclusion is: If money is not a tool, it will rule.

ASSIGNMENT: *Assess how you are using your money as a tool in each of these categories.*

DISCUSSION: *Discuss what "living simply" might look like in a prosperous context.*

56

Stewarding Our Money with Giving

THE COMMAND

Why Share? Why Give? The answer is simple: The Bible commands us to give over and over.

> *Give, and it will be given to you: good measure, pressed down, shaken together, and running over will be put into your bosom. For with the same measure that you use, it will be measured back to you.* (Luke 6:38, NKJV)

It is also a command followed by a blessing.

> *Now concerning the collection for the saints, as I have given orders to the churches of Galatia, so you must do also: On the first day of the week let each one of you lay something aside, storing up as he may prosper, that there be no collections when I come.* (1 Corinthians 16:1-2, NKJV)

We are also commanded to give with regularity and thoughtful planning. There should be no coercion or manipulation involved.

> *Command those who are rich in this present age not to be haughty, nor to trust in uncertain riches but in the living God, who gives us richly all things to enjoy. Let them do good, that they be rich in good works, ready to give, willing to share.* (1 Timothy 6:17 18, NKJV)

Here the word command is even used. Obeying God should be a motivation alone, but nevertheless, let's ask why. Why should we give? Why should we share? Why is giving commanded?

GIVING IS AN ACT OF WORSHIP

The theme of Malachi is a rebuke of Israel for its lack of worship and lack of gratitude.

> *"From the days of your fathers you have turned aside from My statutes and have not kept them. Return to Me, and I will return to you," says the Lord of hosts. "But you say, 'How shall we return?' Will a man rob God? Yet you are robbing Me! But you say, 'How have we robbed You?' In tithes and offerings. You are cursed with a curse, for you are robbing Me, the whole nation of you!*
> *"Bring the whole tithe into the storehouse, so that there may be food in My house, and test Me now in this," says the Lord of hosts, "if I will not open for you the windows of heaven and pour out for you a blessing until it overflows.*
> *"Then I will rebuke the devourer for you, so that it will not destroy the fruits of the ground; nor will your vine in the field cast its grapes," says the Lord of hosts.* (Malachi 3:7-11, NASB)

Giving grows out of gratitude. It is a way of saying thank you, no matter how small. The situation here was that Israel's heart was far from God. God invites them back, but the people say, "How?" God says, "Well, let's start with worship and with your giving as a means of worship." God looks for sacrifice. God looks for devotion. In the Old Testament there was a standard of the "tithe," or 10%, that was expected. However, the people were not even giving their tithe, and God says, "You are robbing me."

When we become disappointed or angry with a church or a ministry and we withhold our giving from them, we are actually robbing God.

> *Honor the Lord with your wealth and with the firstfruits of all your produce; then your barns will be filled with plenty, and your vats will be bursting with wine.* (Proverbs 3:9-10, ESV)

Giving is an expression of worship, but giving also invites the blessing of God. Do you want to show God authentic worship? Do you want the blessing of God? A generous spirit with money has that effect.

GIVING IS AN ACT OF COMPASSION

Paul was writing the Corinthian church, reminding them how generous the poor Macedonian believers were. During a time of great need that the Corinthians were enduring, the Macedonian believers came through with great compassion. Now the Corinthian believers were being challenged to show compassion to the believers in Jerusalem who were going through a hard time.

> *We want you to know, brothers, about the grace of God that has been given among the churches of Macedonia, for in a severe test of affliction, their abundance of joy and their extreme poverty have overflowed in a wealth of generosity on their part. For they gave according to their means, as I can testify, and beyond their means, of their own accord, begging us earnestly for the favor of taking part in the relief of the saints.* (2 Corinthians 8:1-4, ESV)

For I do not mean that others should be eased and you burdened, but that as a matter of fairness your abundance at the present time should supply their need, so that their abundance may supply your need, that there may be fairness. As it is written, "Whoever gathered much had nothing left over, and whoever gathered little had no lack." (2 Corinthians 13-15, ESV)

Paul reminds the Corinthians, "When you had a need, others helped you. Now that others have a need, help them." In this way, there is a sense of equality. This is not an imposed socialism, but it is conscientious, intentional sharing, motivated out of compassion.

GIVING IS AN ACT OF SELF-CONTROL

And He told them a parable, saying, "The land of a rich man was very productive. And he began reasoning to himself, saying, 'What shall I do, since I have no place to store my crops?' Then he said, 'This is what I will do: I will tear down my barns and build larger ones, and there I will store all my grain and my goods. And I will say to my soul, "Soul, you have many goods laid up for many years to come; take your ease, eat, drink and be merry."'

"But God said to him, 'You fool! This very night your soul is required of you; and now who will own what you have prepared?'

"So is the man who stores up treasure for himself, and is not rich toward God." (Luke 12:16-21, NASB)

Here was a man who owned a lot of money, or perhaps I should say a lot of money owned him. He was wealthy, but not in control. Recall, if money is not a tool, it will rule. We must control money, not the other way around. We must manage money.

The rich rule over the poor, and the borrower is servant to the lender. (Proverbs 22:7, NIV)

The point of this proverb is that the lender is in control and the borrower is under control. Do not let money control you with its power, or through debt. You control it! You manage it! If not, it can become a curse. When you and I give freely, generously, and compassionately, we are asserting our positive control over money.

GIVING IS AN ACT OF INVESTMENT IN VISION

In 1 Chronicles 29, King David is speaking before his people in the capital, Jerusalem. He was seeking to set an example of his tremendous belief in building a Temple for God.

> *"Moreover, in my delight in the house of my God, the treasure I have of gold and silver, I give to the house of my God, over and above all that I have already provided for the holy temple, namely, 3,000 talents of gold, of the gold of Ophir, and 7,000 talents of refined silver, to overlay the walls of the buildings; of gold for the things of gold and of silver for the things of silver, that is, for all the work done by the craftsmen. Who then is willing to consecrate himself this day to the Lord?"*
>
> *Then the rulers of the fathers' households, and the princes of the tribes of Israel, and the commanders of thousands and of hundreds, with the overseers over the king's work, offered willingly; and for the service for the house of God they gave 5,000 talents and 10,000 darics of gold, and 10,000 talents of silver, and 18,000 talents of brass, and 100,000 talents of iron.*
>
> *Whoever possessed precious stones gave them to the treasury of the house of the Lord, in care of Jehiel the Gershonite.*
>
> *Then the people rejoiced because they had offered so willingly, for they made their offering to the Lord with a whole heart, and King David also rejoiced greatly.* (1 Chronicles 29:3-9, NASB)

The phrase, "They gave for the work of the house of God..." (verse 7) indicates how much they were motivated by David's speech and example. They wanted to participate. They were investing in a dream, a vision. This building would symbolize the presence of God. God cannot be housed, but this represented God's home in their midst, there in Jerusalem. The people were motivated to give toward that investment.

Paul echoes a similar situation.

> But this I say: He who sows sparingly will also reap sparingly, and he who sows bountifully will also reap bountifully. So let each one give as he purposes in his heart, not grudgingly or of necessity; for God loves a cheerful giver. And God is able to make all grace abound toward you, that you, always having all sufficiency in all things, may have an abundance for every good work. As it is written: "He has dispersed abroad, He has given to the poor; His righteousness endures forever."
>
> Now may He who supplies seed to the sower, and bread for food, supply and multiply the seed you have sown and increase the fruits of your righteousness, while you are enriched in everything for all liberality, which causes thanksgiving through us to God. For the administration of this service not only supplies the needs of the saints, but also is abounding through many thanksgivings to God, while, through the proof of this ministry, they glorify God for the obedience of your confession to the Gospel of Christ, and for your liberal sharing with them and all men. (2 Corinthians 9:6-13, NKJV)

Note the superlatives of verse 8: "And God is able to make all grace abound toward you, that you, always having all sufficiency in all things, may have an abundance for every good work." We are stewards, managers of God's resources. Here Paul tells the Corinthian believers to give. He even says, "Give to get." But not to get rich, like some prosperity evangelists teach. Rather, we are to give to get, to give, to get, to give, etc. When we give, God uses our giving. He multiplies our giving. He multiplies the investment for His kingdom purposes.

ASSIGNMENT: *Look at your budget. Set a financial target and plan to increase your systematic giving.*

DISCUSSION: *Discuss the principle of the "tithe." Is it relevant for today? Are there transferable principles at work?*

——— 57 ———

Stewarding Our Talents and Gifts

YOU HAVE A SPIRITUAL GIFT

For just as we have many members in one body and all the members do not have the same function, so we, who are many, are one body in Christ, and individually members one of another. Since we have gifts that differ according to the grace given to us, each of us is to exercise them accordingly: if prophecy, according to the proportion of his faith; if service, in his serving; or he who teaches, in his teaching; or he who exhorts, in his exhortation; he who gives, with liberality; he who leads, with diligence; he who shows mercy, with cheerfulness. (Romans 12:4-8, NASB)

Now there are varieties of gifts, but the same Spirit. And there are varieties of ministries, and the same Lord. There are varieties of effects, but the same God who works all things in all persons. But to each one is given the manifestation of the Spirit for the common good. For to one is given the word of wisdom through the

Spirit, and to another the word of knowledge according to the same Spirit; to another faith by the same Spirit, and to another gifts of healing by the one Spirit, and to another the effecting of miracles, and to another prophecy, and to another the distinguishing of spirits, to another various kinds of tongues, and to another the interpretation of tongues. But one and the same Spirit works all these things, distributing to each one individually just as He wills. For even as the body is one and yet has many members, and all the members of the body, though they are many, are one body, so also is Christ. (1 Corinthians 12:4-12, NASB)

And He gave some as apostles, and some as prophets, and some as evangelists, and some as pastors and teachers, for the equipping of the saints for the work of service, to the building up of the body of Christ; until we all attain to the unity of the faith, and of the knowledge of the Son of God, to a mature man, to the measure of the stature which belongs to the fullness of Christ. As a result, we are no longer to be children, tossed here and there by waves and carried about by every wind of doctrine, by the trickery of men, by craftiness in deceitful scheming; but speaking the truth in love, we are to grow up in all aspects into Him who is the head, even Christ, from whom the whole body, being fitted and held together by what every joint supplies, according to the proper working of each individual part, causes the growth of the body for the building up of itself in love. (Ephesians 4:11-16, NASB)

A spiritual gift can be understood as a special or unique ability that God gives us to serve him and others. According to the above passages, such gifts are divinely given and each believer has at least one. These abilities are intended to build up the church, the body of Christ. No gift has greater value than another gift. All are needed for the body of Christ to function as a whole. These gifts are not given to us for our benefit as much as for the benefit of others, and ultimately for the glory of God.

Peter instructs us:

*Each one should use whatever gift he has received to serve others,
faithfully administering God's grace in its various forms.* (1 Peter
4:10, NIV)

UNDERSTANDING THE GIFTS

The following is a list of the gifts identified in Scripture, along with a brief
descriptor for each. They are listed in the order found in Romans, 1 Corinthians, and Ephesians. Some have suggested that, because each list is
slightly different, these gifts are not comprehensive, meaning that there
may still be additional gifts. While that is certainly possible, we will treat
this as a working list to guide us as disciples in serving God to the fullest.

- Prophesy: the ability to receive and communicate divine
  revelation from God to man. Another possible understanding of this is that it is the ability to proclaim truth
  which leads to repentance and correction.
- Service: the ability to identify and fulfill unmet needs.
- Teaching: the ability to communicate truth so that others
  may learn and grow.
- Exhortation: the ability to comfort, console, or encourage
  another.
- Giving: the ability to contribute in a uniquely generous
  and cheerful manner.
- Leadership: the ability to attract, lead, and motivate people
  to accomplish tasks.
- Mercy: the ability to feel compassion and minster to the
  hurting.
- Wisdom: the ability to apply truth to given situations.
- Knowledge: the ability to accumulate and analyze infor-
  mation in order to better understand truth.
- Faith: the ability to trust God for great things.

- Healing: the ability to heal someone who is ill.

- Miracles: the ability to perform an unexplainable event.

- Discerning of spirits: the ability to distinguish between truth and error.

- Tongues: the ability to speak in a language not previously known.

- Interpretation of tongues: the ability to interpret or translate a language not previously known.

- Apostle: the leadership ability given to Christ's Disciples. The word means "sent one." Some have suggested that the gift of apostle differs from the office of apostle. Thus, the gift may be to communicate the Gospel cross-culturally in an effective manner, and is therefore linked to missionary exploits.

- Helps: the ability to identify and fulfill unmet needs.

- Administration: the ability to plan and execute goals and objectives in fulfillment of a vision.

- Evangelist: the ability to communicate the Gospel in a clear and effective manner which produces results.

- Pastor/teacher: the ability to nurture, build up, teach, and care for individuals.

- Celibacy: the ability to remain single with a contented attitude in order to serve the Lord (1 Corinthians 7:7).

- Hospitality: the ability to open up one's home to give of one's resources to minister to someone in need (1 Peter 4:9).

- Craftsmanship: the ability to use one's artistic abilities to draw people's attention toward God (Exodus 28:3, 31:2-11, 35:30-35, 36:1).

DISCOVERING YOUR GIFT

How do we know what our spiritual gift is? While there are numerous spiritual inventories and tests you may want to take advantage of, there is no science to this discovery. Here are some initiatives that will prove helpful:

- Prayer: Ask God to show you what your spiritual gift(s) might be. Remember, when we ask, seek, or knock, God is listening.

- Exposure: Expose yourself to different service opportunities and possibilities. You may be drawn to certain opportunities which may be more familiar to you; however, do not hesitate to expose yourself to completely new experiences.

- Desire: You should enjoy using your spiritual gift. Our desires may not always be defining. However, they will play a role.

- Confirmation: Others should see your spiritual gift at work. Seek feedback from people who know you well and from people who are in leadership of the ministry area you are exploring. The affirmation and confirmation of the church should play a major role in helping you identify your spiritual gift.

- Results: Has the ministry initiative you engaged in produced some significant or measurable results? Usually, the confirmation you receive from others will relate to the evidence of results.

As you seek to discover where you fit in the body of Christ, draw on all five of these principles. Be patient, but be persistent.

DEVELOPING YOUR GIFT

Once we have identified what our spiritual gifts are, we should be careful not to assume that our task is complete. Natural talents need to be cultivated. Someone with musical ability should take music lessons. Someone with language aptitude should learn as many languages as possible. Someone with strong academic skills should pursue advanced education. In the same way, spiritual gifts need to be developed if they are going to accomplish all that they can for God's purposes. Consider the following:

- Education: Read, study, seek out mentoring, and learn as much as you can about the arena of gifting that God has given you. Such education should continue on an ongoing basis.
- Exercise: Use your gift. God intends for us to use our spiritual abilities for the edification of the church. If we are not using our gift, we will not grow, and we are inhibiting the church from attaining the maturity and influence that it is intended to have.
- Evaluation: Seek feedback. Constructive evaluation leads to improvement and increased effectiveness.

A FEW CAUTIONS

While spiritual gifts are from God, we need to remember that our humanity and propensity to pervert truth continues to seek expression. We are capable of taking a good thing and turning it into a dark or damaging thing. Here are some things to keep in mind:

- No gift is more important than another. 1 Corinthians 12 makes this point strongly. However, for those who have more publically recognizable gifts, the temptation can be to think you are indispensible. Furthermore, no gift is evidence of any greater love by God. While we should feel good when we serve, and we should feel joy and gratitude when God uses us, we do need to safeguard ourselves against pride.

- Beware of gift projection. This is the tendency to think that the gift that you have is the priority that everyone else should have. Evangelists may think that others are not sharing their faith enough. Musicians may think that worship should be everyone's central priority. Teachers may think that biblical education should be the highest objective. Administrators may think that everyone else is disorganized. Your gift should edify the whole body, not just some individuals.

ASSIGNMENT: *Work through all the prompts in this chapter. What do you think your top three gifts are?*

DISCUSSION: *Discuss what others think you are good at or effective at.*

—— 58 ——
Stewarding Our Calling and Life

A PERSONAL SENSE OF CALL

We are stewards, managers of God's resources. Our resources, our money, and our time all belong to God and we are expected to use these wisely. Furthermore, we are gifted to accomplish God's mission which, broadly speaking, is the Great Commandment and the Great Commission. While the essential mission and purpose is set before us by God, God then gives us a unique part in this larger agenda. Recall our study of Ephesians 2:10.

> *For we are God's workmanship, created in Christ Jesus to do good works, which God prepared in advance for us to do.* (Ephesians 2:10, NIV)

It is extremely helpful for us to be able to package that sense of call into a defined statement: "What is God calling me to become and to do?" The answer to this question is God's more specific "call" upon our lives. The call of God for me personally may be understood as a sense that this is what God wants me uniquely to become and do (the divine element) coupled with the affirmation of people (the human element). With this in view, I must seek out God's "call" for my life through personal spiritual pursuits while embracing sensitivity to God's leading, and through the affirmation of the body. Being able to verbalize one's call into a concise mission or vision statement is a way of clarifying and focusing one's call in a very specific way. Having a sense of call, or a sense of focus, is valuable for a number of reasons.

First, it confirms our obedience to God's purposes for our life. We have a conviction that we are doing what the Master desires us to do. Second, it brings us a sense of fulfillment, knowing that we are doing God's work. Human nature is such that we long for connection in relationship and for impact and significance. Feeling unloved and useless is the curse of low self-esteem. When we experience God's love and we have a confidence that we are serving his kingdom purposes, we feel whole. Direction gives purpose and confidence. Third, it keeps us responsible. We have a job to do within Christ's body and we cannot be negligent in keeping our commitments. Fourth, it holds us accountable. A vision statement gives us something objective with which to measure our life and activities. Fifth, a vision statement can serve to keep us going when we feel like quitting.

The actual exercise of developing a mission or vision statement is a mixture of the subjective and the objective. A vision statement will be made concise as we keep paring down our answers by asking increasingly more specific questions. Allow the following exercise to help you focus.

- What is my personality type? If you have never taken a personality inventory, you will find this to be a helpful and insightful exercise.
- What is my leadership style? There are leadership

assessment tools that can assist you.

- What keeps me awake at night?
- If I could do anything I wanted (money not being an issue) what would I choose to do?
- In what areas have people most affirmed me?
- What are my spiritual gifts, natural strengths, and learned competencies?
- What are my greatest weaknesses and fears?
- What has pain in my life taught me and made me particularly sensitive toward?
- What do I spend discretionary money on?
- In moments of quiet reflection before God, what do I believe God is nudging me toward?

Take some time to prayerfully reflect upon how you have answered the above questions. The final step will be to distill the above observations into a personal vision statement. Begin a rough draft of what you believe God has called you to be, become, and do with your life. Allow the draft to percolate for several days (or even weeks). Evaluate your draft statement by asking yourself the following questions:

- Does it honour God?
- Does it inspire me?
- Does it stretch me?
- Is it timeless?
- Is it focused enough?

Discuss your work with your mentor or with close friends. Keep tweaking and polishing until you have distilled something that grips you with passion. It may take several weeks to digest and then articulate your life calling into a focused statement, but the process will prove invaluable in bringing focus to your life. Once you have a final statement, record it in your journal. Place it at the front of your day-timer. Memorize it! Review it often. Finally, live by it!

PUTTING FLESH ON THE VISION

The next step is to put some action steps to your vision statement. Nothing could be more futile than going through the process of developing a vision statement and then never using it. Your vision needs goals (specific objectives you plan on carrying through) and strategies (specific action steps that will achieve your goals). Some have found value in developing goals that are SMART. This acrostic stands for goals that are Specific, Measurable, Attainable, Realistic, and Timely. This criteria keeps us from being too vague with our goals.

Your vision should point you in the direction of several life goals (likely not less than three, but preferably not more than seven). Each of the goals will require detailed action steps. Take the time to map these out.

- What am I called to? Vision Statement
- What are the basic objectives of my calling? Vision Goals
- How will I accomplish my calling? Vision Strategies

There a wise saying: Plan your work and work your plan. However, working your plan is more difficult than it seems on paper. Self-leadership is required. How will we ensure that we stay on the growing edge of maturity? We will need self-discipline.

There are numerous tragic examples of those who started well, but ended poorly because of the absence of good self-leadership.

CASE STUDY: KING SAUL

So they ran and brought him from there; and when he stood among the people, he was taller than any of the people from his shoulders upward. And Samuel said to all the people, "Do you see him whom the Lord has chosen, that there is no one like him among all the people?"

So all the people shouted and said, "Long live the king!" (1 Samuel 10:23-24, NKJV)

Saul was impressive, without equal, a head taller than others, a warrior, a man's man, a leader of leaders. What happens? He starts well, but quickly embraces his own press releases and places himself above the law. He becomes arrogant and proud, and eventually anxious, fearful of losing the crown, and paranoid of young David, the next anointed King. In the end, he goes down in the annuls of history as a deeply flawed leader.

CASE STUDY: KING SOLOMON

So King Solomon surpassed all the kings of the earth in riches and wisdom. And all the kings of the earth sought the presence of Solomon to hear his wisdom, which God had put in his heart. Each man brought his present: articles of silver and gold, garments, armor, spices, horses, and mules, at a set rate year by year.

Solomon had four thousand stalls for horses and chariots, and twelve thousand horsemen whom he stationed in the chariot cities and with the king at Jerusalem.

So he reigned over all the kings from the River to the land of the Philistines, as far as the border of Egypt. The king made silver as common in Jerusalem as stones, and he made cedar trees as abundant as the sycamores which are in the lowland. And they brought horses to Solomon from Egypt and from all lands. (2 Chronicles 9:22-28, NKJV)

This sounds impressive. Solomon built on the foundation of his father and amassed an incredible inventory of goods. However, this symbol of human strength would become his undoing. Deuteronomy warned against the very practices Solomon willingly engaged in.

> *But he shall not multiply horses for himself, nor cause the people to return to Egypt to multiply horses, for the Lord has said to you, "You shall not return that way again." Neither shall he multiply wives for himself, lest his heart turn away; nor shall he greatly multiply silver and gold for himself.* (Deuteronomy 17:16-17, NKJV)

CASE STUDY: KING UZZIAH

> *Now all the people of Judah took Uzziah, who was sixteen years old, and made him king instead of his father Amaziah. He built Elath and restored it to Judah, after the king rested with his fathers.*
>
> *Uzziah was sixteen years old when he became king, and he reigned fifty-two years in Jerusalem. His mother's name was Jecholiah of Jerusalem. And he did what was right in the sight of the Lord, according to all that his father Amaziah had done. He sought God in the days of Zechariah, who had understanding in the visions of God; and as long as he sought the Lord, God made him prosper.*
>
> *Now he went out and made war against the Philistines, and broke down the wall of Gath, the wall of Jabneh, and the wall of Ashdod; and he built cities around Ashdod and among the Philistines. God helped him against the Philistines, against the Arabians who lived in Gur Baal, and against the Meunites. Also the Ammonites brought tribute to Uzziah. His fame spread as far as the entrance of Egypt, for he became exceedingly strong.*
>
> *And Uzziah built towers in Jerusalem at the Corner Gate, at the Valley Gate, and at the corner buttress of the wall; then he fortified them. Also he built towers in the desert. He dug many wells, for he had much livestock, both in the lowlands and in the plains; he also had farmers and vinedressers in the mountains and*

in Carmel, for he loved the soil.

Moreover Uzziah had an army of fighting men who went out to war by companies, according to the number on their roll as prepared by Jeiel the scribe and Maaseiah the officer, under the hand of Hananiah, one of the king's captains. The total number of chief officers of the mighty men of valor was two thousand six hundred. And under their authority was an army of three hundred and seven thousand five hundred, that made war with mighty power, to help the king against the enemy. Then Uzziah prepared for them, for the entire army, shields, spears, helmets, body armor, bows, and slings to cast stones. And he made devices in Jerusalem, invented by skillful men, to be on the towers and the corners, to shoot arrows and large stones. So his fame spread far and wide, for he was marvelously helped till he became strong.

But when he was strong his heart was lifted up, to his destruction, for he transgressed against the Lord his God by entering the temple of the Lord to burn incense on the altar of incense.
(2 Chronicles. 26:1-16, NKJV)

Uzziah began as perhaps one of the most effective leaders. However, his pride became his undoing. He thought himself above the law. He thought we was above accountability and he threw away all his credibility.

CASE STUDY: KING HEZEKIAH

Thus Hezekiah did throughout all Judah, and he did what was good and right and true before the Lord his God. And in every work that he began in the service of the house of God, in the law and in the commandment, to seek his God, he did it with all his heart. So he prospered. (2 Chronicles 31:20-21, NKJV)

However, regarding the ambassadors of the princes of Babylon, whom they sent to him to inquire about the wonder that was done in the land, God withdrew from him, in order to test him, that He might know all that was in his heart. (2 Chronicles 32:31, NKJV)

Hezekiah also began well. However, he proudly displayed his wealth, his armory, his defenses, and his Achilles heel. The Babylonians learned of the Siloam tunnel, a remarkable engineering feat, and how they brought in water from the Spring of Gihon. This would be their entry point to take Jerusalem. And so, another leader bites the proverbial dust and joins the ranks of fallen, tarnished leaders.

Robert Clinton has observed that 70% of leaders fail to finish well.[54] Self-leadership is difficult. In self-leadership, we fight entropy and we fight internal energy siphons. Indelible family messages, catastrophic experiences, resentment, bitterness, unteachability, toxic organizational experiences, busyness, laziness, undisciplined living, and an uncultured spiritual centre can all limit our growth potential.[55] Finishing well will require a rigorous commitment to our sense of call and to maintaining that commitment.

OWN SELF-LEADERSHIP

> *Watch your life and doctrine closely. Persevere in them, because if you do, you will save both yourself and your hearers.* (1 Timothy 4:16, NIV)

PLAN SELF-LEADERSHIP

> *But the noble man makes noble plans, and by noble deeds he stands.* (Isaiah 32:8, NIV)

ASSIGNMENT: *Work through each of the steps identified, with a view to developing a personal vision statement. Then set a handful of measurable* *goals and some action plans to realize these goals.*

DISCUSSION: *Discuss why so many leaders crash.*

— 59 —

Stewarding Our Time

TIME IS A GIFT

Teach us to number our days aright, that we may gain a heart of wisdom.
(Psalm 90:12, NIV)

> *Lord, make me to know my end, and what is the measure of my days, that I may know how frail I am. Indeed, You have made my days as handbreadths, and my age is as nothing before You; certainly every man at his best state is but vapor. Selah. Surely every man walks about like a shadow; surely they busy themselves in vain; he heaps up riches, and does not know who will gather them. "And now, Lord, what do I wait for? My hope is in You."*
> (Psalm 39:4-7, NKJV)

> *Therefore be careful how you walk, not as unwise men but as wise, making the most of your time, because the days are evil.*
> (Ephesians 5:15-16, NASB)

Everyone is given the gift of time. While life duration differs radically from one person to another, we all have the same minutes in an hour, the same hours in a day, the same days in a week, the same weeks in a month, the same months in a year. While some people may have marginally more energy than others, and some may require slightly less sleep than others, a central observation of life is that productive people know how to manage their time. If we can manage time, we can manage life. The key to managing time is planning.

PLANNING AS A MEANS OF USING TIME WISELY

May he give you the desire of your heart and make all your plans succeed. (Psalm 20:4, NIV)

For lack of guidance a nation falls, but many advisers make victory sure. (Proverbs 11:14, NIV)

Righteousness guards the man of integrity, but wickedness overthrows the sinner. (Proverbs 13:6, NIV)

Plans fail for lack of counsel, but with many advisers they succeed. (Proverbs 15:22, NIV)

By wisdom a house is built, and through understanding it is established; through knowledge its rooms are filled with rare and beautiful treasures. (Proverbs 24:3-4, NIV)

But the noble man makes noble plans, and by noble deeds he stands. (Isaiah 32:8, NIV)

Suppose one of you wants to build a tower. Will he not first sit down and estimate the cost to see if he has enough money to complete it? (Luke 14:28, NIV)

FOUNDATIONAL PLANNING

- Know what your life mission is. Everything we do in life, or plan on doing in life, should be an expression of our sense of call or mission. To live proactively, we must know where we are headed and why. If not, we are cursed with living reactively to the plethora of options and distractions that come our way. People who live this way may be busy, and even overwhelmed, but they seldom accomplish anything of value.

- Know what your life categories are in order to maintain balance.[56] We must all give attention to our physical, spiritual, emotional, social, and mental wellbeing. These are all inseparably connected. When one area is neglected, the other areas of life are shaken.

- Know what your major life roles are.[57] We all shoulder more than one role in life. We are disciples of Christ: we may be a husband or a wife, we may be a parent, we may have an official ministry role, we may have a marketplace or employment role, we may have a role as a citizen.

- What are your goals? Once I understand my mission, my life categories, and my major roles in life, I must ask myself: What goals do I want to see realized in each of these?

DAILY/WEEKLY PLANNING

- Set aside a regular time each week to plan for the upcoming week.

- Review your mission, life categories, major roles, and life goals.

- Establish some goals for this week.

- List activities that you should be engaged in based on your goals and on routine expectations and responsibilities. Prioritize these activities. You may either list these in order of priority or you may assign a value to each activity, such as A for high priority, B for moderate priority, and C for low priority.

- Schedule your time according to your priorities. Place these activities directly into your calendar.

- Follow the plan. Now that you have "planned your work," "work your plan."

ASSIGNMENT: *Obtain a workable calendar or organizer. Complete the assigned task of "foundational planning" and "daily/weekly planning."*

DISCUSSION: *Discuss common time wasters. Discuss when "good" becomes the enemy of the "best."*

—— 60 ——
Stewarding the Message:
The Mission of the Church

OUR CHIEF MISSION

> *So whether you eat or drink or whatever you do, do it all for the glory of God.* (1 Corinthians 10:31, NIV)

The chief end of man and for the church is to bring glory to God. This is our chief and all-encompassing life mission. However, God has given to his church a more specific mission to be realized.

OUR CHURCH MISSION

God is a God of mission. He is constantly pursuing us. The incarnation of Christ is the ultimate example of the missionary heart of God. The intention of God was that he would use the nation of Israel to be his representatives and ambassadors to reach out to the nations of the world. In the New Testament, God calls the church to be his agent of the message of hope. Missions are not merely programs or committees of a local church. They are the church's calling.

> Then Jesus came to them and said, "All authority in heaven and on earth has been given to me. Therefore go and make disciples of all nations, baptizing them in the name of the Father and of the Son and of the Holy Spirit, and teaching them to obey everything I have commanded you. And surely I am with you always, to the very end of the age." (Matthew 28:18-20, NIV)

> But you will receive power when the Holy Spirit comes on you; and you will be my witnesses in Jerusalem, and in all Judea and Samaria, and to the ends of the earth. (Acts 1:8, NIV)

The early church understood this and embraced the responsibility. The book of Acts gives a historical account of the missionary exploits of the early church. The Apostle Paul was a role model in mission's initiatives. He lived out a fourfold emphasis in his missional work.

SPOTLIGHT ON THE UNREACHED

> It has always been my ambition to preach the Gospel where Christ was not known, so that I would not be building on someone else's foundation. (Romans 15:20, NIV)

Of the six billion people on the earth, at least 2.5 billion are completely "unreached." We often talk about the 10/40 Window (the rectangular area encompassing North Africa, the Middle East, and Asia, between the latitudes of 10 degrees north and 40 degrees north) as the largest region of unreached peoples.

SPOTLIGHT ON THE NEWLY REACHED

> *For I long to see you so that I may impart some spiritual gift to*
> *you, that you may be established; that is, that I may be encour-*
> *aged together with you while among you, each of us by the other's*
> *faith, both yours and mine.* (Romans 1:11-12, NASB)

> *But now, with no further place for me in these regions, and since I*
> *have had for many years a longing to come to you whenever I go*
> *to Spain—for I hope to see you in passing, and to be helped on*
> *my way there by you, when I have first enjoyed your company for*
> *a while.* (Romans 15:23-24, NASB)

Paul was committed to helping those who were young in their faith. His
goal was not just to see people place faith in Christ; Paul wanted to see mature, multiplying disciples continue the work of God.

SPOTLIGHT ON THE MISTAKEN

> *I am telling the truth in Christ, I am not lying, my conscience tes-*
> *tifies with me in the Holy Spirit, that I have great sorrow and un-*
> *ceasing grief in my heart. For I could wish that I myself were ac-*
> *cursed, separated from Christ for the sake of my brethren, my*
> *kinsmen according to the flesh.* (Romans 9:1-3, NASB)

> *Brethren, my heart's desire and my prayer to God for them is for*
> *their salvation. For I testify about them that they have a zeal for*
> *God, but not in accordance with knowledge. For not knowing*
> *about God's righteousness and seeking to establish their own,*
> *they did not subject themselves to the righteousness of God. For*
> *Christ is the end of the law for righteousness to everyone who be-*
> *lieves.* (Romans 10:1-4, NASB)

Paul also had compassion for the mistaken and the misguided. In Paul's
day, this would have included those who were being carried off by false

doctrine as well as the Jews who had rejected Jesus as the Messiah. In our context, Christianity means many things to many people. Authentic faith is very different from checking "Christian" on a census form.

SPOTLIGHT ON THE PHYSICALLY NEEDY

> *But now, I am going to Jerusalem serving the saints. For Macedonia and Achaia have been pleased to make a contribution for the poor among the saints in Jerusalem. Yes, they were pleased to do so, and they are indebted to them. For if the Gentiles have shared in their spiritual things, they are indebted to minister to them also in material things. Therefore, when I have finished this, and have put my seal on this fruit of theirs, I will go on by way of you to Spain. I know that when I come to you, I will come in the fullness of the blessing of Christ.* (Romans 15:25-29, NASB)

The Bible has always placed a responsibility on the people of God to concern themselves with justice and issues of social compassion. Israel was to do so, as is the church today. The church is called to minister to the starving, the imprisoned, the unjustly treated, the marginalized, those with mental illness, those with physical illness, the abused, the downtrodden, the motherless, and the widows.

ASSIGNMENT: *Is your church involved in the four categories of ministry highlighted in this chapter? In what area can you be involved?*

DISCUSSION: *Discuss the prospect of engaging in some kind of short-term mission project or cross-cultural experience.*

—— 61 ——
Stewarding the Message: Explaining the Good News

The mission of the church is to make disciples. Evangelism is on one side of the coin, while helping people grow is on the other. Evangelism is the proclamation of the Gospel. Gospel simply means "good news." Evangelism is a privilege and a responsibility for all Christ followers.

THE ESSENCE OF THE GOSPEL

First, let's remind ourselves of the very core of the Gospel, the Good News. We looked at this earlier, but repetition lends clarity.

> *Moreover, brethren, I declare to you the Gospel which I preached to you, which also you received and in which you stand, by which also you are saved, if you hold fast that word which I preached to you—unless you believed in vain.*

For I delivered to you first of all that which I also received:
that Christ died for our sins according to the Scriptures, and that
He was buried, and that He rose again the third day according to
the Scriptures. (1 Corinthians 15:1-4, NKJV)

The Gospel is the Good News, which was that Jesus died for our sins as a substitute. The Good News is activated in our lives when we believe. When we believe, we receive forgiveness. We start a new living and growing relationship with God. We experience eternal life and the hope of an eternal future. We become part of God's kingdom. We also become agents of communication and transformation in our world. This is what a disciple is.

MISCONCEPTIONS

Evangelism has unfortunately been associated with some incorrect expressions. Some have erroneously viewed evangelism as the task of sharing the basic elements of the Gospel. However, evangelism is in fact more about the building of relationships. Furthermore, evangelism has sometimes been seen as an event; however, we are more accurate in viewing it as a process. Finally, evangelism is sometimes seen as the sole duty of a suitably gifted evangelist; however, we would be more accurate to view evangelism as the responsibility of the entire community, and every individual within that community. There are implications which grow out of a correct and biblical attitude. If evangelism is a relationship, then I need to identify some relationships to work on. If evangelism is a process, then I need to nudge my relationships further in the process. If evangelism is done by a community, then I need to think of who else can help me.

Being a witness is sharing how Jesus, the Son of God, forgave us, gave us life, and welcomed us into his family. Being a witness may sound like a single conversation, or even an event, but in actuality it is much more. One

of the metaphors that the New Testament often uses is an agricultural image. Doing evangelism can be compared to farming.

CULTIVATING THE SOIL

Before we can farm, we have to prepare the soil. Similarly, before having a
significant spiritual conversation with someone, we need to build some
kind of relationship with them. Truth is always shared in the flesh. It was
never intended to be abstract, distant, and detached. Truth is transmitted
from person to person, and thus relationships are profoundly significant.

Jesus was always connecting with people, not just talking at them. He
was able to build these relationships quickly, but he did establish bonds. In
those relationships Jesus showed that he cared. Doing good demonstrates
that we truly care about people and their needs.

We also see that evangelism is more of a process than an event. Think
of evangelism as being like courtship. Imagine you are single (some of you
don't have to imagine), and you think, "It's time to get married." You don't
go to the local mall and randomly select a person and propose marriage.
Proposing marriage is the result of a relationship, time, care, communication, and understanding. When we ask someone if they want to trust Christ
with the eternal destiny of their soul, this is a significant question. This requires some time, some friendship, some dialogue, and some trust. It is a
relationship; it is a process.

In the cultivation of the soil, seldom are you the only person involved
in the evangelism process. In fact, involving others is very helpful, because
when our friends who are spiritually seeking meet other Christians it wid-
ens their opportunity to have conversations and draw conclusions.

Demonstrating authentic care and concern for people establishes a
credible platform on which we can build and ultimately speak.

SOWING THE SEED

At some point in our friendships with people, there comes a time to communicate the essence of the message. Sometimes people may ask as a straightforward question: "So, what is it that you believe?" or "What is the heart of this Christianity?" When that happens, we must know what to say. Sometimes, we will feel like the relationship has progressed to the point where we want to introduce the conversation, and so we might ask them, "How do you make life work for you?" "How do you deal with stress, or pain, or heartaches, or guilt?" In these questions, we are trying to provoke conversation related to matters of the soul. Such conversations really should emerge out of the conversations of life, but we need to have a sensitivity that sees and seizes such God-given opportunities.

Once we are in conversation, there is some core content that we need to ensure that will be discussed. While evangelism is a relationship and a process, it is also a set of propositions or truths. In order for a person to be rescued by Jesus, they must understand what they are being rescued from, to, why, and by whom.

The following biblical texts will prove helpful in describing the plight of humanity, the love of God, the work of Jesus, and the necessary response by individuals. We would be wise to commit these passages to memory.

> *For all have sinned and fall short of the glory of God.* (Romans 3:23, NIV)

> *For the wages of sin is death, but the gift of God is eternal life in Christ Jesus our Lord.* (Romans 6:23, NIV)

> *But God demonstrates his own love for us in this: While we were still sinners, Christ died for us.* (Romans 5:8, NIV)

> *Yet to all who received him, to those who believed in his name, he gave the right to become children of God.* (John 1:12, NIV)

Another valuable tool to help us in our understanding and in our communication is the classic mono-mythic cycle. Narrative throughout time has employed this pattern, which is modeled in the theme of God's salvation of humanity.

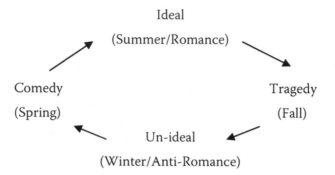

The redemptive story of God begins with everything being good and ideal (summer), but this paradise is soon interrupted with tragedy (fall). The results of the tragedy are un-ideal (a long winter). However, into this long period of longing comes hope and comedy (spring). While this is God's story, many good storylines follow this classic pattern. The human heart resonates with this pattern.

HARVESTING FAITH

Our goal is not just to give information; we should invite people to personally wrestle with the implications of truth. In effect, we are calling for decision. We are challenging them to do something with the information. We are inviting people to believe and follow Jesus.

We certainly need to do so with respect for the person's will (as God does), but yet with clarity and confidence, in order to ensure that they understand that this is not just a cool idea, nor is it just a philosophical worldview to identify with academically. Jesus wants to have a living relationship with us.

ENGLE'S STAGES OF CONVERSION

The following is a chart describing the process of moving from a position of being far from God to trusting Christ, and from there to growth as a disciple of Christ.[58] Engle's stages illustrate the process of evangelism and our need for patience and grace.

-8	Awareness of supreme being; no knowledge of the Gospel.
-7	Initial awareness of the Gospel.
-6	Awareness of fundamentals of the Gospel.
-5	Grasp of implications of the Gospel.
-4	Positive attitude toward the Gospel.
-3	Personal problem recognition.
-2	Decision to act.
-1	Repentance and faith in Christ.
0	Conversion.
+1	Post-decision evaluation.
+2	Incorporation into the body of Christ.
+3	A lifetime of conceptual and behavioural growth in Christ.

ASSIGNMENT: *All spiritual conversations should flow naturally out of the routines and questions of life. However, being able to succinctly explain the Good News is critical. Write out an explanation of the Gospel that you could commit to memory (including biblical passages). Incorporate verses that you have memorized.*

DISCUSSION: *Discuss illustrations that help explain the Good News.*

62

Stewarding the Message: Telling Our Story

Witnesses tell their story: what they saw, what they heard, and what they experienced. Acts 1:8 calls us to be Christ's witnesses. In Mark 5, Jesus tells a man whom he has just healed:

> *Go home to your family and tell them how much the Lord has done for you, and how he has had mercy on you.* (Mark 5:19, NIV)

Being a witness is explaining who Jesus is and what he has done for you. Being a witness is explaining how the story of Christ has changed your story. Being a witness is the essence of evangelism, a responsibility that God places on all of us. Telling one's story is modeled clearly by the Apostle Paul.

Paul's Story

Agrippa spoke directly to Paul: "Go ahead—tell us about yourself."

Paul took the stand and told his story. "I can't think of anyone, King Agrippa, before whom I'd rather be answering all these Jewish accusations than you, knowing how well you are acquainted with Jewish ways and all our family quarrels. "From the time of my youth, my life has been lived among my own people in Jerusalem. Practically every Jew in town who watched me grow up—and if they were willing to stick their necks out they'd tell you in person—knows that I lived as a strict Pharisee, the most demanding branch of our religion. It's because I believed it and took it seriously, committed myself heart and soul to what God promised my ancestors—the identical hope, mind you, that the twelve tribes have lived for night and day all these centuries—it's because I have held on to this tested and tried hope that I'm being called on the carpet by the Jews. They should be the ones standing trial here, not me! For the life of me, I can't see why it's a criminal offense to believe that God raises the dead.

"I admit that I didn't always hold to this position. For a time I thought it was my duty to oppose this Jesus of Nazareth with all my might. Backed with the full authority of the high priests, I threw these believers—I had no idea they were God's people!— into the Jerusalem jail right and left, and whenever it came to a vote, I voted for their execution. I stormed through their meeting places, bullying them into cursing Jesus, a one-man terror obsessed with obliterating these people. And then I started on the towns outside Jerusalem.

"One day on my way to Damascus, armed as always with papers from the high priests authorizing my action, right in the middle of the day a blaze of light, light outshining the sun, poured out of the sky on me and my companions. Oh, King, it was so bright! We fell flat on our faces. Then I heard a voice in Hebrew:

'Saul, Saul, why are you out to get me? Why do you insist on going against the grain?'

"I said, 'Who are you, Master?'

"The voice answered, 'I am Jesus, the One you're hunting down like an animal. But now, up on your feet—I have a job for you. I've handpicked you to be a servant and witness to what's happened today, and to what I am going to show you.

I'm sending you off to open the eyes of the outsiders so they can see the difference between dark and light, and choose light, see the difference between Satan and God, and choose God. I'm sending you off to present my offer of sins forgiven, and a place in the family, inviting them into the company of those who begin real living by believing in me.'

"What could I do, King Agrippa? I couldn't just walk away from a vision like that! I became an obedient believer on the spot. I started preaching this life-change—this radical turn to God and everything it meant in everyday life—right there in Damascus, went on to Jerusalem and the surrounding countryside, and from there to the whole world.

"It's because of this 'whole world' dimension that the Jews grabbed me in the Temple that day and tried to kill me. They want to keep God for themselves. But God has stood by me, just as he promised, and I'm standing here saying what I've been saying to anyone, whether king or child, who will listen. And everything I'm saying is completely in line with what the prophets and Moses said would happen: One, the Messiah must die; two, raised from the dead, he would be the first rays of God's daylight shining on people far and near, people both godless and God-fearing."

That was too much for Festus. He interrupted with a shout: "Paul, you're crazy! You've read too many books, spent too much time staring off into space! Get a grip on yourself, get back in the real world!"

But Paul stood his ground. "With all respect, Festus, Your Honor, I'm not crazy. I'm both accurate and sane in what I'm say-

*ing. The king knows what I'm talking about. I'm sure that nothing
of what I've said sounds crazy to him. He's known all about it for
a long time. You must realize that this wasn't done behind the
scenes. You believe the prophets, don't you, King Agrippa? Don't
answer that—I know you believe."*

*But Agrippa did answer: "Keep this up much longer and
you'll make a Christian out of me!"*

*Paul, still in chains, said, "That's what I'm praying for,
whether now or later, and not only you but everyone listening today, to become like me—except, of course, for this prison jewelry!"*

*The king and the governor, along with Bernice and their ad-
visors, got up and went into the next room to talk over what they
had heard. They quickly agreed on Paul's innocence, saying,
"There's nothing in this man deserving prison, let alone death."*

*Agrippa told Festus, "He could be set free right now if he
hadn't requested the hearing before Caesar."* (Acts 26:1-32, MSG)

There are five movements in Paul's presentation:

- Gracious preamble or introduction (26:1-3).
- Life before following Christ (26:4-11).
- The event of starting to follow Christ (26:12-18).
- The journey of following Christ (26:19-23).
- Gracious invitation to his listeners in his conclusion
  (26:24-29).

ASSIGNMENT: *Write out your story (testimony) in less than five hundred
words.*

DISCUSSION: *Tell your story (in your discipleship group) and discuss it. Is it
clear? Is it compelling?*

63

Servant Leadership in Our World: Doing Good

GOOD WORKS

Many wealthy, well-known individuals have been commended for their generous philanthropy. They, along with others, have experienced the joy of giving away time, money, and resources in order to alleviate suffering and bring benefit to others. The activity of doing good deeds and performing good works has a purposeful place in God's agenda for his disciples.

DOING GOOD GIVES OUR LIVES PURPOSE

This is more than just feeling good, or being healthy. Doing good actually is a part of why we were created. Let's review yet again:

For we are God's workmanship, created in Christ Jesus to do good works, which God prepared in advance for us to do. (Ephesians 2:10, NIV)

We are created in relationship with Christ for a purpose: to do good work. The word "vocation" is a Latin word which meant "calling." We have since given it the meaning of paid work, but the more fundamental truth is that we have a vocation, a calling from God, and when we discover and do it, we are doing what we were made to do. When we do good works for others, even if there is no immediate benefit, or payback, we are fulfilling a divine purpose. When you and I do what we were designed to do, we feel complete, whole, meaningful, and purposeful.

DOING GOOD INSPIRES SPIRITUAL GROWTH AND MATURITY

And let us consider how to stir up one another to love and good works. (Hebrews 10:24, ESV)

The context here is that the author is speaking to followers of Christ and challenging them to be engaged in each other's lives. Do not withdraw and do not fly solo. Be involved and, furthermore, challenge each other to do good deeds.

And he gave the apostles, the prophets, the evangelists, the shepherds and teachers, to equip the saints for the work of ministry, for building up the body of Christ. (Ephesians 4:11-12, ESV)

This passage tells us that God gives gifted leaders to the church, not to do all the work, but to "prepare" or literally "equip" all the people for "works of service." The result is that the whole body matures and is built up. When we serve, we grow. We do not grow in a balanced fashion when we fail to serve. However, when we serve, the whole church benefits and grows. When we do not serve, we become part of the problem that holds the church back from becoming what God is calling us to become.

DOING GOOD DRAWS ATTENTION TO GOD

> *You are the salt of the earth; but if the salt loses its flavor, how*
> *shall it be seasoned? It is then good for nothing but to be thrown*
> *out and trampled underfoot by men. You are the light of the*
> *world. A city that is set on a hill cannot be hidden. Nor do they*
> *light a lamp and put it under a basket, but on a lampstand, and it*
> *gives light to all who are in the house. Let your light so shine be-*
> *fore men, that they may see your good works and glorify your Fa-*
> *ther in heaven.* (Matthew 5:13-16, NKJV)

Christ's followers are salt. We act as a preserving agent. We create thirst, like salt does, and salt also acts as a cleansing agent. We are also called "the light of the world." Light speaks of truth, and knowledge. Light shows what's really there and as such light dispels darkness, ignorance, fear, and evil. When we are acting as light and doing good deeds, people will see this and their attention will be drawn to God.

> *Keep your conduct among the Gentiles honorable, so that when*
> *they speak against you as evildoers, they may see your good deeds*
> *and glorify God on the day of visitation.* (1 Peter 2:12, ESV)

According to Peter, unbelievers will accuse believers of all kinds of things including religious intolerance, philosophical narrow-mindedness, academic anti-intellectualism, and moral legalism. This may be unfair, but we will hear it. However, Peter says, when they see you doing good by aiding the economically disadvantaged, the physically disabled, and the socially marginalized, people will be drawn to God. When the world sees us doing something about poverty, HIV-AIDS, the sex trade, unemployment, social injustice, loneliness, and addictions, people will think differently about Christianity because of the good deeds of Christians.

DOING GOOD GIVES EVIDENCE OF AUTHENTIC FAITH

> *What good is it, my brothers, if someone says he has faith but does not have works? Can that faith save him? If a brother or sister is poorly clothed and lacking in daily food, and one of you says to them, "Go in peace, be warmed and filled," without giving them the things needed for the body, what good is that? So also faith by itself, if it does not have works, is dead.*
>
> *But someone will say, "You have faith and I have works." Show me your faith apart from your works, and I will show you my faith by my works.* (James 2:14-18, ESV)

Our faith is not just in our head, nor is it is what comes out of our mouths. Our faith acts. Our faith works, displays itself, and demonstrates its authenticity. We do this because Christ modeled it to us:

> *But when the kindness of God our Savior and His love for mankind appeared, He saved us, not on the basis of deeds which we have done in righteousness, but according to His mercy, by the washing of regeneration and renewing by the Holy Spirit, whom He poured out upon us richly through Jesus Christ our Savior, so that being justified by His grace we would be made heirs according to the hope of eternal life.*
>
> *This is a trustworthy statement; and concerning these things I want you to speak confidently, so that those who have believed God will be careful to engage in good deeds. These things are good and profitable for men.* (Titus 3:4-8, NASB)

Our faith is not just something we talk about; it is something we show. St. Francis of Assisi said, "Preach the Gospel at all times. If necessary, use words." This has always been at the heart of orthodox Christianity, but in recent decades we have thought that all we need to do is talk about our faith. Yes, we do need to talk about our faith, but we first need to show it.

ASSIGNMENT: *Identify a need that you could meet. Make a plan. Put the plan into action.*

DISCUSSION: *Discuss how good deeds extend the platform of our witnessing.*

—— 64 ——

Servant Leadership in the Church

"ONE ANOTHER" MINISTRY

The church of Jesus Christ is God's family, Christ's bride, and a community in which we share, and minister to. Servant leadership is all about meeting needs. Servant leadership takes initiative. The Bible calls believers to show utmost care and concern for one another. Mature disciples take seriously their responsibility to one another. Consider this complete list of New Testament "one another's" and our responsibility to serve.

> *Now that I, your Lord and Teacher, have washed your feet, you also should wash one another's feet.* (John 13:14, NIV)

> *A new command I give you: Love one another. As I have loved you, so you must love one another. By this all men will know that you are my disciples, if you love one another.* (John 13:34-35, NIV)

Be devoted to one another in brotherly love. Honor one another above yourselves. (Romans 12:10, NIV)

Live in harmony with one another. Do not be proud, but be willing to associate with people of low position. Do not be conceited. (Romans 12:16, NIV)

Let no debt remain outstanding, except the continuing debt to love one another, for he who loves his fellowman has fulfilled the law. (Romans 13:8, NIV)

Therefore let us stop passing judgment on one another. Instead, make up your mind not to put any stumbling block or obstacle in your brother's way. (Romans 14:13, NIV)

Accept one another, then, just as Christ accepted you, in order to bring praise to God. (Romans 15:7, NIV)

I myself am convinced, my brothers, that you yourselves are full of goodness, complete in knowledge and competent to instruct one another. (Romans 15:14, NIV)

Greet one another with a holy kiss. All the churches of Christ send greetings. (Romans 16:16, NIV)

I appeal to you, brothers, in the name of our Lord Jesus Christ, that all of you agree with one another so that there may be no divisions among you and that you may be perfectly united in mind and thought. (1 Corinthians 1:10, NIV)

You, my brothers, were called to be free. But do not use your freedom to indulge the sinful nature; rather, serve one another in love. (Galatians 5:13, NIV)

Be completely humble and gentle; be patient, bearing with one another in love. (Ephesians 4:2, NIV)

Be kind and compassionate to one another, forgiving each other, just as in Christ God forgave you. (Ephesians 4:32, NIV)

Speak to one another with psalms, hymns and spiritual songs. Sing and make music in your heart to the Lord. (Ephesians 5:19, NIV)

Submit to one another out of reverence for Christ. (Ephesians 5:21, NIV)

Bear with each other and forgive whatever grievances you may have against one another. Forgive as the Lord forgave you. (Colossians 3:13, NIV)

Let the word of Christ dwell in you richly as you teach and admonish one another with all wisdom, and as you sing psalms, hymns and spiritual songs with gratitude in your hearts to God. (Colossians 3:16, NIV)

Therefore encourage one another and build each other up, just as in fact you are doing. (1 Thessalonians 5:11, NIV)

But encourage one another daily, as long as it is called Today, so that none of you may be hardened by sin's deceitfulness. (Hebrews 3:13, NIV)

And let us consider how we may spur one another on toward love and good deeds. (Hebrews 10:24, NIV)

Let us not give up meeting together, as some are in the habit of doing, but let us encourage one another—and all the more as you see the Day approaching. (Hebrews 10:25, NIV)

Brothers, do not slander one another. Anyone who speaks against his brother or judges him speaks against the law and judges it. When you judge the law, you are not keeping it, but sitting in judgment on it. (James 4:11, NIV)

Finally, all of you, live in harmony with one another; be sympa-

thetic, love as brothers, be compassionate and humble. (1 Peter 3:8, NIV)

Offer hospitality to one another without grumbling. (1 Peter 4:9, NIV)

Young men, in the same way be submissive to those who are older. All of you, clothe yourselves with humility toward one another, because, "God opposes the proud but gives grace to the humble." (1 Peter 5:5, NIV)

But if we walk in the light, as he is in the light, we have fellowship with one another, and the blood of Jesus, his Son, purifies us from all sin. (1 John 1:7, NIV)

This is the message you heard from the beginning: We should love one another. (1 John 3:11, NIV)

And this is his command: to believe in the name of his Son, Jesus Christ, and to love one another as he commanded us. (1 John 3:23, NIV)

Dear friends, let us love one another, for love comes from God. Everyone who loves has been born of God and knows God. (1 John 4:7, NIV)

Dear friends, since God so loved us, we also ought to love one another. (1 John 4:11, NIV)

No one has ever seen God; but if we love one another, God lives in us and his love is made complete in us. (1 John 4:12, NIV)

Above all, love each other deeply, because love covers over a multitude of sins. (1 Peter 4:8, NIV)

Therefore confess your sins to each other and pray for each other so that you may be healed. The prayer of a righteous man is powerful and effective. (James 5:16, NIV)

Don't grumble against each other, brothers, or you will be judged. The Judge is standing at the door! (James 5:9, NIV)

Keep on loving each other as brothers. (Hebrews 13:1, NIV)

We ought always to thank God for you, brothers, and rightly so, because your faith is growing more and more, and the love every one of you has for each other is increasing. (2 Thessalonians 1:3, NIV)

Make sure that nobody pays back wrong for wrong, but always try to be kind to each other and to everyone else. (1 Thessalonians 5:15, NIV)

Hold them in the highest regard in love because of their work. Live in peace with each other. (1 Thessalonians 5:13, NIV)

Therefore encourage one another and build each other up, just as in fact you are doing. (1 Thessalonians 5:11, NIV)

Therefore encourage each other with these words. (1 Thessalonians 4:18, NIV)

Now about brotherly love we do not need to write to you, for you yourselves have been taught by God to love each other. (1 Thessalonians 4:9, NIV)

May the Lord make your love increase and overflow for each other and for everyone else, just as ours does for you. (1 Thessalonians 3:12, NIV)

Bear with each other and forgive whatever grievances you may have against one another. Forgive as the Lord forgave you. (Colossians 3:13, NIV)

Do not lie to each other, since you have taken off your old self with its practices. (Colossians 3:9, NIV)

I plead with Euodia and I plead with Syntyche to agree with each other in the Lord. (Philippians 4:2, NIV)

Be kind and compassionate to one another, forgiving each other, just as in Christ God forgave you. (Ephesians 4:32, NIV)

Let us not become conceited, provoking and envying each other. (Galatians 5:26, NIV)

Carry each other's burdens, and in this way you will fulfill the law of Christ. (Galatians 6:2, NIV)

...so that there should be no division in the body, but that its parts should have equal concern for each other. (1 Corinthians 12:25, NIV)

If you keep on biting and devouring each other, watch out or you will be destroyed by each other. (Galatians 5:15, NIV)

So then, my brothers, when you come together to eat, wait for each other. (1 Corinthians 11:33, NIV)

...that is, that you and I may be mutually encouraged by each other's faith. (Romans 1:12, NIV)

From him the whole body, joined and held together by every supporting ligament, grows and builds itself up in love, as each part does its work. (Ephesians 4:16, NIV)

Do nothing out of selfish ambition or vain conceit, but in humility consider others better than yourselves. Each of you should look not only to your own interests, but also to the interests of others. Your attitude should be the same as that of Christ Jesus. (Philippians 2:3-5, NIV)

GIFT-ORIENTED MINISTRY

God gives gifted leaders to the church to equip the body so that each member of the body does his or her part in fulfilling their calling. The goal is to build up the body and bring it to maturity. Ephesians 4:11-16 addresses this, as does 1 Peter 4:10:

> *Each one should use whatever gift he has received to serve others, faithfully administering God's grace in its various forms.* (1 Peter 4:10, NIV)

CONTEXT-SPECIFIC MINISTRY

Most ministry settings employ some kind of structure and program. These are tools and tracks for doing ministry. Servant leadership is expressed in the more formal ministry leadership roles such as:

- Board ministries (elder, deacon)
- Staff ministries (pastoral, administrative, operations)
- Small group ministries
- Teaching ministries
- Life Stage specific ministries (children, youth, young adult, single adult, senior adult)
- Worship ministries
- Recovery ministries
- Community and outreach ministries
- International missions ministries
- Greeting, ushering, hospitality ministries
- Special event ministries
- Operations ministries (facility, grounds, finance)

ASSIGNMENT: *Reflect on the prospective responsibilities of each of the above ministries. How is "servant leadership" central? Are there needs in your church that you could meet through service?*

DISCUSSION: *How does servant leadership challenge our culture's view of leadership?*

—— 65 ——
Servant Leadership Skill:
Think Biblically

We all have value systems, assumptions, pictures, and images that shape how we perceive reality and how we relate to our world. Sometimes we are aware of these attitudes at work, but often they just surface without us even realizing it. These attitudes or thought processes are mental models. Our thinking affects our behaviour unconsciously. We may act aloof with others without ever realizing that at the core we have a mental model that says, "Don't trust people. Don't get close to people. They will betray you and always let you down."

Leaders have a powerful influence on the organizations they are called to lead. Parents have an enormously pivotal role in the lives of their children. These are awesome stewardships. Because our mental models shape how we think and how we behave, leaders must learn how to think biblically. Reflecting on one's mental models does not come naturally. It is a discipline that must be learned. Leaders, however, must be willing to make the commitment to unlearn incorrect mental models and replace them with correct mental models. Thus, leaders must *learn* (discipline) *to think* (critical leadership skill) *biblically* (with new, true, creative mental models).

DEVELOPING A BIBLICAL THEOLOGY AND CHRISTIAN WORLDVIEW

How we think determines what we believe, how we live, and how we lead. What are the mental models and paradigms by which we both read the problem and provide a prospective solution? Our mental models are the grid, thought process, or even value system by which we interpret reality and events. Mental models are deeply ingrained assumptions, generalizations, or even pictures that shape how we view our world, our organization, and how we relate to them.

In Western contexts, we live in a culture where truth is perceived to be relative and rooted in subjective tastes and experiences. It is of utmost importance that Christians know what truth is and what the Bible says about the world in which we live. Our feelings, opinions, and experiences can deceive us into thinking and living contrary to the way God would want us to think and live. We all have mental models and ways of perceiving reality. As we are immersed in biblical truth, our mental models will slowly be shaped and conformed to biblical thinking.

The book of Daniel provides an ideal case study for thinking biblically in a cultural context that did not reflect a biblical worldview or biblical values.

THE BIBLICAL THINKING OF DANIEL

While personal life experiences provide gripping and memorable lessons, much can be learned from the life experiences of others. Case studies allow

us to objectify experiences into principles. It will be our goal to ask ourselves: What can I learn about how God works in us and through us as
leaders from what I have observed in God's dealings with others?

A case study of the leadership practice of Daniel will offer some helpful
insights for church leaders, even though his leadership task was not specifically prophetic or ministry oriented. Daniel was an exemplary statesman in
the courts of ungodly monarchs. His impact was far reaching, as he influ-
enced kings and rulers who would in turn shape entire nations.

Daniel, along with his three colleagues—Hananiah, Mishael, and
Azariah—were initially taken as captives to Babylon when they were young
men (perhaps even teenagers). The Babylonian strategy was to take young,
bright men, saturate them with Babylonian culture (change their language
and context), Babylonian religion (change their names), Babylonian education (change their training), and Babylonian morality (change their menu),
and then commission them as vassal leaders of their former homelands. In
so doing, Babylon would ensure control, while allowing for some national
sensitivity. How did these young leaders respond to these environmental
conditions?

> *But Daniel determined that he would not defile himself by eating
> the king's food or drinking his wine, so he asked the head of the
> palace staff to exempt him from the royal diet. The head of the
> palace staff, by God's grace, liked Daniel, but he warned him, "I'm
> afraid of what my master the king will do. He is the one who as-
> signed this diet and if he sees that you are not as healthy as the
> rest, he'll have my head!"*
>
> *But Daniel appealed to a steward who had been assigned by
> the head of the palace staff to be in charge of Daniel, Hananiah,
> Mishael, and Azariah: "Try us out for ten days on a simple diet of
> vegetables and water. Then compare us with the young men who
> eat from the royal menu. Make your decision on the basis of what*

you see."

The steward agreed to do it and fed them vegetables and wa-ter for ten days. At the end of the ten days they looked better and more robust than all the others who had been eating from the royal menu. So the steward continued to exempt them from the royal menu of food and drink and served them only vegetables.

God gave these four young men knowledge and skill in both books and life. In addition, Daniel was gifted in understanding all sorts of visions and dreams. At the end of the time set by the king for their training, the head of the royal staff brought them in to Nebuchadnezzar. When the king interviewed them, he found them far superior to all the other young men. None were a match for Daniel, Hananiah, Mishael, and Azariah.

And so they took their place in the king's service. Whenever the king consulted them on anything, on books or on life, he found them ten times better than all the magicians and enchant-ers in his kingdom put together.

Daniel continued in the king's service until the first year in the reign of King Cyrus. (Daniel 1:8-21, MSG)

WISDOM

On the matter of education, the young Hebrews accepted the additional instruction. No doubt they were already grounded in solid biblical truths. On the matter of being given different names, they too accepted these new designations, as names cannot change heart. However, on the matter of menu, these men determined not to violate their convictions rooted in the law of Moses, as it did address diet.

Wisdom emerges here. Amidst pressure to compromise, these follow-ers of Jehovah sought for acceptable ways of maintaining their relationship with God while not jeopardizing their beliefs.

The pressures continued when King Nebuchadnezzar erected an

enormous idol and called on the entire nation to worship before it. Hananiah, Mishael, and Azariah (now called Shadrach, Meshach, and Abednego) all refused to follow the king's orders (Daniel appears to be strangely absent). Nebuchadnezzar responded with an irrational rage and had the three young leaders thrown into a flaming inferno. The story unfolds:

> Shadrach, Meshach, and Abednego answered King Nebuchadnezzar, "Your threat means nothing to us. If you throw us in the fire, the God we serve can rescue us from your roaring furnace and anything else you might cook up, O king. But even if he doesn't, it wouldn't make a bit of difference, O king. We still wouldn't serve your gods or worship the gold statue you set up."
>
> Nebuchadnezzar, his face purple with anger, cut off Shadrach, Meshach, and Abednego. He ordered the furnace fired up seven times hotter than usual. He ordered some strong men from the army to tie them up, hands and feet, and throw them into the roaring furnace. Shadrach, Meshach, and Abednego, bound hand and foot, fully dressed from head to toe, were pitched into the roaring fire. Because the king was in such a hurry and the furnace was so hot, flames from the furnace killed the men who carried Shadrach, Meshach, and Abednego to it, while the fire raged around Shadrach, Meshach, and Abednego.
>
> Suddenly King Nebuchadnezzar jumped up in alarm and said, "Didn't we throw three men, bound hand and foot, into the fire?"
>
> "That's right, O king," they said.
>
> "But look!" he said. "I see four men, walking around freely in the fire, completely unharmed! And the fourth man looks like a son of the gods!"
>
> Nebuchadnezzar went to the door of the roaring furnace and called in, "Shadrach, Meshach, and Abednego, servants of the High God, come out here!"

Shadrach, Meshach, and Abednego walked out of the fire.

All the important people, the government leaders and king's counselors, gathered around to examine them and discovered that the fire hadn't so much as touched the three men—not a hair singed, not a scorch mark on their clothes, not even the smell of fire on them!

Nebuchadnezzar said, "Blessed be the God of Shadrach, Meshach, and Abednego! He sent his angel and rescued his servants who trusted in him! They ignored the king's orders and laid their bodies on the line rather than serve or worship any god but their own.

"Therefore I issue this decree: Anyone anywhere, of any race, color, or creed, who says anything against the God of Shadrach, Meshach, and Abednego will be ripped to pieces, limb from limb, and their houses torn down. There has never been a god who can pull off a rescue like this."

Then the king promoted Shadrach, Meshach, and Abednego in the province of Babylon. (Daniel 3:16-30, MSG)

COURAGE

In this case, no alternatives could be found. Raw, unbending courage prevailed. Fearlessness in the face of death triumphed. What was particularly noteworthy was that the three young Hebrews trusted God regardless of whether they would experience deliverance or not. No demands were made of God. They remained firmly established in their convictions regardless of the potential consequences. This response deeply impacted King Nebuchadnezzar, who seemingly softened to the rule of God in his life. Nebuchadnezzar experiences a wild dream, which Daniel interprets. This resulted in a season of temporary insanity, which upon conclusion caused Nebuchadnezzar to express faith and submission to God. Thus, Daniel was strategically used to touch the heart of a king.

"At the end of the seven years, I, Nebuchadnezzar, looked to heaven. I was given my mind back and I blessed the High God, thanking and glorifying God, who lives forever:

"His sovereign rule lasts and lasts, his kingdom never declines and falls. Life on this earth doesn't add up to much, but God's heavenly army keeps everything going. No one can interrupt his work, no one can call his rule into question.

"At the same time that I was given back my mind, I was also given back my majesty and splendor, making my kingdom shine. All the leaders and important people came looking for me. I was reestablished as king in my kingdom and became greater than ever. And that's why I'm singing—I, Nebuchadnezzar—singing and praising the King of Heaven:

"Everything he does is right, and he does it the right way. He knows how to turn a proud person into a humble man or woman." (Daniel 4:34-37, MSG)

FAITHFULNESS

Years passed and Babylon weakened until it fell to the Medes and a new regime took power. God providentially retained Daniel in his strategic role as a statesman and again used him to impact this new world power of the Medo-Persians.

The Medo-Persian administrators soon became jealous of Daniel's breadth of influence and determined to have him removed. Daniel's faith became the point of accusation and his faithful worship of God was met with attack. The result was that Daniel is placed in a den of hungry lions. God supernaturally protected Daniel and this had a powerful effect on Darius, the king of the empire.

King Darius published this proclamation to every race, color, and creed on earth:

Peace to you! Abundant peace! I decree that Daniel's God

*shall be worshiped and feared in all parts of my kingdom. He is
the living God, world without end. His kingdom never falls. His
rule continues eternally. He is a savior and rescuer. He performs
astonishing miracles in heaven and on earth. He saved Daniel
from the power of the lions.*

*From then on, Daniel was treated well during the reign of
Darius, and also in the following reign of Cyrus the Persian.*
(Daniel 6:25-28, MSG)

In the biblical episode of Daniel and his friends, God raised up leaders
to impact other leaders. Daniel and his associates must have stood out
among the others like fine bone china amidst plastic picnic dishes. They
were different. They were men of integrity and conviction. They were
committed to doing what was right, regardless of the consequences. Daniel
was deeply committed to routine faithfulness and when opposition came
his way, his response was like a reflex. Right responses came naturally.

Wisdom, courage, and devotion are values that leap off the pages of
this book of the Bible. Such are the qualities of high-impact, high-profile
leaders who trust God. These qualities are all rooted in biblical mental
models. Daniel and his colleagues had learned to think biblically in an environment of radically divergent mental models.

Thus, leaders must *learn* (discipline) *to think* (critical leadership skill)
biblically (with new, true, creative mental models).

ASSIGNMENT: *As you reflect on your employment environment or community context, what worldview challenges are you facing?*

DISCUSSION: *What do Christians in political life today have to face?*

— 66 —
Servant Leadership Skill:
Serve Purposefully

"Servant leadership" has become another leadership "buzz" concept found in current management leadership. While contemporary research has taken place through the exploration of the effectiveness of this principle, the ultimate model and pioneer of "servant leadership" is Jesus Christ. Jesus said:

> And Jesus called them to him and said to them, "You know that those who are considered rulers of the Gentiles lord it over them, and their great ones exercise authority over them. But it shall not be so among you. But whoever would be great among you must be your servant, and whoever would be first among you must be slave of all. For even the Son of Man came not to be served but to serve, and to give his life as a ransom for many." (Mark 10:42-45, ESV)

Serving, we have discovered, is all about meeting needs. Throughout Jesus' entire ministry, he served the needs of people. Jesus would usually first identify the felt need and, while meeting the felt need, point the individual to the deeper spiritual need at work. Consider these episodes in the life of Christ.[59]

- People felt pain, but needed spiritual healing (the man brought to Jesus on a pallet in Mark 2:1-12; the woman with a bleeding problem in Mark 5:21-34; the man who was healed at the pool in John 5:1-18).
- People felt fear, but needed a sense of spiritual security (the disciple amidst a storm in Matthew 8:23-27; Jairus' fear of losing his daughter in Mark 5:21-43).
- People felt alienated, but needed spiritual intimacy (the tax collector in Luke 19:1-10; the leper in Mark 1:40-45; Peter in John 21:15-25).
- People felt guilty, but needed spiritual forgiveness (the man brought to Jesus on a pallet in Mark 2:1-12; the woman who washed Jesus' feet in Luke 7:36-50; the thief on the cross in Luke 23:32-43; the woman caught in adultery in John 8:1-11).
- People felt a sense of emptiness, but needed spiritual wholeness (the woman at the well in John 4:1-42).
- People felt a need for happiness, but needed a deeper sense of spiritual joy (Jesus' teaching on the Beatitudes in Matthew 5:1-12).
- People felt insignificant, but needed to feel a sense of spiritual meaning (the calling of the disciples in Luke 5:1-11; children coming to Jesus in Matthew 19:13-15).

The act of serving peoples' needs is radically different from serving peoples' desires. A waiter in a restaurant serves my desires and appetites.

Christ serves my needs: my need for forgiveness, my need for peace with God, my need for connection in community. What Jesus modeled was strategic or purposeful servanthood. Jesus knows our real needs at the moment. He knows that some need salvation, while others need recovery and healing. Some need to be confronted, while others need to be trained.

STRATEGIC REFLECTIONS

- Reflect on some of the needs that surface in a marriage, and how they can be met.
- Reflect on some of the needs that surface in children, and how they can be met.
- Reflect on some of the needs that surface in a church, and how they can be met.
- Reflect on some of the needs that surface in the workplace, and how they can be met.
- Reflect on some of the needs that surface in a community, and how they can be met.
- Reflect on some of the needs that surface in society, and how they can be met.
- Reflect on some of the needs that surface in other international, cultural contexts, and how they can be met.

Servant leaders must *learn* (discipline) *to serve* (critical leadership skill rooted in humility) *strategically* (with purpose, understanding that everyone does not have the same need at the same time).

ASSIGNMENT: *Make a list of all the ways in which a leader should be a servant.*

DISCUSSION: *How can you cultivate your powers of observation in order to more accurately recognize needs around you?*

67

Servant Leadership Skill: Equip Systematically

The analogy of the church as a body beautifully describes the wonder of the church in terms of an organism. It is alive, made up of cells and systems. As a body, it can be healthy and thereby accomplish great feats. It can grow and reproduce. However, it can similarly become ill, full of viruses, infections, or worse, disease. Physician Paul Brand offers a unique insight:

> Sometimes a dreaded thing occurs in the body—a mutiny—resulting in a tumor...
>
> A tumor is called benign if its effect is fairly localized and it stays within membrane boundaries. But the most traumatizing condition in the body occurs when disloyal cells defy inhibition. They multiply without any checks on growth, spreading rapidly throughout the body, choking out normal cells. White cells, armed against foreign invaders, will not attack the body's own

mutinous cells. Physicians fear no other malfunction more deeply: it is called cancer. For still mysterious reasons, these cells—and they may be cells from the brain, liver, kidney, bone, blood, skin, or other tissues—grow wild, out of control. Each is a healthy, functioning cell, but disloyal, no longer acting in regard for the rest of the body.

Even the white cells, the dependable palace guard, can destroy the body through rebellion. Sometimes they recklessly reproduce, clogging the bloodstream, overloading the lymph system, strangling the body's normal functions—such as in leukemia.

Because I am a surgeon and not a prophet, I tremble to make the analogy between cancer in the physical body and mutiny in the spiritual body of Christ. But I must. In His warnings to the church, Jesus Christ showed no concern about the shocks and bruises His Body would meet from external forces. "The gates of hell shall not prevail against my church," He said flatly (Matthew 16:18). He moved easily, unthreatened, among sinners and criminals. But He cried out against the kind of disloyalty that comes from within.[60]

Biblical theology paints a picture of the church as a living organism more than a lifeless organization. Leaders need to heighten their awareness and understanding of the systemic nature of the church, and may therefore need to unlearn some old mental models about how to equip. Equipping is not something that is exclusively done for the individual, but it must also be done for the whole.

Servant leaders seeking to lead the body of Christ need to *learn* (discipline) *to equip* (critical leadership and development skill) *systemically* (with a new, mental model of viewing the church as a system).

UNDERSTANDING SYSTEMS THEORY

Systems theory was first proposed in the 1920s by the biologist Ludwig von

Bertalanffy and grew out of a philosophy of science.[61] "He recognized that biological organisms could not be adequately understood by the classical Newtonian method in science, which regarded each object as a collection of distinct and disconnected parts."[62] The then classic approach was that the whole could be understood by examining the individual parts. Bertalanffy believed that this approach was inadequate and inaccurate and sought to examine the relationships between the parts that created the whole.[63]

While systems theory was initially promoted by von Bertalanffy in the mid 1940s, it continues to be a significant paradigm for both the hard and soft sciences today. Systems thinking now impacts not only biology, but also mathematics, transportation, national financial planning, space exploration, psychology, leadership, and management theory.

Systems theory fundamentally promotes the long held belief that the whole is more significant than the sum of the parts. The human body is an ideal illustration of this.

Organs and members stand in specific relationship with other organs and members so that each is dependent on the other, and the health of one member is dependent on the health of another. Kidney disease affects the whole body. The body is a marvellously self-regulating organism that is obviously more than a collection of functioning members.[64]

A *system* then, "involves the relationship patterns between the subsystems of an organism... Since the whole is greater than the sum of its parts, we cannot thoroughly comprehend a system by reducing it into separate parts."[65]

DEVELOPING A SYSTEMS VIEW OF THE CHURCH

Using the Bible's description of the church as a living body introduces a natural standard or measurement that proves useful. The goal of that which is living should be to achieve health, so that successful reproduction can take place. This is the essence of the Great Commission. A lack of health and a lack of reproduction are clear signs that the system is not working properly.

How will health be achieved within the body of Christ? Systems thinking provides the diagnostic tools and healing solutions. "Health is wholeness. Health means all the parts are working together to maintain balance. Health means all the parts are interacting to function as a whole. Health is a continuous process, the ongoing interplay of multiple forces and conditions."[66]

Health is the result of balance. Balance occurs when you have a strategy and a structure to fulfill every one of what I believe are the five New Testament purposes for the church—worship, evangelism, fellowship, discipleship, and ministry. If you don't have a strategy and a structure that intentionally balances the purposes of the church, the church tends to overemphasize the purpose the pastor feels most passionate about.[67]

EQUIPPING

One of the objectives of leadership teaching is described in the unique task of "equipping" or "preparing God's people for works of service" (Ephesians 4:11-12, NIV). This word, prepare, equip, or perfect (*katartismos*), carries the concept of putting in order, restoring, mending, or healing. Training and discipline is also in view.[68] William Barclay explains how this word may be applied in diverse contexts when he states, "This word's military usage speaks of fully furnishing an army. Its civic usage speaks of pacifying a city, which is torn by factions. Its medical usage speaks of setting a broken bone or putting a joint back into place. The basic idea of the word is that of putting a thing into the condition in which it ought to be."[69] As leaders train individuals to use their gifts and fulfill their particular calling, the entire body is "built up" (4:12).

When leaders think of equipping, they often think of individual training or a seminar for a class. While equipping certainly can and should be applied personally and with groups, this principle is rooted in the understanding that leaders must provide appropriate equipping for the whole body in a community and organic manner. While problems affect the whole, so do solutions, the advancement of health and wholeness.

Case Study: Israel in the Promised Land

The people gazed nervously and yet desirously at the Promised Land. Joshua, their leader, no doubt was reflecting on that day forty years earlier when he and eleven others had been sent on a covert mission to spy on the land of Canaan. When they returned, ten brought back a report full of fear and doubt. Only Joshua and Caleb had the confidence and faith to suggest that they could and should proceed. Now, four decades later, it was time to inherit that which God had promised. Joshua was concerned that once again fear would rule the day. God, knowing the power of fear in weak humanity, issued a powerful message to Joshua and the people.

> *Be strong and courageous, for you shall cause this people to inherit the land that I swore to their fathers to give them. Only be strong and very courageous, being careful to do according to all the law that Moses my servant commanded you. Do not turn from it to the right hand or to the left, that you may have good success wherever you go. This Book of the Law shall not depart from your mouth, but you shall meditate on it day and night, so that you may be careful to do according to all that is written in it. For then you will make your way prosperous, and then you will have good success. Have I not commanded you? Be strong and courageous. Do not be frightened, and do not be dismayed, for the Lord your God is with you wherever you go.* (Joshua 1:6-9, ESV)

Indeed, fear has tremendous power. It can obsess us, paralyze us, and immobilize us. God, however, commands, "Be strong and courageous!" It is a command. It is an act of volition that issues from a mind that trusts. The trust has three objects. First, trust is in the reality that God is present. We are never alone. Second, trust is in the historical fact that God has promised. The veracity of God will be in question if God does not come through with his promises. Third, trust is in the secure thought that God has the power. As God delivered Israel from the Egyptians, so too can God deliver Israel from the hand of the Canaanites.

Joshua and the people chose to trust and they proceeded to take that which God had given them. Along the way, the people celebrated God's leading and provision and reinstated ancient worship practices that had been long ignored. The first significant test was taking the city of Jericho. God gave exact procedural steps for the securing of victory, but God added one vitally significant restriction.

> *But you, keep yourselves from the things devoted to destruction, lest when you have devoted them you take any of the devoted things and make the camp of Israel a thing for destruction and bring trouble upon it. But all silver and gold, and every vessel of bronze and iron, are holy to the Lord; they shall go into the treasury of the Lord.* (Joshua 6:18-19, ESV)

The actual taking of Jericho unfolded as God said it would. Jericho crumbled and victory was the Lord's. However, the next exploit met with disastrous results. The soldiers of Ai routed some three thousand Israelites, killing thirty-six of them. Why the sudden change? It is soon discovered that a virus had surfaced in the camp of Israel.

> *But the people of Israel broke faith in regard to the devoted things, for Achan the son of Carmi, son of Zabdi, son of Zerah, of*

the tribe of Judah, took some of the devoted things. And the an-
ger of the Lord burned against the people of Israel...

Then Joshua tore his clothes and fell to the earth on his face
before the ark of the Lord until the evening, he and the elders of
Israel. And they put dust on their heads. And Joshua said, "Alas, O
Lord God, why have you brought this people over the Jordan at
all, to give us into the hands of the Amorites, to destroy us?
Would that we had been content to dwell beyond the Jordan! O
Lord, what can I say, when Israel has turned their backs before
their enemies! For the Canaanites and all the inhabitants of the
land will hear of it and will surround us and cut off our name
from the earth. And what will you do for your great name?"

The Lord said to Joshua, "Get up! Why have you fallen on
your face? Israel has sinned; they have transgressed my covenant
that I commanded them; they have taken some of the devoted
things; they have stolen and lied and put them among their own
belongings. Therefore the people of Israel cannot stand before
their enemies. They turn their backs before their enemies, be-
cause they have become devoted for destruction. I will be with
you no more, unless you destroy the devoted things from among
you. Get up! Consecrate the people and say, 'Consecrate your-
selves for tomorrow; for thus says the Lord, God of Israel, "There
are devoted things in your midst, O Israel. You cannot stand be-
fore your enemies until you take away the devoted things from
among you.""" (Joshua 7:1, 6-13, ESV)

The lesson here again confirms the nature of systems and the power of
systemic viruses. One person never sins in isolation. There is always residual impact or collateral damage. The sin of Achan had affected the whole
nation. Addressing this decisively and severely would send a message on
how we are all connected relationally, spiritually, and morally. The health
of the whole had to be preserved.

Joshua was faithful to his assignment as a leader. He demonstrated perseverance and good judgment through his tenure as an agent of change. In his own farewell challenge to the community of Israel, he pleaded for their good judgment.

> *You have not forsaken your brothers these many days, down to this day, but have been careful to keep the charge of the Lord your God. And now the Lord your God has given rest to your brothers, as he promised them. Therefore turn and go to your tents in the land where your possession lies, which Moses the servant of the Lord gave you on the other side of the Jordan. Only be very careful to observe the commandment and the law that Moses the servant of the Lord commanded you, to love the Lord your God, and to walk in all his ways and to keep his commandments and to cling to him and to serve him with all your heart and with all your soul.* (Joshua 22:3-5, ESV)

> *And with him ten chiefs, one from each of the tribal families of Israel, every one of them the head of a family among the clans of Israel. And they came to the people of Reuben, the people of Gad, and the half-tribe of Manasseh, in the land of Gilead, and they said to them, "Thus says the whole congregation of the Lord, 'What is this breach of faith that you have committed against the God of Israel in turning away this day from following the Lord by building yourselves an altar this day in rebellion against the Lord? Have we not had enough of the sin at Peor from which even yet we have not cleansed ourselves, and for which there came a plague upon the congregation of the Lord, that you too must turn away this day from following the Lord? And if you too rebel against the Lord today then tomorrow he will be angry with the whole congregation of Israel.'"* (Joshua 22:14-18, ESV)

The nation of Israel must be viewed here as a whole. While it is true that God works in the lives of individuals and individuals will give an account before God, God longs to work in entire communities. Thus, Israel as a whole could be healthy or it could be ill (as with Achan). The church can be viewed in the same way, as can a family. We succeed in community. We grow as a community. We contract viruses as a community. The church is a living system, a body. Leaders must learn to view the church as a whole, address challenges by looking at the whole, inspire the whole, care for the whole, and equip the whole.

Servant leaders seeking to lead the body of Christ will need to *learn* (discipline) *to equip* (critical leadership skill) *systemically* (with a new, mental model of viewing the church as a system).

ASSIGNMENT: *Examine the health of your church and your family. What issues are affecting the whole and what unique "equipping" does it require?*

DISCUSSION: *Tease out all the implications of viewing church as a living organism?*

68

Servant Leadership Skill: Inspire Continuously

When Disney World in Orlando opened some years ago, the widow of the great entrepreneur stood with one of the engineers of the expansive entertainment center, gazing at its magnificence and beauty. The engineer, in a genuine effort to honor one of our country's greatest innovators, turned toward Mrs. Disney and remarked, "Boy, I wish Walt could have seen this!" Without taking her eyes off the sprawling playland, she replied, "He did. That's why it's here."[70]

All leaders have vision. They then cast that vision relentlessly until it is embraced and lived out by all. Effective leaders are always casting a vision of a preferred future. This is a discipline that must be learned. Servant leaders must *learn* (discipline) *to inspire* (critical leadership skill of vision-casting) *continuously* (unceasingly sharing with others).

UNDERSTANDING THE POWER OF MISSION AND VISION

The mission or purpose of any organization answers the question, "Why?" "Why does this group, organization, association, or entity exist?" The core answer is the mission or purpose statement. The church of Christ locally and universally has a very clearly articulated mission. Jesus gave the church two critical mandates. The first was essentially relational, while the second was a task.

> *Jesus said to him, "'You shall love the Lord your God with all your heart, with all your soul, and with all your mind.' This is the first and great commandment. And the second is like it: 'You shall love your neighbor as yourself.'"* (Matthew 22:37-39, NKJV)

> *Go therefore and make disciples of all the nations, baptizing them in the name of the Father and of the Son and of the Holy Spirit, teaching them to observe all things that I have commanded you; and lo, I am with you always, even to the end of the age.* (Matthew 28:19-20, NKJV)

A disciple is a learner and follower of Jesus Christ who loves God and people and who helps others become disciples who love God and people. Thus, the mission of the church is to make disciples (the Great Commission) who live out the supreme expression of love (the Great Commandment). An examination of Acts 2:42-47 will surface the more specific functions of worship, witness, fellowship, and instruction. However, these may be more broadly expressed under the mandate of the above Great Commission and Great Commandment.

Regardless of the nature of the Christian organization, whether it is a church, a school, a mission, a relief agency, a parachurch ministry, or a campus ministry, if it is a part of the body of Christ it should have some expression of a biblical mission or purpose. In this, we are all united and made one.

When we seek to identify and articulate our own personal vision statement (as we did earlier), it is critical for it to reflect a subordinate, yet complementary relationship to Christ's Great Commission and Great Commandment.

The King James Version describes the destructive nature of the lack of vision.

Where there is no vision, the people perish. (Proverbs 29:18, KJV)

"The New International Version renders the verse, 'Where there is no revelation, the people cast off restraint.' The Hebrew work *khazon* in Proverbs 29:18 is variously translated 'vision' *(KJV, NASB)*, 'prophecy' *(RSV)*, and 'revelation' *(NIV)*. Each of these translations underscores the fact that true vision comes only from the Lord."[71] When a vision is from God and people are motivated out of a sense of call, there is a real power and energy at work.

There are numerous biblical examples of visionary leaders.

- Noah had a vision of an ark that would deliver his family.
- Abraham had a vision of a family, a nation, and a homeland.
- Moses had a vision of a free Israel dwelling in the Promised Land.
- Joshua carried out Moses' vision.
- David had a vision of a safe and united nation serving God.
- Jeremiah had a vision to confront the elders of Judah.
- Nehemiah had a vision of a revived, safe, and secure Jerusalem.
- Ezra had a vision of a spiritually revived people dwelling in Jerusalem.

- Jesus cast a vision of the kingdom of God.

- Peter and the disciples sought to fulfill Jesus' vision among the Jewish people.

- Paul's vision was to be a pioneer in reaching the Gentiles.

CASE STUDY: PAUL

Perhaps the most noticeable leadership quality, associated with the Apostle Paul, is the characteristic of single-mindedness. Paul was consumed with a clear and uncompromising call to live out the Great Commandment and fulfill the Great Commission. Everything in him bowed in submission to this responsibility. He would not be dissuaded or distracted. He was a man who *inspired* others *continuously* with the power of the Gospel. Consider some of these passionate texts.

> *I am a debtor both to Greeks and to barbarians, both to wise and to unwise. So, as much as is in me, I am ready to preach the Gospel to you who are in Rome also.*
>
> *For I am not ashamed of the Gospel of Christ, for it is the power of God to salvation for everyone who believes, for the Jew first and also for the Greek. For in it the righteousness of God is revealed from faith to faith; as it is written, "The just shall live by faith."* (Romans 1:14-17, NKJV)

Paul was gripped with the power of the redemptive work of Christ. Note also his sense of focus and target in these later passages.

> *Therefore I have reason to glory in Christ Jesus in the things which pertain to God. For I will not dare to speak of any of those things which Christ has not accomplished through me, in word and deed, to make the Gentiles obedient—in mighty signs and wonders, by the power of the Spirit of God, so that from Jerusalem and round about to Illyricum I have fully preached the Gos-*

pel of Christ. And so I have made it my aim to preach the Gospel, not where Christ was named, lest I should build on another man's foundation. (Romans 15:17-20, NKJV)

Do you not know that those who run in a race all run, but only one receives the prize? Run in such a way that you may win. Everyone who competes in the games exercises self-control in all things. They then do it to receive a perishable wreath, but we an imperishable. Therefore I run in such a way, as not without aim; I box in such a way, as not beating the air; but I discipline my body and make it my slave, so that, after I have preached to others, I myself will not be disqualified. (1 Corinthians 9:24-27, NASB)

But whatever things were gain to me, those things I have counted as loss for the sake of Christ. More than that, I count all things to be loss in view of the surpassing value of knowing Christ Jesus my Lord, for whom I have suffered the loss of all things, and count them but rubbish so that I may gain Christ, and may be found in Him, not having a righteousness of my own derived from the Law, but that which is through faith in Christ, the righteousness which comes from God on the basis of faith, that I may know Him and the power of His resurrection and the fellowship of His sufferings, being conformed to His death; in order that I may attain to the resurrection from the dead. Not that I have already obtained it or have already become perfect, but I press on so that I may lay hold of that for which also I was laid hold of by Christ Jesus. Brethren, I do not regard myself as having laid hold of it yet; but one thing I do: forgetting what lies behind and reaching forward to what lies ahead, I press on toward the goal for the prize of the upward call of God in Christ Jesus. (Philippians 3:7-14, NASB)

Paul left behind power, influence, prestige and reputation all to simply know Christ.

I solemnly charge you in the presence of God and of Christ Jesus,

who is to judge the living and the dead, and by His appearing and
His kingdom: preach the word; be ready in season and out of sea-
son; reprove, rebuke, exhort, with great patience and instruction.
For the time will come when they will not endure sound doctrine;
but wanting to have their ears tickled, they will accumulate for
themselves teachers in accordance to their own desires, and will
turn away their ears from the truth and will turn aside to myths.
But you, be sober in all things, endure hardship, do the work of an
evangelist, fulfill your ministry. (2 Timothy 4:1-5, NASB)

Paul was committed to reproducing himself and his single-mindedness in others.

Therefore we also, since we are surrounded by so great a cloud of
witnesses, let us lay aside every weight, and the sin which so easily
ensnares us, and let us run with endurance the race that is set be-
fore us, looking unto Jesus, the author and finisher of our faith,
who for the joy that was set before Him endured the cross, de-
spising the shame, and has sat down at the right hand of the
throne of God. (Hebrews 12:1-2, NKJV)

While the book of Hebrews has not been conclusively attributed to being one of Paul's works, the spirit of Paul's values emerges here also.

VISION CREATES ENERGY AND ALIGNMENT

Vision casting is needed because of human nature's propensity to level out. Energy leaks and entropy sets in. Vision provides energy and motivation, which are critical to the maintaining of direction and effort. Thus leadership must constantly hold the organization accountable to the mission, vision, values, and strategy of the organization. Therefore, leaders must be communicators, promoters, and inspirers.

Communicating the vision also ensures the creation and maintenance of alignment. When an automobile lacks wheel alignment, the performance of the entire vehicle is negatively affected. Similarly, if an organization lacks alignment with its vision, the organization will not function with the desired synergy and effectiveness. Wayne Cordeiro observes:

> The strength of any vision lies in alignment—that is, vision that is caught and shared by every person involved. A common vision is the product of every person living a life of character and hearing the same call—a shared picture of a preferred, God-designed future. Everyone pulling together for the cause is one of the most powerful concepts in building teams… Vision means little without alignment.[72]

Alignment is the uniting of functioning parts or members under one purpose. When an organization has multiple visions, it lacks focus. An old Greek proverb wisely states, "If you pursue two hares, both will escape you."[73] The following diagrams illustrate the power of alignment:[74]

An organization with alignment

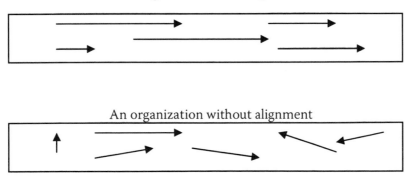

An organization without alignment

Too often, ministries within the same organization compete with each other. A common vision unites and connects these complementary ministries.

VISION CASTING SPECIFICS

How can leaders share the vision? There are numerous avenues available to
the ministry leader. The following is a list to catalyze ideas.

- Personal example
- Messages or series of messages on vision (Nehemiah,
  Joshua, Gospel)
- Staffing according to vision
- Budgeting according to vision
- Vision nuggets in all leadership meetings
- Small groups on vision, or based on Sunday messages
- Slogans (e.g. "Give me liberty or give me death")
- Logos
- Newsletters
- Analogies (e.g. "The kingdom of heaven is like…")
- Weekly Programs
- Music
- Drama
- Testimony
- Story
- Recognition of accomplishments of vision expressions
- One-on-one inspiration
- Retreats
- The use of symbols (communion, baptism, postures in
  prayer)
- Vision woven into the fibre of daily ministry and
  communication
- Profiled on Web pages and blogs

Kouzes and Posner suggest a helpful principle that unites people with
vision. In their book, *The Leadership Challenge,* they advise:

Always say we. When thinking and talking about what you plan to accomplish and have accomplished, it is essential that you think and talk in terms of *our* goals. Your task as a leader is to help other people to reach mutual goals, not your goals. You never accomplish anything alone, so your attitude can never be "here's what I did" but rather, "here's what we did." This language reinforces the belief that goals are truly collaborative, not exploitive.[75]

Servant leaders must *learn* (discipline) *to inspire* (critical leadership skill of vision-casting) *continuously* (unceasingly sharing with others).

ASSIGNMENT: *Reflect on three successful organizations or ministries. What is their vision and how is it communicated?*

DISCUSSION: *How can you contribute to the casting of a Great Commission vision in your church?*

69

Servant Leadership Skill: Collaborate Synergistically

Jazz-band leaders must choose the music, find the right musicians, and perform—in public. But the effect of the performance depends on so many things—the environment, the volunteers playing in the band, the need for everybody to perform as individuals and as a group, the absolute dependence of the leader on the members of the band, the need for the followers to play well. What a summary of an organization![76]

Music is made when each instrumentalist is contributing to the whole. This is collaboration, a working together which creates something beautiful.

George Cladis defines collaboration as "the art and skill of negotiating community, networking gifts, and focusing individual contributions to fit into the larger movement of the faithful fellowship."[77] Effective collaboration takes place when there is dialogue, discussion, learning, cooperating, problem solving, and strategic planning. The result of this kind of collaboration is synergy. Synergy is the force and influence that is generated or created from a working whole that is far greater than the sum of its parts.

Thus, servant leaders must *learn* (discipline) *to collaborate* (critical leadership skill of functioning in team) *synergistically* (with a view that together more is accomplished than alone).

UNDERSTANDING THE POWER OF TEAMS

As iron sharpens iron, so one man sharpens another. (Proverbs 27:17, NIV)

Given the biblical data of our previous studies on the nature of the body of Christ and how we are all to work together, it is not surprising to note that teams are highly valued in Scripture. When studying leadership in the New Testament, there is almost always the acknowledgement of leadership as a plurality or team. Elders and deacons are consistently spoken of as pluralities (1 Timothy 3; Titus 1). Working with others brings out the best in all. While there may be sparks (iron on iron), there will certainly be a sharpening. A collective benefit takes place for all. Thus, the whole body, or system, benefits.

We would be wise to again remind ourselves that community and team lie at the core of the identity of God himself. God as a Trinity is a divine community. Three persons exist and function eternally as three persons, yet one God. There is unity and differentiation. This image is helpful as church leaders function in teams or small ministry communities. Each member is equal, important, and different. However, as they function together as one an increased benefit and strength is realized.

The Bible describes numerous mentoring and team relationships:

- Moses training Joshua and Caleb.

- David and his friendship with Jonathan.

- David and his mighty men of valour.

- Elijah working with and training Elisha.

- Jesus training his twelve disciples.

- Paul working with Barnabas, Silas, Luke, Mark, and others.

- Barnabas working with Mark.

- Peter also working with Mark.

- Wherever elders are sighted, it is always in the plural form, implying a team.

CASE STUDY: THE JERUSALEM CONFLICT

It wasn't long before some Jews showed up from Judea insisting that everyone be circumcised: "If you're not circumcised in the Mosaic fashion, you can't be saved." Paul and Barnabas were up on their feet at once in fierce protest. The church decided to resolve the matter by sending Paul, Barnabas, and a few others to put it before the apostles and leaders in Jerusalem.

After they were sent off and on their way, they told everyone they met as they traveled through Phoenicia and Samaria about the breakthrough to the non-Jewish outsiders. Everyone who heard the news cheered—it was terrific news!

When they got to Jerusalem, Paul and Barnabas were graciously received by the whole church, including the apostles and leaders. They reported on their recent journey and how God had used them to open things up to the outsiders. Some Pharisees stood up to say their piece. They had become believers, but continued to hold to the hard party line of the Pharisees. "You have to circumcise the pagan converts," they said. "You must make them keep the Law of Moses."

The apostles and leaders called a special meeting to consider the matter. The arguments went on and on, back and forth, get-

ting more and more heated. Then Peter took the floor: "Friends, you well know that from early on God made it quite plain that he wanted the pagans to hear the Message of this good news and embrace it—and not in any secondhand or roundabout way, but firsthand, straight from my mouth. And God, who can't be fooled by any pretense on our part but always knows a person's thoughts, gave them the Holy Spirit exactly as he gave him to us. He treated the outsiders exactly as he treated us, beginning at the very center of who they were and working from that center outward, cleaning up their lives as they trusted and believed him.

"So why are you now trying to out-god God, loading these new believers down with rules that crushed our ancestors and crushed us, too? Don't we believe that we are saved because the Master Jesus amazingly and out of sheer generosity moved to save us just as he did those from beyond our nation? So what are we arguing about?"

There was dead silence. No one said a word. With the room quiet, Barnabas and Paul reported matter-of-factly on the miracles and wonders God had done among the other nations through their ministry. The silence deepened; you could hear a pin drop.

James broke the silence. "Friends, listen. Simeon has told us the story of how God at the very outset made sure that racial outsiders were included. This is in perfect agreement with the words of the prophets:

After this, I'm coming back; I'll rebuild David's ruined house; I'll put all the pieces together again; I'll make it look like new so outsiders who seek will find, so they'll have a place to come to, all the pagan peoples included in what I'm doing.

"God said it and now he's doing it. It's no afterthought; he's always known he would do this.

"So here is my decision: We're not going to unnecessarily burden non-Jewish people who turn to the Master. We'll write them a letter and tell them, 'Be careful to not get involved in activities connected with idols, to guard the morality of sex and

marriage, to not serve food offensive to Jewish Christians—blood,
for instance.' This is basic wisdom from Moses, preached and
honored for centuries now in city after city as we have met and
kept the Sabbath."

Everyone agreed: apostles, leaders, all the people. They
picked Judas (nicknamed Barsabbas) and Silas—they both carried
considerable weight in the church—and sent them to Antioch
with Paul and Barnabas with this letter:

From the apostles and leaders, your friends, to our friends in
Antioch, Syria, and Cilicia:

Hello! We heard that some men from our church went to
you and said things that confused and upset you. Mind you, they
had no authority from us; we didn't send them. We have agreed
unanimously to pick representatives and send them to you with
our good friends Barnabas and Paul. We picked men we knew
you could trust, Judas and Silas—they've looked death in the face
time and again for the sake of our Master Jesus Christ. We've sent
them to confirm in a face-to-face meeting with you what we've
written. It seemed to the Holy Spirit and to us that you should not
be saddled with any crushing burden, but be responsible only for
these bare necessities: Be careful not to get involved in activities
connected with idols; avoid serving food offensive to Jewish
Christians (blood, for instance); and guard the morality of sex and
marriage. These guidelines are sufficient to keep relations conge-
nial between us. And God be with you! (Acts 15:1-29, MSG)

This episode in the life of the church provides a positive example of church
leadership functioning as a team and a learning organization that grew
through conflict and collaboration. Understanding the context is significant. The church was changing from a predominantly Jewish makeup toward including an ever-increasing number of Gentiles. This rapid change
finally came to a head. While Gentile disciples were welcoming the news of
"grace through faith," some Jews were struggling with whether or not Gen-

tiles should embrace Jewish culture and values. Additionally, some moral issues had arisen, given the introduction of sexual purity into the Gentile's absence of sexual morality.

These theological and moral issues had to be tackled. A core understanding of the Gospel was critical, but moral issues had to be addressed also. As to the message of clarity to the Gentiles, "No, you don't have to become Jewish. You don't have to become circumcised." But as to specific prohibitions, the council identified three key areas of concern—not that these were the only concerns, but they were certainly major concerns. These issues were: food polluted by idols, sexual immorality, and issues related to blood. The Council was not going to cater to Jewish legalists, but they were going to address real, transcultural moral issues.

In the process, we see "sharp dispute and debate" (15:2), reporting of information (15:4), "much discussion" (15:6), historical reflection (15:7-18), and decision (15:19; 28).

The result of this council was profound and cannot be overstated. First, the Gospel of divine grace was affirmed. Second, the unity of the church was safeguarded. Three, the evangelization of the Gentiles could proceed without hindrance. While the theological result was of significance to the expansion of the church, the process is also revealing. The conclusion to the council was: "it seemed good to the Holy Spirit and to us..." (15:28). This statement indicates that significant dialogue, learning, and discussion must have taken place before there was a sense of unity. Thus, the early church demonstrated the capacity to learn from its challenges and change contextual factors in a way that allowed it to continue moving forward in its mission. They collaborated as a team. The conflict and collaboration forged truth, beliefs, and relationships.

DEVELOPING TEAMS

Gathering colleagues together in a room does not constitute a team. Oftentimes such assemblies only create a working group. Working groups, while serving a place, are less effective than teams. Katzenbach and Smith draw the following differentiations between working groups and teams.[78]

Working groups may be well-run meetings where there is discussion, decision, and delegation, but teams are to encourage dynamic, open-ended discussions and active problem solving toward the achievement of a stated objective. Such teams discuss, decide, and do real work.

While most teams are, in fact, working groups, true teams function at a higher level. A team functions as one entity with one common purpose. Working groups tend to be made up of individuals who come to the meeting with their portfolios and their own concerns, often unable or unwilling to see and embrace the larger picture. Teams are made up of individuals who, though holding various portfolios, come to the meeting concerned with the united whole. Teams are committed to functioning as one unit in order to accomplish the uniting purpose.

Working groups "happen" when people are put together. Teams, however, do not just happen. They are cultivated and developed. "One of the most important aspects of successful leadership is putting together a group of people to carry out the mission. Great athletic coaches know they must have talent to win and therefore they take an active part in choosing players. Teams that just happen get happenstance results."[79]

It is noteworthy that Jesus prayed before selecting his discipleship team (see Luke 6:12-16). Jesus desired there to be a divinely appointed selection of members to this group. After he prayed, he proceeded with confidence. Jesus then called people who were committed to following him, who believed in his message and mission. It should be observed that Jesus did not select individuals from one homogenous group. Jesus selected individuals who were common fishermen (Peter, James, John, and Andrew), political zealots (Simon), business-oriented individuals (Judas), and social outcasts (Matthew). Some had wealth (Matthew, Judas), while others were relatively poor (fishermen). What united them was Christ and his vision.

TEAM COVENANT

I love the church that I serve and am a part of. I also have the privilege of being a part of a wonderful staff team. We have united around the following team covenant. We do not practice it perfectly (just ask the rest of the team), but we do strive to honour these values. I have included it here for your pondering.

> Believing that God has called each of us to serve Christ as a member of the leadership team of this church, we unite in a covenant of relationship and mission. We look to the very nature of our Triune God, who eternally exists as one God and yet three persons. This eternal community of love, equality, differentiation, and interconnection serves as a model for the functioning of teams and the development of community within the body of Christ. We therefore agree to unite in a covenant around the following values and practices:
>
> Together we will seek to fulfill our mission, vision, values, and strategy. We value each other's unique personalities, character, and calling. We value each other's families, time, and personal lives. We value affirmation and encouragement. We value the development of authentic friendships. We value interconnection, collaboration, and cooperation. We value individual and team learning. We value open and truthful communication. We value feedback and constructive evaluation. We value conflict resolution. We value accountability. We value faith-stretching risks. We value appropriate loyalty.[80]

Servant leaders must *learn* (discipline) *to collaborate* (critical leadership skill of functioning in team) *synergistically* (with a view that together more is accomplished than alone).

ASSIGNMENT: *If you are presently involved in a team ministry, does it operate as a team or a working group? How can you bring improvement to your collaboration?*

DISCUSSION: *Discuss the genius of effective sports teams.*

70

Servant Leadership Skill:
Shepherd Tenderly

CASE STUDY: PETER

After this, Jesus appeared again to the disciples, this time at the Tiberias Sea (the Sea of Galilee). This is how he did it: Simon Peter, Thomas (nicknamed "Twin"), Nathanael from Cana in Galilee, the brothers Zebedee, and two other disciples were together. Simon Peter announced, "I'm going fishing."

The rest of them replied, "We're going with you." They went out and got in the boat. They caught nothing that night. When the sun came up, Jesus was standing on the beach, but they didn't recognize him.

Jesus spoke to them: "Good morning! Did you catch anything for breakfast?"

They answered, "No."

He said, "Throw the net off the right side of the boat and see what happens."

They did what he said. All of a sudden there were so many fish in it, they weren't strong enough to pull it in.

Then the disciple Jesus loved said to Peter, "It's the Master!"

When Simon Peter realized that it was the Master, he threw on some clothes, for he was stripped for work, and dove into the sea. The other disciples came in by boat for they weren't far from land, a hundred yards or so, pulling along the net full of fish. When they got out of the boat, they saw a fire laid, with fish and bread cooking on it.

Jesus said, "Bring some of the fish you've just caught." Simon Peter joined them and pulled the net to shore—153 big fish! And even with all those fish, the net didn't rip.

Jesus said, "Breakfast is ready." Not one of the disciples dared ask, "Who are you?" They knew it was the Master.

Jesus then took the bread and gave it to them. He did the same with the fish. This was now the third time Jesus had shown himself alive to the disciples since being raised from the dead.

After breakfast, Jesus said to Simon Peter, "Simon, son of John, do you love me more than these?"

"Yes, Master, you know I love you."

Jesus said, "Feed my lambs."

He then asked a second time, "Simon, son of John, do you love me?"

"Yes, Master, you know I love you."

Jesus said, "Shepherd my sheep."

Then he said it a third time: "Simon, son of John, do you love me?"

Peter was upset that he asked for the third time, "Do you love me?" so he answered, "Master, you know everything there is to know. You've got to know that I love you."

Jesus said, "Feed my sheep. I'm telling you the very truth now: When you were young you dressed yourself and went wherever you wished, but when you get old you'll have to stretch out your hands while someone else dresses you and takes you where you don't want to go." He said this to hint at the kind of death by which Peter would glorify God. And then he commanded, "Follow me."

Turning his head, Peter noticed the disciple Jesus loved following right behind. When Peter noticed him, he asked Jesus, "Master, what's going to happen to him?"

Jesus said, "If I want him to live until I come again, what's that to you? You—follow me." That is how the rumor got out among the brothers that this disciple wouldn't die. But that is not what Jesus said. He simply said, "If I want him to live until I come again, what's that to you?"

This is the same disciple who was eyewitness to all these things and wrote them down. And we all know that his eyewitness account is reliable and accurate.

There are so many other things Jesus did. If they were all written down, each of them, one by one, I can't imagine a world big enough to hold such a library of books. (John 21:1-25, MSG)

Jesus appears to his followers at the sea of Tiberias. The disciples had been fishing all night, but had not caught anything (verses 1-3). They were no doubt discouraged by the unexpected turn of events and had returned to what they knew best, fishing. They were questioning their "calling." Jesus calls them to cast out their nets again and they are overwhelmed with a load of fish (verses 4-6). When Peter realizes who it is, he swims to shore, while the others paddle in by boat (verses 7-8). Jesus then takes some of the 153 fish and some bread and the group enjoys breakfast (verses 9-13). John, the author, reflects on this being the third time Jesus appears to the disciples, affirming the reality of the resurrection.

Jesus then deals with Peter on an individual level. The last significant conversation Jesus had with Peter revolved around Peter's promise not to forsake Jesus, but you will recall, Peter denied Jesus.

Jesus asks, "Do you love me more than these?" What or who are "these"? Some have suggested, "Do you love me more than the other disciples love me?" This is unlikely. "Do you love me more than you love your friends, the disciples?" This is possible, but consider, "Do you love me more than these fish?" This is the likely intention of Jesus. Because these fish had taken Peter off of his calling, Jesus was asking him if his work and career were more important than his relationship with Jesus himself. This was really a question of priorities. Peter lost sight of his priorities and Jesus pointed it out.

Jesus is likely saying, "I know you like me, but I will know you love me, really love me, when you care about what I care about (namely, my people… feeding the sheep)." Your first priority must be your God and service to the mission and priorities of God. This sounds strangely familiar to Matthew 22: "Love the Lord your God… love your neighbor as yourself." The penetrating question that Jesus asks Peter, he asks of all of us. Do you love me? Do you care about the things that I care about? If so, take care of my people.

FEED GOD'S SHEEP

Leaders and influencers love God by loving people and feeding God's sheep. This implies caring for them, building into their lives, protecting them, training them, guiding them, correcting them, and supporting them. This again parallels the command to make disciples (Matthew 28:18-20). Teaching was also a significant measurement of maturity, as evidenced in Hebrews.

> For though by this time you ought to be teachers, you need someone to teach you again the first principles of the oracles of God; and you have come to need milk and not solid food. For everyone who partakes only of milk is unskilled in the word of right-

eousness, for he is a babe. But solid food belongs to those who are
of full age, that is, those who by reason of use have their senses
exercised to discern both good and evil. (Hebrews 5:12-14, NKJV)

Therefore, leaving the discussion of the elementary principles of
Christ, let us go on to perfection, not laying again the foundation
of repentance from dead works and of faith toward God, of the
doctrine of baptisms, of laying on of hands, of resurrection of the
dead, and of eternal judgment. And this we will do if God permits.
(Hebrews 6:1-3, NKJV)

The author of Hebrews rebukes his readers because of their spiritual
growth plateau. He challenges them with the expectation, "You ought to be
teachers" (5:12). There are times when leaders hear people say, "I am just
not being fed. I need meat. I need deeper truths." While such may be the
case, the writer of Hebrews is reminding us that teaching and reproducing
is the intended evidence of maturity. Anyone who says that they are not
being fed is likely not teaching or feeding God's flock.

Jesus says, "If you love me, really love me, care about what I care
about—my sheep, my lambs, my flock, my children, my disciples, my small
group and my church." This is what matters. This is what fulfills. This is
what satisfies. It is not high-octane, adrenalin-pumping, testosterone-
flowing energetic programs that lift us. We are most fulfilled when we engage in simple discipleship, simple shepherding, and simple feeding. When
we love our flock and feed our flock—like Jesus loves us and feeds us—we
are showing that we love Jesus.

Servant leaders must *learn* (discipline) *to shepherd* (critical leadership
skill of feeding) *tenderly* (with love, care, sensitivity, and resilience).

ASSIGNMENT: *Are you feeding anyone? How are you building into his or*
her life?

DISCUSSION: *Discuss what ancient "shepherding" may have looked like. Why was this an appropriate metaphor?*

— 71 —
Servant Leadership Skill: Communicate Clearly

There is an old saying that preachers have used: "If there is a mist in the pulpit, there is a fog in the pew." The meaning of this saying is self-evident. If the teacher or communicator is confused or unclear, the likelihood of the students understanding the message is slim. Clarity in communication is not always easy, but it must be one of the servant leader's objectives. If as leaders we are going to cast vision, equip the body, and feed the flock, we must be clear.

> Then teach them the statutes and the laws, and make known to them the way in which they are to walk and the work they are to do. (Exodus 18:20, NASB)

> It is a trustworthy statement: if any man aspires to the office of overseer, it is a fine work he desires to do. An overseer, then,

must be above reproach, the husband of one wife, temperate, prudent, respectable, hospitable, able to teach, not addicted to wine or pugnacious, but gentle, peaceable, free from the love of money. He must be one who manages his own household well, keeping his children under control with all dignity (but if a man does not know how to manage his own household, how will he take care of the church of God?), and not a new convert, so that he will not become conceited and fall into the condemnation incurred by the devil. And he must have a good reputation with those outside the church, so that he will not fall into reproach and the snare of the devil. (1 Timothy 3:1-7, NASB)

I solemnly charge you in the presence of God and of Christ Jesus, who is to judge the living and the dead, and by His appearing and His kingdom: preach the word; be ready in season and out of season; reprove, rebuke, exhort, with great patience and instruction. For the time will come when they will not endure sound doctrine; but wanting to have their ears tickled, they will accumulate for themselves teachers in accordance to their own desires, and will turn away their ears from the truth and will turn aside to myths. But you, be sober in all things, endure hardship, do the work of an evangelist, fulfill your ministry. (2 Timothy 4:1-5, NASB)

Continue steadfastly in prayer, being watchful in it with thanksgiving. At the same time, pray also for us, that God may open to us a door for the word, to declare the mystery of Christ, on account of which I am in prison—that I may make it clear, which is how I ought to speak. (Colossians 4:2-4, ESV)

PRINCIPLES OF GOOD COMMUNICATION

Teaching is something we do all the time. Leaders are constantly instructing in one way or another. We ought to be looking for "teachable moments" throughout life in order to capitalize on opportunities to learn. Parents do this with children, mentors do this with their protégés, servant leaders do this with their people, and disciples do this with other disciples.

However, there will be times when a more formal teaching presentation is required. The following will provide a basic grid for clarity in a teaching outline.

Every lesson (study, class, message) should follow a simple outline:

- The introduction (say what you are going to say).
- The body (say it).
- The conclusion (say what you have just said).

A good introduction should:

- Introduce the subject.
- Create a need.
- Arouse interest.

An accurate Bible study should:

- Thoroughly explore the Biblical event or lesson in its historical cultural context.
- Determine the transferable principle that transcends time and culture. This is your thesis statement, but should be packaged in a memorable fashion. All sub-points should support the essential thesis.
- Make appropriate application for the listener/reader/participant to current situations.

A good conclusion will:

- Review your thesis.
- Appeal to decision and application.

Artistic considerations:

- Use stories. People relate to stories, especially when they are personal.
- Use illustrations. Illustrations are like windows allowing you to look inside the truth.
- Use culturally appropriate memory hooks (alliterations, acrostics, images, repetition).
- Use quotes, statistics, and sources where applicable. Cite sources.

Aristotle observed the power of these three qualities in rhetoric and persuasive communication:

- Ethos: the credibility of the speaker.
- Logos: the logic or reasoning of our presentation.
- Pathos: the emotional pull in our presentation.

Servant leaders must *learn* (discipline) *to communicate* (critical leadership skill) *clearly* (understandably, accurately, creatively, and relevantly).

ASSIGNMENT: *Select a Bible text. Use the above outline to prepare a ten to fifteen minute lesson. Find an opportunity to present your lesson.*

DISCUSSION: *What did you find difficult with this assignment? What did you find enlightening?*

——— 72 ———
Servant Leadership Skill:
Decide Wisely

Teach me knowledge and good judgment, for I believe in your commandments. (Psalm 119:66, NIV)

As leaders, we understand that the quality of our decisions is the determining factor in our leadership effectiveness. Good judgment is rooted in biblical thinking and wise, godly character. However, there are some principles, skill sets, and perspectives that can aid us in the cultivation of good judgment.

OBJECTIVE CRITERIA

While we are emotional beings, decision-making should be anchored in ruthless objectivity. While God may prompt us, and we may from time to time get those "gut hunches," the quality of our decisions will be measured by their conformity to the values of God.

A general observation of life is that: People do what they want to do. People buy what they want. People act the way they want. People choose what they want. Disciplined disciples and servant leaders have cultivated the self-control to bring these desires under the authority of moral and biblical truth.

If we want to be wise, discerning, prudent, disciplined and thoughtful in our decision-making, objective criteria will serve us well. Among the many voices we hear, here are some voices to which we should be listening.

VOICE OF TRUTH: WHAT DOES GOD'S WORD TELL ME?

This is an objective voice. This is the voice of truth—objective, absolute truth. This is the life roadmap, the blueprint, the operations manual. This is the Bible. This is God's message to us. The Bible is God's letter, God's heart to us. God wants us to know him and to know truth. We could say that the will of God is in the Word of God. Do you want to know the will of God for your life? Start with the Word of God.

> *For this is the will of God, your sanctification: that you should abstain from sexual immorality.* (1 Thessalonians 4:3, NKJV)

This verse speaks of our sexuality, our sexual appetites, and practices. God here is telling us that he wants us to live in sexual purity, honouring only the exclusive marriage relationship. This is God's will. It is God's will that we live pure lives! The same is true of all the teachings of Scripture. This voice must be listened to.

VOICE OF DATA: WHAT DO ALL THE FACTS TELL ME?

This, too, is an objective voice.

For which of you, intending to build a tower, does not sit down first and count the cost, whether he has enough to finish it—lest, after he has laid the foundation, and is not able to finish, all who see it begin to mock him, saying, "This man began to build and was not able to finish"? (Luke 14:28-30, NKJV)

Research data and gather the facts. Get as many facts as you can. Make a pro and con list. It may not prove conclusive, but it will help. The voice of data will aid us in our pursuit of objectivity. Listen up.

VOICE OF COUNSEL: WHAT DO WISE ADVISORS TELL ME?

This is yet another critical voice. While the voice of advisors appears slightly less objective, it is in their agreement and alignment that confirmation is discovered.

Where there is no counsel, the people fall; But in the multitude of counselors there is safety. (Proverbs 11:14, NKJV)

Without counsel, plans go awry, But in the multitude of counselors they are established. (Proverbs 15:22, NKJV)

We are being foolish if we are making a significant, life-determining decision without seeking the counsel of people we trust.

VOICE OF CONSEQUENCES: WHAT DO THE IMPLICATIONS TELL ME?

This is the objective voice of exploring consequences.

And if you faithfully obey the voice of the Lord your God, being careful to do all his commandments that I command you today, the Lord your God will set you high above all the nations of the earth... But if you will not obey the voice of the Lord your God or be careful to do all his commandments and his statutes that I command you today, then all these curses shall come upon you and overtake you. (Deuteronomy 28:1, 15, ESV)

If we understand Deuteronomy 28 and 30, we will understand the Old Testament. This is the law of cause and effect. This is the principle that we reap what we sow. There are implications and consequences to every decision. These implications must be considered. This is the repeated theme of the Proverbs.

VOICE OF TIMING: WHAT DOES MY SITUATION TELL ME?

This is a combination of an objective voice and a subjective voice, but is still useful.

> *To everything there is a season, a time for every purpose under heaven.* (Ecclesiastes 3:1, NKJV)

John Maxwell has observed that the wrong decision at the wrong time leads to disaster, the wrong decision at the right time is a mistake, the right decision at the wrong time results in unacceptance, and the right decision at the right time brings success.[81] Sometimes we need to wait. Sometimes we need to seize an opportunity quickly.

VOICE OF DIVINE GUIDANCE: WHAT DO GOD'S LEADINGS TELL ME?

While this is a subjective voice, God never leads us to do anything that is contrary to his revealed will. Further, God's promptings may be less frequent, but they should be no less valid. Consider this episode in Paul's ministry.

> *They went to Phrygia, and then on through the region of Galatia. Their plan was to turn west into Asia province, but the Holy Spirit blocked that route. So they went to Mysia and tried to go north to Bithynia, but the Spirit of Jesus wouldn't let them go*

there either. Proceeding on through Mysia, they went down to the seaport Troas.

That night Paul had a dream: A Macedonian stood on the far shore and called across the sea, "Come over to Macedonia and help us!" The dream gave Paul his map. We went to work at once getting things ready to cross over to Macedonia. All the pieces had come together. We knew now for sure that God had called us to preach the good news to the Europeans. (Acts 16:6-10, MSG)

In this story, God's will came through a vision. Sometimes God uses circumstances and situations to open and close doors to guide us. Sometimes God uses gentle, inner promptings. Sometimes we speak of having "peace" about a decision.

Be anxious for nothing, but in everything by prayer and supplication with thanksgiving let your requests be made known to God. And the peace of God, which surpasses all comprehension, will guard your hearts and your minds in Christ Jesus. (Philippians 4:6-7, NASB)

Is this peace purely emotional? The peace here is deeper, wider, more solid than "It just feels right!" We need caution here, but nevertheless God does nudge us. Let's have a listening ear, but we must ensure that it conforms to and complements objective truth.

VOICE OF PERSONAL ASPIRATION: WHAT DOES MY SPIRIT TELL ME?

This is also is a subjective voice, but it is significant.

Delight yourself in the Lord; and He will give you the desires of your heart. (Psalm 37:4, NASB)

When we are walking with God in a dynamic, intimate, trust-based relationship, and we are celebrating God and life, listen to your desires. They

may be God-instilled. This is the voice of personal aspiration and it is not
an insignificant one.

WISE PROBLEM-SOLVING

*Solomon arranged a marriage contract with Pharaoh, king of
Egypt. He married Pharaoh's daughter and brought her to the
City of David until he had completed building his royal palace and
God's Temple and the wall around Jerusalem. Meanwhile, the
people were worshiping at local shrines because at that time no
temple had yet been built to the Name of God. Solomon loved
God and continued to live in the God-honoring ways of David his
father, except that he also worshiped at the local shrines, offering
sacrifices and burning incense.*

*The king went to Gibeon, the most prestigious of the local
shrines, to worship. He sacrificed a thousand Whole-Burnt-
Offerings on that altar. That night, there in Gibeon, God appeared to Solomon in a dream: God said, "What can I give you?
Ask."*

*Solomon said, "You were extravagantly generous in love with
David my father, and he lived faithfully in your presence, his relationships were just and his heart right. And you have persisted in
this great and generous love by giving him—and this very day!—a
son to sit on his throne.*

*"And now here I am: God, my God, you have made me, your
servant, ruler of the kingdom in place of David my father. I'm too
young for this, a mere child! I don't know the ropes, hardly know
the 'ins' and 'outs' of this job. And here I am, set down in the middle of the people you've chosen, a great people—far too many to
ever count.*

*"Here's what I want: Give me a God-listening heart so I can
lead your people well, discerning the difference between good and
evil. For who on their own is capable of leading your glorious peo-*

ple?"

God, the Master, was delighted with Solomon's response. And God said to him, "Because you have asked for this and haven't grasped after a long life, or riches, or the doom of your enemies, but you have asked for the ability to lead and govern well, I'll give you what you've asked for—I'm giving you a wise and mature heart. There's never been one like you before; and there'll be no one after. As a bonus, I'm giving you both the wealth and glory you didn't ask for—there's not a king anywhere who will come up to your mark. And if you stay on course, keeping your eye on the life-map and the God-signs as your father David did, I'll also give you a long life."

Solomon woke up—what a dream! He returned to Jerusalem, took his place before the Chest of the Covenant of God, and worshiped by sacrificing Whole-Burnt-Offerings and Peace-Offerings. Then he laid out a banquet for everyone in his service.

The very next thing, two prostitutes showed up before the king. The one woman said, "My master, this woman and I live in the same house. While we were living together, I had a baby. Three days after I gave birth, this woman also had a baby. We were alone—there wasn't anyone else in the house except for the two of us. The infant son of this woman died one night when she rolled over on him in her sleep. She got up in the middle of the night and took my son—I was sound asleep, mind you!—and put him at her breast and put her dead son at my breast. When I got up in the morning to nurse my son, here was this dead baby! But when I looked at him in the morning light, I saw immediately that he wasn't my baby."

"Not so!" said the other woman. "The living one's mine; the dead one's yours."

The first woman countered, "No! Your son's the dead one; mine's the living one."

They went back and forth this way in front of the king.

The king said, "What are we to do? This woman says, 'The

*living son is mine and the dead one is yours,' and this woman
says, 'No, the dead one's yours and the living one's mine.'"*

*After a moment the king said, "Bring me a sword." They
brought the sword to the king.*

*Then he said, "Cut the living baby in two—give half to one
and half to the other."*

*The real mother of the living baby was overcome with emo-
tion for her son and said, "Oh no, master! Give her the whole
baby alive; don't kill him!"*

*But the other one said, "If I can't have him, you can't have
him—cut away!"*

*The king gave his decision: "Give the living baby to the first
woman. Nobody is going to kill this baby. She is the real mother."*

*The word got around—everyone in Israel heard of the king's
judgment. They were all in awe of the king, realizing that it was
God's wisdom that enabled him to judge truly.* (1 Kings 3:1-28,
MSG)

Solomon's reputation for wise problem solving became widely celebrated.
Problem solving is a critical arena where judgment is tested. Solutions begin with an accurate diagnosis of the problem. Most problems, however,
are extremely complex. Leaders all too often approach problems simplisti-
cally and in a one-dimensional fashion. The temptation is to perceive the
problem from one vantage point and offer a similarly narrow solution.
Judgments are made, but they frequently fail to make the grade when they
are rooted in simplistic analysis.

Authors Lee Bolman and Terrence Deal point out that organizations
(problems) are full of complexity, surprise, deception, and ambiguity. To
illustrate how complexity creates ambiguity, they cite the following dilemmas with which many leaders wrestle:

We are not sure what the problem is. Definitions of the problem
are vague or competing, and any given problem is intertwined

with other messy problems.

We are not sure what is really happening. Information is incomplete, ambiguous, and unreliable, and people disagree on how to interpret the information that is available.

We are not sure what we want. We have multiple goals that are unclear or conflicting. Different people want different things, leading to political and emotional conflict.

We do not have the resources we need. Shortages of time, attention, or money make a difficult situation even more chaotic.

We are not sure who is supposed to do what. Roles are unclear, there is disagreement about who is responsible for what, and things keep shifting as players come and go.

We are not sure how to get what we want. Even if we agree on what we want, we are not sure (or we disagree) about how to make it happen.

We are not sure how to determine if we have succeeded. We are not sure what criteria to use in evaluating success. Or if we do know the criteria, we are not sure how to measure them.[82]

Bolman and Deal suggest that all issues should be analyzed from four potential viewpoints called frames: the Political Frame, the Human Resources Frame, the Symbolic Frame, and the Structural Frame.[83] Thus, a controversy may be rooted in structural violation, but it may be compounded by the failure to honour significant symbols of the organization. Some key players with strategic leverage have perhaps been overlooked, thus identifying the Human Resources Frame. There may also have been some political naiveté at work.

One more frame could be added to heighten the excellence of our judgment that could be called the Bird's-Eye-View Frame. This is the perspective of being able to assess or project the implications or consequences of a decision that is made or not made. Together, these five frames can serve as an ensemble to assist us in making quality decisions. While good judgment is value-based, it is cultivated with the skill of perceptive analysis.

Servant leaders must *learn* (discipline) *to decide* (critical leadership skill) *wisely* (with ruthless objectivity, appropriately, and sensitively).

ASSIGNMENT: *Identify a major decision that you must make. Place it through the grid and determine what the best decision should be.*

DISCUSSION: *Discuss Bolman and Deal's four-fold lens. How might employing these lenses spare us from poor choices and unintended consequences?*

——— 73 ———
Servant Leadership Skill:
Plan Strategically

But the noble man makes noble plans, and by noble deeds he stands. (Isaiah 32:8, NIV)

CASE STUDY: NEHEMIAH

Nehemiah was a surprise leader who seemed to come out of the shadows to be used by God for the rebuilding of the morale, identity, and safety of the nation of Israel. Initially, he was an advisor to the powerful King Artaxerxes I during the time when the Jews were being allowed to return to Israel from exile in Babylon. Although Nehemiah was a man of influence in Artaxerxes' court, his call to leadership was born out of need. Nehemiah in the end stumbled into leadership. Nehemiah tells his story:

The memoirs of Nehemiah son of Hacaliah.

It was the month of Kislev in the twentieth year. At the time I was in the palace complex at Susa. Hanani, one of my brothers, had just arrived from Judah with some fellow Jews. I asked them about the conditions among the Jews there who had survived the exile, and about Jerusalem.

They told me, "The exile survivors who are left there in the province are in bad shape. Conditions are appalling. The wall of Jerusalem is still rubble; the city gates are still cinders."

When I heard this, I sat down and wept. I mourned for days, fasting and praying before the God-of-Heaven.

I said, "God, God-of-Heaven, the great and awesome God, loyal to his covenant and faithful to those who love him and obey his commands: Look at me, listen to me. Pay attention to this prayer of your servant that I'm praying day and night in interces-sion for your servants, the People of Israel, confessing the sins of the People of Israel. And I'm including myself, I and my ancestors, among those who have sinned against you.

"We've treated you like dirt: We haven't done what you told us, haven't followed your commands, and haven't respected the decisions you gave to Moses your servant. All the same, remem-ber the warning you posted to your servant Moses: 'If you betray me, I'll scatter you to the four winds, but if you come back to me and do what I tell you, I'll gather up all these scattered peoples from wherever they ended up and put them back in the place I chose to mark with my Name.'

"Well, there they are—your servants, your people whom you so powerfully and impressively redeemed. O Master, listen to me, listen to your servant's prayer—and yes, to all your servants who delight in honoring you—and make me successful today so that I get what I want from the king."

I was cupbearer to the king. (Nehemiah 1:2-10, MSG)

It was the month of Nisan in the twentieth year of Artaxerxes the king. At the hour for serving wine I brought it in and gave it to the king. I had never been hangdog in his presence before, so he asked me, "Why the long face? You're not sick are you? Or are you depressed?"

That made me all the more agitated. I said, "Long live the king! And why shouldn't I be depressed when the city, the city where all my family is buried, is in ruins and the city gates have been reduced to cinders?"

The king then asked me, "So what do you want?"

Praying under my breath to the God-of-Heaven, I said, "If it please the king, and if the king thinks well of me, send me to Judah, to the city where my family is buried, so that I can rebuild it."

The king, with the queen sitting alongside him, said, "How long will your work take and when would you expect to return?"

I gave him a time, and the king gave his approval to send me.

Then I said, "If it please the king, provide me with letters to the governors across the Euphrates that authorize my travel through to Judah; and also an order to Asaph, keeper of the king's forest, to supply me with timber for the beams of The Temple fortress, the wall of the city, and the house where I'll be living."

The generous hand of my God was with me in this and the king gave them to me. When I met the governors across The River (the Euphrates) I showed them the king's letters. The king even sent along a cavalry escort.

When Sanballat the Horonite and Tobiah the Ammonite official heard about this, they were very upset, angry that anyone would come to look after the interests of the People of Israel.

And so I arrived in Jerusalem. After I had been there three days, I got up in the middle of the night, I and a few men who were with me. I hadn't told anyone what my God had put in my heart to do for Jerusalem. The only animal with us was the one I was riding.

Under cover of night I went past the Valley Gate toward the Dragon's Fountain to the Dung Gate looking over the walls of Je-

rusalem, which had been broken through and whose gates had
been burned up. I then crossed to the Fountain Gate and headed
for the King's Pool but there wasn't enough room for the donkey I
was riding to get through. So I went up the valley in the dark continuing my inspection of the wall. I came back in through the Valley Gate. The local officials had no idea where I'd gone or what I
was doing—I hadn't breathed a word to the Jews, priests, nobles,
local officials, or anyone else who would be working on the job.

Then I gave them my report: "Face it: we're in a bad way
here. Jerusalem is a wreck; its gates are burned up. Come—let's
build the wall of Jerusalem and not live with this disgrace any
longer." I told them how God was supporting me and how the
king was backing me up.

They said, "We're with you. Let's get started." They rolled up
their sleeves, ready for the good work.

When Sanballat the Horonite, Tobiah the Ammonite official,
and Geshem the Arab heard about it, they laughed at us, mocking, "Ha! What do you think you're doing? Do you think you can
cross the king?"

I shot back, "The God-of-Heaven will make sure we succeed.
We're his servants and we're going to work, rebuilding. You can
keep your nose out of it. You get no say in this—Jerusalem's none
of your business!" (Nehemiah 2:1-20, MSG).

The high priest Eliashib and his fellow priests were up and at
it: They went to work on the Sheep Gate; they repaired it and
hung its doors, continuing on as far as the Tower of the Hundred
and the Tower of Hananel. The men of Jericho worked alongside
them; and next to them, Zaccur son of Imri.

The Fish Gate was built by the Hassenaah brothers; they re-
paired it, hung its doors, and installed its bolts and bars.
Meremoth son of Uriah, the son of Hakkoz, worked; next to him
Meshullam son of Berekiah, the son of Meshezabel; next to him
Zadok son of Baana; and next to him the Tekoites (except for
their nobles, who wouldn't work with their master and refused to

get their hands dirty with such work).

The Jeshanah Gate was rebuilt by Joiada son of Paseah and Meshullam son of Besodeiah; they repaired it, hung its doors, and installed its bolts and bars. Melatiah the Gibeonite, Jadon the Meronothite, and the men of Gibeon and Mizpah, which was under the rule of the governor from across the Euphrates, worked alongside them. Uzziel son of Harhaiah of the goldsmiths' guild worked next to him, and next to him Hananiah, one of the perfumers. They rebuilt the wall of Jerusalem as far as the Broad Wall. (Nehemiah 3:1-6, MSG)

This story is full of inspiring leadership qualities that revolve around the need for a plan. Observe:

- *Leaders are first servants.* Nehemiah saw a tremendous need. The people of Jerusalem were vulnerable because of the condition of the walls. Something had to be done and someone would have to do it. Rather than wait for a hero, Nehemiah steps into the gap as a servant meeting a need.
- *Leaders care.* Nehemiah was a man of compassion for his own people. He left his own position of security and opulent living to serve in any way he could, even if it meant risking his relationship with the king.
- *Leaders act.* Nehemiah was a man of initiative. Where were the prophets, priests, noblemen, and elders of the city? Their silence is deafening.
- *Leaders pray.* Nehemiah had a deep devotion and trust in God and although he was a man of action, he knew his success depended on God.
- *Leaders connect.* Nehemiah entered the system as a relative outsider, but quickly related to the people and thus became part of the system. He did not enter in with a "you need to..." but rather a "we need to..."

- *Leaders inspire.* "Let us start rebuilding!" (2:18) was Nehemiah's rallying cry and the people of Jerusalem responded with excitement and diligence.

- *Leaders model character.* Honesty and integrity marked Nehemiah's life, whether in the king's court or on the construction site. This gave Nehemiah credibility and greatly extended his leadership platform.

- *Leaders employ planning and good judgment.* Nehemiah researched, assessed, reflected, planned, and then acted. Nehemiah understood the gravity of each of his decisions.

- *Leaders multiply.* The job was immense and the only way it would get done was through delegation. Nehemiah was able to multiply himself to advance efficiency.

As the work got underway, Nehemiah discovered yet more leadership challenges. He found that leadership initiative invites opposition. Mockery (4:1-3), aggression (4:7-8), opportunists (5:1-12), distraction with the view to assassination (6:1-4), and slander (6:5-9) all came Nehemiah's way. Initially, the people began to lose heart, but Nehemiah provided the necessary inspiration for them to continue.

> But soon word was going around in Judah, The builders are pooped, the rubbish piles up; We're in over our heads, we can't build this wall.
>
> And all this time our enemies were saying, "They won't know what hit them. Before they know it we'll be at their throats, killing them right and left. That will put a stop to the work!" The Jews who were their neighbors kept reporting, "They have us surrounded; they're going to attack!" If we heard it once, we heard it ten times.
>
> So I stationed armed guards at the most vulnerable places of the wall and assigned people by families with their swords, lances,

and bows. After looking things over I stood up and spoke to the nobles, officials, and everyone else: "Don't be afraid of them. Put your minds on the Master, great and awesome, and then fight for your brothers, your sons, your daughters, your wives, and your homes." (Nehemiah 4:10-14, MSG)

Nehemiah and the people of Jerusalem ultimately succeeded in their mission. After essential safety was provided for the city, Nehemiah turned his attention to deeper issues of spirituality and a right relationship with God. Ezra was called upon to read from the long forgotten law and Nehemiah led the people in a response of repentance and renewal of their covenant responsibilities.

Servant leaders must *learn* (discipline) *to plan* (critical leadership skill) *strategically* (with purpose, with the right people, and in the right time).

ASSIGNMENT: *Study this case thoroughly. What additional qualities of planning do you see that Nehemiah employed. How could you become a better planner?*

DISCUSSION: *What happens when we don't plan?*

74

Servant Leadership Skill: Manage Carefully

Management is the organization of the parts to accomplish the whole. The need for careful management surfaces early in the biblical text.

CASE STUDY: MOSES AND JETHRO

> *The next day Moses took his place to judge the people. People were standing before him all day long, from morning to night. When Moses' father-in-law saw all that he was doing for the people, he said, "What's going on here? Why are you doing all this, and all by yourself, letting everybody line up before you from morning to night?"*
>
> *Moses said to his father-in-law, "Because the people come to me with questions about God. When something comes up, they come to me. I judge between a man and his neighbor and teach*

them God's laws and instructions."

Moses' father-in-law said, "This is no way to go about it. You'll burn out, and the people right along with you. This is way too much for you—you can't do this alone. Now listen to me. Let me tell you how to do this so that God will be in this with you. Be there for the people before God, but let the matters of concern be presented to God. Your job is to teach them the rules and instructions, to show them how to live, what to do. And then you need to keep a sharp eye out for competent men—men who fear God, men of integrity, men who are incorruptible—and appoint them as leaders over groups organized by the thousand, by the hundred, by fifty, and by ten. They'll be responsible for the everyday work of judging among the people. They'll bring the hard cases to you, but in the routine cases they'll be the judges. They will share your load and that will make it easier for you. If you handle the work this way, you'll have the strength to carry out whatever God commands you, and the people in their settings will flourish also."

Moses listened to the counsel of his father-in-law and did everything he said. Moses picked competent men from all Israel and set them as leaders over the people who were organized by the thousand, by the hundred, by fifty, and by ten. They took over the everyday work of judging among the people. They brought the hard cases to Moses, but in the routine cases they were the judges. Then Moses said good-bye to his father-in-law who went home to his own country. (Exodus 18:13-26, MSG)

When leadership is defined, at its simplest level, as an influence, we see leadership emerging with Adam. However, the first significant example of a leader of a large organization is Moses. Moses became the reluctant leader of the nation of Israel. Thankfully, he had a teachable heart and when Jethro spoke into his life and role, Moses listened. Jethro could see that Moses needed to manage, administrate, and delegate if he was to survive his leadership mandate.

There are all kinds of leadership styles, shapes, qualities, and techniques. Indeed, good leaders are flexible and versatile in their approach; however, there are different kinds of leaders and these leaders do gravitate to a particular approach. I will suggest three: directional leaders, managing leaders, and disciple-making leaders. All are necessary. All need to be strategically placed. All need to be suitably empowered.

- Directional leaders—Setting direction (determining and casting vision)
- Managing leaders—Planning and budgeting
- Disciple-making leaders—Executing the plan

- Directional leaders—Coping with environmental change
- Managing leaders—Coping with complexity
- Disciple-making leaders—Providing active, constructive feedback

- Directional leaders—Aligning people
- Managing leaders—Organizing and staffing
- Disciple-making leaders—Actively cooperating

- Directional leaders—Motivating people
- Managing leaders—Controlling and problem-solving
- Disciple-making leaders—Maintaining strategic movement

- Directional leaders—Leading the whole
- Managing leaders—Connecting and interrelating the parts
- Disciple-making leaders—Collaborating with the parts

- Directional leaders—Attention to effectiveness (doing the right things)
- Managing leaders—Attention to efficiency (doing things right)

- Disciple-making leaders—Attention to execution (doing the plan)

- Directional leaders—Emphasis on multiplication
- Managing leaders—Emphasis on the plan leading to multiplication
- Disciple-making leaders—Emphasis on the task of multiplication

SUMMARY

- Directional leaders—Initiate a vision
- Managing leaders—Initiate a plan
- Disciple-making leaders—Initiate the work

Servant leaders must *learn* (discipline) *to manage* (critical leadership and administrative skill) *carefully* (conscious of their role and responsibility, conscious of their place in the larger organizational context).

ASSIGNMENT: *What kind of a leader are you? What can you do to contribute to the effective management of your church or ministry?*

DISCUSSION: *Discuss the implications of: (1) not knowing your place, (2) not being empowered to act consistently with your gifting, and (3) not having all three types of leaders at work in your organization.*

75

Servant Leadership Skill:
Innovate Suitably

*[The] men of Issachar, who understood the times and knew what
Israel should do.* (1 Chronicles 12:32, NIV)

The men of Issachar were strategists and innovators. They were able to
analyze the environment and their own organizational strengths with accuracy and were then able to innovate a suitable and appropriate action plan.

Max Depree observes that the first order of leadership is to define reality.[84] No doubt, this is where the men of Issachar began. A common tool
used to assess the organization in its context on the environmental landscape is a SWOT analysis.[85]

- Strengths: What are the strengths and uniquely effective
  abilities of the organization? This is an internal question
  for the organization.

- Weaknesses: What are the weaknesses and drawbacks of the organization? This is also an internal question for the organization.

- Opportunities: What are the opportunities that are presented before the organization? This is an external question. How does the organization interact with the environment?

- Threats: What are the presenting and prospective threats against the success of the organization? This too is an external question.

While this exercise is technical, it will aid in "understanding the times" and "defining reality." The action plans growing out of this observation may, however, draw on a different set of skills—namely, creativity. Creativity and innovation are frequently at the core of significant advancements. Creativity and innovation have given us such advancements as:

- Shelter: from caves and tents in the wilderness to high-rise condominiums in mega cities.

- Travel: from donkeys to automobiles and space shuttles.

- Weapons: from spears for hunting to missiles of war, guided with precision.

- Medicine: from plants and herbs to transplants and genetic manipulation.

- Science: from observing the stars to exploring DNA.

- Technology: from the wheel to the internet.

- Communication: from papyrus to cell phones.

- Ministry methods: from speaking on hillsides to home groups and mega structures.

Jesus addressed the role of the old and the new when he said:

But no one puts a patch of unshrunk cloth on an old garment; for

the patch pulls away from the garment, and a worse tear results.
Nor do people put new wine into old wineskins; otherwise the
wineskins burst, and the wine pours out and the wineskins are ru-
ined; but they put new wine into fresh wineskins, and both are
preserved. (Matthew 9:16-17, NASB)

Jesus was preparing his followers for a transition to take place. The kingdom of God was going to look very different from what was expected. A political takeover was envisioned by Israel, but Jesus' objective began with the transformation of hearts and souls. Transformation would begin from the inside and move outward into families, communities, cultures, and societies. Jesus warned that this transition would require some new ways of thinking, and some new methods.

MESSAGE OR METHOD

Throughout the history of the church, we have seen both message and method change. Some of these changes were positive and brought about significant Great Commission progress. Others, however, brought harm and injury to the work of the church.

One of the objectives of *Disciple* is to anchor us with biblical, historic, orthodox Christianity that has survived hundreds of years of pressure, opposition, assaults, heresies, and attacks. While biblical scholars and everyday students of the Word continue to draw fresh insights from the bottomless well of Scripture, the core message has remained the same. The nature of God, the sufficiency of Christ, and the authority of Scripture all continue as bedrocks of the message.

In the nineteenth century, European universities and seminaries began to employ a critical approach to the Scriptures which resulted in a lower view of Scripture and its authority. This diluted message would impact Europe and North America into the early twentieth century and the result was a notable floundering of several mainline denominations. When we change the message, we invariably lose the message. Such temptations to adapt the message or somehow make it more culturally palpable continue. However, we must remain students of truth and Berean-like in our approach.

> The brothers immediately sent Paul and Silas away by night to Berea, and when they arrived they went into the Jewish synagogue. Now these Jews were more noble than those in Thessalonica; they received the word with all eagerness, examining the Scriptures daily to see if these things were so. (Acts 17:10-11, ESV)

While the message of the Gospel has power and relevance to all people, in all cultural settings, throughout all historic times, the methods employed in delivering the message have often changed. Missiologists have this as one of their chief objectives: to find how to contextualize the Gospel in a meaningful and clear way without compromising its substance. Thus, we have seen the church throughout history and around the world function in highly structured ways, and in more undefined organic ways. We have seen large cathedrals and modern mega-churches, as well as small house churches. We have seen midsized groups, age-appropriate groups, life-stage groups, generationally mixed groups, generationally divided groups, traditionally oriented groups, along with current and culturally relevant groups. We have seen orphanages, schools, hospitals, universities, bus ministries, seeker services, alpha groups, recovery ministries, blogs, and web-based ministries. Which are the best? The question is foolish. Some were more effective than others. Some were more enduring than others. Some were more target-focused than others. Methods may change, but where the message has endured, Great Commission ministry has endured.

Servant leaders must *learn* (discipline) *to innovate* (critical creative leadership skill) *suitably* (carefully protecting the message, but creatively exploring new methods).

ASSIGNMENT: *Assess the present ministry structures and programs in which you are involved. Were these programs present fifty years ago? Will they be here ten years from now?*

DISCUSSION: *In what ways are some seeking to change the message in your cultural context?*

76

Servant Leadership Skill: Initiate Tirelessly

Moses was a leader who followed the purposes of God in his life with faith, resilience, and endurance. Sometimes he was passionately excited, while at other times he was reluctant and discouraged. In all, he was faithful to the discipline of following God's vision for his life. Examining Moses as a leader surfaces some valuable insights. At the centre of his leadership was initiative. While his emotions sometimes pulled him toward reluctance, he nevertheless gave himself tirelessly to initiating servant leadership. Leaders are not passive. Leaders are not spectators. Leaders make things happen.

CASE STUDY: MOSES

The people of Israel had initially moved to Egypt due to a famine in their own land. For many years, they were tolerated and even accepted because of the leadership influence of Joseph. However, with time, the people of Israel prospered and increased in population, causing concern within the circles of power in Egypt. Something would have to be done.

> *A new king came to power in Egypt who didn't know Joseph. He spoke to his people in alarm, "There are way too many of these Israelites for us to handle. We've got to do something: Let's devise a plan to contain them, lest if there's a war they should join our enemies, or just walk off and leave us."*
>
> *So they organized them into work-gangs and put them to hard labor under gang-foremen. They built the storage cities Pithom and Rameses for Pharaoh. But the harder the Egyptians worked them the more children the Israelites had—children everywhere! The Egyptians got so they couldn't stand the Israelites and treated them worse than ever, crushing them with slave labor. They made them miserable with hard labor—making bricks and mortar and back-breaking work in the fields. They piled on the work, crushing them under the cruel workload.*
>
> *The king of Egypt had a talk with the two Hebrew midwives; one was named Shiphrah and the other Puah. He said, "When you deliver the Hebrew women, look at the sex of the baby. If it's a boy, kill him; if it's a girl, let her live."*
>
> *But the midwives had far too much respect for God and didn't do what the king of Egypt ordered; they let the boy babies live. The king of Egypt called in the midwives. "Why didn't you obey my orders? You've let those babies live!"* (Exodus 1:8-17, MSG)

When death by attrition didn't work, Pharaoh attempted death by annihilation. However, God's people could not be annihilated. Even amidst tremendous opposition and hostility, God was at work. God's plan for freeing Israel from bondage would begin with a deliverer. Somehow, God would have to sovereignly produce a leader to deliver his people out of great danger.

> *A man from the family of Levi married a Levite woman. The woman became pregnant and had a son. She saw there was something special about him and hid him. She hid him for three months. When she couldn't hide him any longer she got a little basket-boat made of papyrus, waterproofed it with tar and pitch, and placed the child in it. Then she set it afloat in the reeds at the edge of the Nile.*
>
> *The baby's older sister found herself a vantage point a little way off and watched to see what would happen to him. Pharaoh's daughter came down to the Nile to bathe; her maidens strolled on the bank. She saw the basket-boat floating in the reeds and sent her maid to get it. She opened it and saw the child—a baby crying! Her heart went out to him. She said, "This must be one of the Hebrew babies."*
>
> *Then his sister was before her: "Do you want me to go and get a nursing mother from the Hebrews so she can nurse the baby for you?"*
>
> *Pharaoh's daughter said, "Yes. Go." The girl went and called the child's mother.*
>
> *Pharaoh's daughter told her, "Take this baby and nurse him for me. I'll pay you." The woman took the child and nursed him.*
>
> *After the child was weaned, she presented him to Pharaoh's daughter who adopted him as her son. She named him Moses (Pulled-Out), saying, "I pulled him out of the water."* (Exodus 2:1-10, MSG)

Deliverance came in the form of the Pharaoh's own daughter. Moses was raised in the king's court, learned the king's language, ate the king's food, and sat under the teaching of the king's scholars, yet he was nursed by his own mother and no doubt had the seeds of faith in Jehovah planted within him. Moses spent forty years in the world of the man who would become his foe.

Time passed. Moses grew up. One day he went and saw his brothers, saw all that hard labor. Then he saw an Egyptian hit a Hebrew—one of his relatives! He looked this way and then that; when he realized there was no one in sight, he killed the Egyptian and buried him in the sand.

The next day he went out there again. Two Hebrew men were fighting. He spoke to the man who started it: "Why are you hitting your neighbor?"

The man shot back: "Who do you think you are, telling us what to do? Are you going to kill me the way you killed that Egyptian?"

Then Moses panicked: "Word's gotten out—people know about this."

Pharaoh heard about it and tried to kill Moses, but Moses got away to the land of Midian. He sat down by a well.

The priest of Midian had seven daughters. They came and drew water, filling the troughs and watering their father's sheep. When some shepherds came and chased the girls off, Moses came to their rescue and helped them water their sheep. (Exodus 2:11-17, MSG)

In a moment of passion and poor judgment, Moses committed a foolish act. He did initiate, but he initiated out of impulse and not purpose. Flight was necessary and Moses spent the next forty years as a shepherd in obscurity.

So God heard their groaning, and God remembered His covenant with Abraham, with Isaac, and with Jacob. And God looked upon the children of Israel, and God acknowledged them. (Exodus 2:24-25, NKJV)

Indeed, God was listening to his people and was preparing a leader. Finally, God called Moses, at the age of eighty, into strategic leadership.

God said, "I've taken a good, long look at the affliction of my people in Egypt. I've heard their cries for deliverance from their slave masters; I know all about their pain. And now I have come down to help them, pry them loose from the grip of Egypt, get them out of that country and bring them to a good land with wide-open spaces, a land lush with milk and honey, the land of the Canaanite, the Hittite, the Amorite, the Perizzite, the Hivite, and the Jebusite.

"The Israelite cry for help has come to me, and I've seen for myself how cruelly they're being treated by the Egyptians. It's time for you to go back: I'm sending you to Pharaoh to bring my people, the People of Israel, out of Egypt."

Moses answered God, "But why me? What makes you think that I could ever go to Pharaoh and lead the children of Israel out of Egypt?"

"I'll be with you," God said. "And this will be the proof that I am the one who sent you: When you have brought my people out of Egypt, you will worship God right here at this very mountain."

Then Moses said to God, "Suppose I go to the People of Israel and I tell them, 'The God of your fathers sent me to you'; and they ask me, 'What is his name?' What do I tell them?"

God said to Moses, "I-AM-WHO-I-AM. Tell the People of Israel, 'I-AM sent me to you.'"

God continued with Moses: "This is what you're to say to the Israelites: 'God, the God of your fathers, the God of Abraham, the God of Isaac, and the God of Jacob sent me to you.' This has always been my name, and this is how I always will be known.
(Exodus 3:7-15, MSG)

Moses responded by arguing with God, protesting God's selection and wallowing in self-abasement and self-doubt. This story is full of wonderful observations, as God used a unique upbringing, painful experiences, time alone in reflection and obscurity, personal passions, strengths, deficiencies, and inabilities to prepare and call a servant to an enormous and profoundly significant task.

Moses finally, but reluctantly, obeyed God. Through Exodus 5-14, Moses encountered numerous hurdles in his leadership. He experienced the challenge of the raw task itself, the ongoing challenge of self-doubt, the challenge of internal opposition, and the challenge of external opposition. What emerges for our learning is that while God is working *through* Moses (entering into conflict with Pharaoh in order to free Israel from oppressive slavery), God is equally working *in* Moses (taking him through pain and triumphs in order to grow a character and draw Moses closer to God). What, in fact, becomes evident is that Moses encountered more leadership conflict following Israel's deliverance from Pharaoh. Consider the following:[86]

POINT OF CONFLICT	MOSES' RESPONSE	GOD'S RESPONSE	REFERENCE
Complaint re: Pharaoh's Army	Encouraged Israel	Divided Red Sea	Exodus. 14:1-31
Complaint re: bitter water	Prayer	Made water drinkable	Exodus 15:22-27
Complaint re: lack of food	Confrontation/rebuke	Sent manna from heaven	Exodus 16:1-36
Complaint re: lack of water	Prayer	Supplied water from rock	Exodus 17:1-7
Return to idolatry	Pray/mediate/confront	Forgiveness	Exodus 32-34
Complaint re: hardships	Discouragement/prayer	Sent fire	Numbers 11:1-3
Complaint re: lack of meat	Frustration/prayer	Sent quail and plague	Numbers 11:4-35
Undermining of Moses' leadership	Prayer/mediation	Accused become leprous	Numbers 12:1-13
Complaint re: potential enemy	Prayer	Wander for forty years	Numbers 14:1-25
Complaint re: Moses' leadership	Rebuke/anger/prayer	Death of Korah	Numbers 16:1-35

Complaint re: lack of water	Rebuke/struck rock	Moses denied land	Numbers 20:1-13
Complaint re: manna/desert	Made bronze snake	Sent poisonous snakes	Numbers 21:4-9
Immorality, then idolatry	Confrontation	Death of ringleaders	Numbers 25:1-13

A thorough analysis of the above experiences of Moses could potentially discourage a new, prospective leader. First, people who have issues with God invariably take it out on the leader. Leaders must constantly face the accumulation of grievances. Second, being an agent of change seems to invite a disproportionate amount of conflict. Conflict is a part of leadership; thus, no leader should be surprised when it surfaces. Third, most conflict comes from within. This is consistent with the biblical imagery of a group or body being more like a living system or organism. The leader's biggest job is to understand, work within, and lead the entire system.

In the end, after forty years, the people of Israel were brought to the edge of the promised land. Moses' assignment was complete. God worked through Moses. However, throughout Moses' enduring leadership, God had been working in Moses, growing the character of one of his children. Thus, it was said of Moses:

> (Now the man Moses was very humble, more than any man who was on the face of the earth.)... He said, "Hear now My words: If there is a prophet among you, I, the Lord, shall make Myself known to him in a vision. I shall speak with him in a dream. Not so, with My servant Moses, he is faithful in all My household; with him I speak mouth to mouth, even openly, and not in dark sayings, and he beholds the form of the Lord. Why then were you not afraid to speak against My servant, against Moses?" (Numbers 12:3, 6-8, NASB)

Moses' reluctance makes him human. We can relate to him. However,

in spite of the power of his fears, insecurities, and self-doubts, Moses tirelessly initiated, even in the face of continued opposition. Leaders initiate.
Leaders start things. While there are occasions when leaders do need to
respond and react, leaders must never lose sight of the responsibility of
initiative, even when they do not feel like it.

Servant leaders must *learn* (discipline) *to initiate* (critical life and leadership skill) *tirelessly* (with discipline, determination, resilience, and endurance).

ASSIGNMENT: *Reflect on the ways you have had your leadership challenged.
What did you learn?*

DISCUSSION: *Why are some leaders prone to reaction, or worse, passivity?*

77

Servant Leadership Skill: Follow Relentlessly

This chapter is, in many ways, a continuation of the preceding chapter. Leaders may naturally have a high expectation of seeing God work in and through them. However, leaders also need to expect to face significant hardships and challenges. In spite of it all, leaders follow relentlessly. They do not quit, because Jesus never quite.

In this chapter, we want to ensure that we have realistic expectations of leadership. Ministry has highs and lows, successes and stresses, joys and heartaches, benefits and burdens. The gap between our expectations and reality as we experience it is what we call disappointment. If we can enter leadership with realistic expectations and an emotional sense of readiness, we will reduce our disappointments.

MINISTRY LEADERSHIP BLESSINGS

- We grow. It is just that simple. When we eat, we take in energy. But when we move, when we work, and when we exercise, we draw on that energy and get strong. The spiritual life follows the same axiom. If all we do is take in (more Bible studies, more sermons, more Christian books, more classes) and we never exercise our faith, we become imbalanced and unhealthy. To grow and become strong, we must serve. Ephesians 4:12 commands leaders "to prepare God's people for works of service, so that the body of Christ may be built up" (NIV). 1 Peter 4:10 states, "Each one should use whatever gift he has received to serve others, faithfully administering God's grace in its various forms" (NIV). If we want to grow, we need to be in God's Word. We also need the support of Christian community. But we additionally need to get involved in service.

- We see lives change. With every conversion, with every bad habit that ends, with every new virtue that is embraced, with every step forward, we have the honour of seeing a life changed. When we are a spectator on the sidelines, we miss the opportunity of seeing lives change.

- We bear witness to miracles. Seeing lives changed impacts us, but there are those times when we witness something so surprising, so out of the ordinary, and so spectacular, that we realize we are witness to a miracle. It may be an addiction suddenly exercised, or a marriage so devastated but is now full of life, or it may be a healing, or a reconciled relationship. These are the benefits of ministry.

- We have the satisfaction of being a partner in God's kingdom work. We all want our lives to have meaning. We can fritter away a lifetime searching for meaning and purpose.

What could be more satisfying, more self-actualizing, more fulfilling, than being in on God's divine purposes for humanity?

- We experience the forging of our characters. We grow when we press ourselves and when we push and stretch ourselves. We have to tear muscle to build muscle. We have to work the heart to make it resilient and strong. In the same way, ministry shapes our character into a more attractive image. Forging brings out the image of Christ.

MINISTRY LEADERSHIP WEIGHTS

Jesus told us to expect challenges, but to be assured of our ultimate eternal victory.

> Let not your heart be troubled; you believe in God, believe also in Me. In My Father's house are many mansions; if it were not so, I would have told you. I go to prepare a place for you. And if I go and prepare a place for you, I will come again and receive you to Myself; that where I am, there you may be also. (John 14:1-3, NKJV).

> These things I have spoken to you, that in Me you may have peace. In the world you will have tribulation; but be of good cheer, I have overcome the world. (John 16:33, NKJV)

Paul invites leaders in particular to be strong and ready to face difficulties.

> So, my son, throw yourself into this work for Christ. Pass on what you heard from me—the whole congregation saying Amen!—to reliable leaders who are competent to teach others. When the going gets rough, take it on the chin with the rest of us, the way Jesus did. A soldier on duty doesn't get caught up in making deals at the marketplace. He concentrates on carrying out orders. An ath-

lete who refuses to play by the rules will never get anywhere. It's the diligent farmer who gets the produce. Think it over. God will make it all plain.

Fix this picture firmly in your mind: Jesus, descended from the line of David, raised from the dead. It's what you've heard from me all along. It's what I'm sitting in jail for right now—but God's Word isn't in jail! That's why I stick it out here—so that everyone God calls will get in on the salvation of Christ in all its glory. This is a sure thing. (2 Timothy 2:3-10, MSG)

Consider these very real weights of ministry leadership.[87]

- The weight of initiative. The ultimate responsibility for every endeavour (budget, personal, programs, etc.) rests on the leader. The leader therefore is constantly initiating. Leaders must be self-starters. Energy needs actually increase with the complexity of the organization. We cannot wait for someone else to get things started. It's up to the leader, and this can become tiresome.

- The weight of decision. As Paul said to Timothy, "Keep your head in all situations." Literally, Paul was saying, "Abstain from wine." The meaning, however, is, "Be sober in all your judgment." Good judgment is crucial to good leadership. The constant need for decision-making can certainly create pressure. We have to decide when to start, when to stop, who to enlist, who to release, who to affirm, who to confront, what to say, and what not to say. The weight of decision can intensify and prove wearisome.

- The weight of contradictory expectations. Everyone wants a piece of the leader. We spend time with the group and time with individuals. We have family and we have work. We need to focus on the big picture while not neglecting the details. There is the symbolic and there is the strategic.

Some will say, "You spoke too long"; others, "Not long enough." Some will say, "It's not deep enough"; others, "You are not practical enough." We hear, "Delegate and empower more," and then we hear, "You are not asserting enough control!" Sometimes these tensions pull hard on us. We must wrestle with this tension.

- The weight of time. Frontline ministry and leadership implies responsibility. With increased responsibilities come greater demands on time. These time demands will control us if we do not control them. Time will need to be allocated for personal matters, family, other leaders, the flock itself, and certainly for personal reflection, devotion, and self-leadership. If not, fatigue will set in and we risk the temptation of falling, quitting, or burning out.

- The weight of accumulated grievances. All the "junk" eventually ends up on the leader's desk---it doesn't matter whether you are a board member, small group leader, worship team leader, head usher, or volunteer coordinator. The leader will, in time, hear it all. Not only do people lay their concerns with leadership before the leader, but they also usually deposit some of their own issues with God before the leader. When leaders are constantly hearing the negative, continuously mediating and resolving conflict, endlessly defending and explaining, the temptation to become cynical becomes exceedingly forceful.

- The weight of loneliness. As hard as we strive to uphold the value of fellowship and the priesthood of all believers, there will be seasons when the leader feels very much alone. We are not really alone, but we will feel this way. There may be a real aloneness, in that people feel awkward in reaching out to the leader, or it may be a perceived aloneness, the kind that comes from feeling like your deci-

sion was necessary though not popular. Furthermore, it is
often difficult to be friends with someone you are leading
(or supervising). Leaders must intentionally seek out
friendships.

- The weight of obsolescence. Most programs eventually
  run their course. It is expedient for the leader to address
  obsolete programs which no longer serve a useful purpose.
  As someone insightfully observed, "When the horse is
  dead, dismount." These changes, however, invariably meet
  with opposition. The pressure and pain of obsolescence
  finds its ultimate suffering when the leader himself is no
  longer effective. Having the grace to recognize when one's
  role has been realized is crucial.

- The weight of success. The pressures of failure are a given,
  and naturally we should learn from our failures. However,
  success brings about a unique stress all its own. What do
  we do next? Tragically, many leaders have self-destructed
  at the peak of leadership due to an inability to cope with
  success. This is a curious, but often evidenced observation.
  In some cases, people self-destruct because of the pressure
  of success itself. Other times, the leader feels unworthy,
  and thus pulls the plug.

- The weight of temptations. Temptations upon leaders are
  plentiful. They may come to us in the obvious forms of desire, greed, lust, and power, or they may gradually seep
  into our lives as laziness or a gradual pull to slow down or
  even quit. Sometimes, in states of exhaustion, we look for
  quick fixes, experiences to make us feel alive. Such pursuits are usually loaded with danger and folly. While
  temptation is not unique to leadership, often leaders who
  are running close to empty and have not taken care of
  their soul are more susceptible to temptation. Self-

leadership and soul care will guard against temptation.

Servant leaders must *learn* (discipline) *to follow* (critical leadership skill) *relentlessly* (with discipline, determination, resilience, and endurance).

ASSIGNMENT: *What excites you most about ministry leadership? What creates the most stress?*

DISCUSSION: *Discuss the list of leadership burdens. Which ones do you feel the most? What additional burdens would you add to the list?*

— 78 —
Servant Leadership Skill:
Retire Gracefully

CASE STUDY: MOSES

*Moses went on and addressed these words to all Israel. He said,
"I'm 120 years old today. I can't get about as I used to. And God
told me, 'You're not going to cross this Jordan River.' God, your
God, will cross the river ahead of you and destroy the nations in
your path so that you may dispossess them. (And Joshua will
cross the river before you, as God said he would.) God will give
the nations the same treatment he gave the kings of the Amorites,
Sihon and Og, and their land; he'll destroy them. God will hand
the nations over to you, and you'll treat them exactly as I have
commanded you.*

*"Be strong. Take courage. Don't be intimidated. Don't give
them a second thought because God, your God, is striding ahead
of you. He's right there with you. He won't let you down; he won't*

leave you."

Then Moses summoned Joshua. He said to him with all Israel watching, "Be strong. Take courage. You will enter the land with this people, this land that God promised their ancestors that he'd give them. You will make them the proud possessors of it. God is striding ahead of you. He's right there with you. He won't let you down; he won't leave you. Don't be intimidated. Don't worry." (Deuteronomy 31:1-8, MSG)

When the people of Israel finally reached their destination of the Promised Land, and the generation that was under God's discipline had passed away, Moses knew his leadership was complete. Although now aged, Moses still demonstrated humility and a willingness to relinquish and transfer power to the next generation. While this appears normal, in actuality many leaders find it difficult to perceive when their formal leadership is complete and when it is time to retire gracefully but decisively.

One of the values of the plurality of leadership is that every leader should be accountable to others. Ideally, this leadership body should cultivate the transparency and honesty that is needed to help a colleague identify when their contribution is complete. This does not imply that there can be no ministry or leadership contributions afterwards. Retirement is not a biblical concept. However, the form and position which the leader once held will now change.

J. Robert Clinton has engaged in an extensive analysis of leadership phases. He observes that there are six stages or phases that every leader travels through.[88] These are:

- Sovereign foundations: where God is at work through family of origin, experiences, etc.
- Inner-life growth: where faith and values begin to take shape.
- Ministry maturity: where ministry skills are formed.

- Life maturity: where ministry and life brings a feedback of learning and mature reflection.
- Convergence: where all of one's learnings and experience converge in a strategic manner.
- Afterglow: where formal roles exist no longer, but passing on jewels of wisdom occurs.

The leader who has retired gracefully from his or her role now enjoys the season of "afterglow." This is a real phase, but it is not usually characterized by formal position or responsibility. Often the retiring leader will have to physically leave the organizational context in order to allow for new leadership to bond with the organization and sculpt a new vision or ministry ethos. Such decisions need to be made delicately and sensitively for all.

It is the secure, but humble leader who decides what is best for the organization, not for himself or herself. The legacy left behind will be measured by the health of the organization and the disciples that have been reproduced. Such leaders have a clear grip of their role in God's economy. The glory goes to God. The epitaph of David is exemplary:

> For David, after he had served the purpose of God in his own generation, fell asleep, and was laid among his fathers and underwent decay. (Acts 13:36, NASB)

Servant leaders must *learn* (discipline) *to retire* (critical life and leadership skill) *gracefully* (in humility, blessing the next generation).

ASSIGNMENT: *What phase of leadership do you think you are in?*

DISCUSSION: *Discuss a situation where a leader appeared to "stay too long." What happened to the leader? What happened to the organization?*

79

Commencement and Commissioning

As we began *Disciple,* we set out to achieve some essential outcomes and measurable goals. These milestones were:

- We will love God with our entire being, love our neighbour as we love ourselves, and have a passionate love for the work of Christ (Matthew 22:37-39; 28:19-20).
- We will be able to articulate what God has done for us as his witness (Mark 5:19; Acts 3:5).
- We will be regular participants in worship (Hebrews 10:24-25; Acts 2:42).
- We will engage in a discipleship relationship (Matthew 28:19-20; Acts 2:46).
- We will publically identify with Christ in baptism (Matthew 28:19-20).
- We will establish habits that promote spiritual growth, life

transformation, and the development of Christian character. Such habits include Bible reading, meditation, prayer, service, and giving.

- We will maintain a balanced lifestyle that promotes growth mentally, physically, spiritually, and socially (Luke 2:52).
- We will engage in acts of service within the body of Christ and within the community that God has placed us in (Mark 10:45; Ephesians 4:11-12).
- We will pray for service and evangelistic opportunities and seize such opportunities as they arise (Colossians 4:2-4; Acts 1:8).
- We will engage in the intentional act of making disciples with a view to reproduction and multiplication (Matthew 28:19-20).

I hope that these are all now true of you. Perhaps you have just completed *Disciple* as more of a learner than a mentor. The chief objective of this material and the discipleship relationship that you have shared in was to transform you, as a disciple, into a disciple-maker. You may not feel ready, but with the completion of this material you should view this as your "commencement" to the task of reproduction and multiplication. You are now "commissioned" to invite others into a discipleship relationship through this discipleship material. You will only continue to grow as you now aid others in their realization of becoming a disciple. The most significant legacy that you can leave behind is the development of disciples. In so doing, we ensure that Christ's work will continue into the next generation, that the mission of Christ is honoured, and that God is glorified.

THE ASSIGNMENTS CONTINUE

Now that you have completed *Disciple*, write out a twelve-month personal spiritual growth plan that includes goals and action steps that will keep you on the path of continuous growth. This will make you an intentional re-producer and multiplier for the work of Christ.

Welcome to the continuing journey of entering into the kingdom agenda of God, which is making disciples of Jesus Christ.

I hereby accept my commission to continue learning as a disciple and to "make disciples."

_____

Name

_____

Date

APPENDIX

Romans 3:23, NIV

"For all have sinned and fall short of the glory of God."

Romans 5:8, NIV

"But God demonstrates his own love for us in this: While we were still sinners, Christ died for us."

Romans 6:23, NIV

"For the wages of sin is death, but the gift of God is eternal life in Christ Jesus our Lord."

John 3:16, NIV

"For God so loved the world that he gave his one and only Son, that whoever believes in him shall not perish but have eternal life."

John 1:12, NIV

"Yet to all who received him, to those who believed in his name, he gave the right to become children of God."

Luke 9:23, NIV

"Then he said to them all: "If anyone would come after me, he must deny himself and take up his cross daily and follow me.""

2 Corinthians 5:17, NIV

"Therefore, if anyone is in Christ, he is a new creation; the old has gone, the new has come!""

John 5:24, NIV

"I tell you the truth, whoever hears my word and believes him who sent me has eternal life and will not be condemned; he has crossed over from death to life."

Ephesians 2:8-10, NIV

"For it is by grace you have been saved, through faith—and this not from yourselves, it is the gift of God—not by works, so that no one can boast. For we are God's workmanship, created in Christ Jesus to do good works, which God prepared in advance for us to do."

Romans 12:1-2, NIV

"Therefore, I urge you, brothers, in view of God's mercy, to offer your bodies as living sacrifices, holy and pleasing to God—this is your spiritual act of worship. Do not conform any longer to the pattern of this world, but be transformed by the renewing of your mind. Then you will be able to test and approve what God's will is—his good, pleasing and perfect will."

1 Peter 5:7, NIV

"Cast all your anxiety on him because he cares for you."

Isaiah 26:3, NIV

"You will keep in perfect peace him whose mind is steadfast, because he trusts in you."

2 Timothy 3:16-17, NIV

"All Scripture is God-breathed and is useful for teaching, rebuking, correcting and training in righteousness, so that the man of God may be thoroughly equipped for every good work."

Psalm 119:9-11, NIV

"How can a young man keep his way pure? By living according to your word. I seek you with all my heart;
do not let me stray from your commands. I have hidden your word in my heart that I might not sin against you."

Philippians 4:6-7, NIV

"Do not be anxious about anything, but in everything, by prayer and petition, with thanksgiving, present your requests to God. And the peace of God, which transcends all understanding, will guard your hearts and your minds in Christ Jesus."

Matthew 22:37-39, NIV

"Jesus replied: 'Love the Lord your God with all your heart and with all your soul and with all your mind.' This is the first and greatest commandment. And the second is like it: 'Love your neighbor as yourself.'"

Matthew 28:19-20, NIV

"Therefore go and make disciples of all nations, baptizing them in the name of the Father and of the Son and of the Holy Spirit, and teaching them to obey everything I have commanded you. And surely I am with you always, to the very end of the age."

1 Corinthians 10:31, NIV

"So whether you eat or drink or whatever you do, do it all for the glory of God."

John 13:34-35, NIV

"A new command I give you: Love one another. As I have loved you, so you must love one another. By this all men will know that you are my disciples, if you love one another."

Mark 10:45, NIV

"For even the Son of Man did not come to be served, but to serve, and to give his life as a ransom for many."

ABOUT THE AUTHOR

Michael Pawelke is the Senior Pastor of Compass Point Bible Church. Michael, with his wife Linda and two children, Breanna and Matthew, first came to serve in Burlington, Ontario in 1994. Compass Point Bible Church is committed to Great Commission outreach and discipleship, serving its community, and growth through multiplication. Its history includes multiplying worship services, planting two churches, entering into strategic mergers, embracing a multi-site paradigm, and restarting an urban work which had been in decline.

Michael periodically teaches at the college and seminary level and enjoys speaking at Bible conferences and family camps. Michael has also served as a church planter in Winnipeg, Manitoba, and as a youth pastor in Toronto, Ontario. Michael is a graduate of Briercrest Bible College (BRE), Dallas Theological Seminary (MABS), Gordon-Conwell Theological Seminary (D.Min), has an honorary doctorate from Briercrest Biblical Seminary (D.D), and is a graduate of the Arrow Leadership Program. He is ordained with the Associated Gospel Churches of Canada and has a volunteer portfolio as chair of the Canada East Church Health and Leadership Commission. He is on the Advisory Board for McMaster Divinity College and is on the Board of Directors for Briercrest College and Seminary.

Michael began following Jesus as a young teen through reading a Gideon New Testament that he had been given in elementary school. Today, Michael loves studying and teaching God's Word, takes tremendous joy in strategic leadership and equipping disciples, and is deeply passionate with how the Gospel can bring transformational impact to our world.

ENDNOTES

[1] The Greek word *ecclesia*, translated *church*.

[2] The Greek word *mathatas*, translated *disciple*.

[3] W.F. Arndt, and F.W. Gingrich, *A Greek-English Lexicon of the New Testament and Other Early Christian Literature* (Chicago, Ill.: University Press, 1952), 486.

[4] The Greek word *matheteuo*, which is the verb form of *mathatas*, also translated *disciple*.

[5] Bill Hull, *The Complete Book of Discipleship* (Colorado Springs, CO.: NavPress, 2006), 29.

[6] The following are also recommended: Robert E. Colman, *The Master Plan of Evangelism* (Old Tappan, New Jersey, Flemming H. Revell Company, 1963). A.B. Bruce, *The Training of the Twelve* Grand Rapids, Mich.: Kregel Publications, 1971). Leroy Eims, *The Lost Art of Disciple Making* (Grand Rapids, Mich.: Zondervan, 1978).

[7] A. B. Bruce, *The Training of the Twelve* Grand Rapids, Mich.: Kregel Publications, 1971), 11, 12.

[8] Ibid.

[9] I am indebted to George Boyd and Dan Barber for their identification of these milestones.

[10] Ibid.

[11] Wayne Cordeiro, *Doing Church as a Team* (Ventura, CA: Regal Books, 2001), 32-33.

[12] Marjorie Williams, *How Toys Become Real* (London: Heinemann, 1922).

[13] Ibid.

[14] Protagorus was a pre-Socratic Greek philosopher.

[15] Joseph Fletcher founded the theory of situational ethics in the 1960's and become a shaper of bioethics.

[16] Epicurus was a Greek philosopher who developed the school of philosophy called Epicureanism.

[17] This was but one aspect of Aristotle's ethical system.

[18] Frederick Nietzsche was a German philosopher of the late 19th century who profoundly shaped existentialism and postmodernism.

[19] See Genesis 1-3.

[20] This aphorism has been attributed to other Greek sages as well.

[21] Paul Lee Tan, *Encyclopedia of 7700 Illustrations* (Garland, Texas: Bible Communications, 1991), 185.

[22] You can read more about the meaning of baptism in chapter 36; the nature of the church.

[23] We will explore the Trinity as we examine the nature of God the Father, God the Son, and God the Holy Spirit.

[24] Stephen R. Covey *The Seven Habits of Hightly Effective People* (New York, New York: Simon and Schuster, 1989), 145.

[25] C.S. Lewis *Letters of C.S. Lewis,* (San Francisco: Harper Collins, 1951), 228.

[26] I am indebted to George Boyd and Dan Barber for the use of these anchor words: Surrender, Sacrifice and Service.

[27] Soren Kierkegaard viewed the worship service as an unfolding drama.

[28] Fritz Rienecker, *Linguistic Key to the Greek New Testament* (Grand Rapids: Zondervan, 1982), 574.

[29] Focus on the Family, "Resentment: Cancer of the Emotions," Dr. Archibald Hart, guest, 20 December 1982.

[30] Neil Anderson, *The Bondage Breaker*, (Eugene, Oregon: Harvest House Publishers, 2000).

[31] William J. Bennett, *The Book of Virtues* (New York, New York: Simon and Schuster, 1993), 192.

[32] Charles Caldwell Ryrie, *Balancing the Christian Life* (Chicago, Ill.: Moody Press, 1969), 13.

[33] Ephesians develops this significantly.

[34] Charles Caldwell Ryrie, *The Holy Spirit* (Chicago, Illinois: Moody Press, 1965), 33.

[35] Adapted from Charles Caldwell Ryrie, *The Holy Spirit* (Chicago, Illinois: Moody Press, 1965), 33.

[36] The doctrine of the Trinity is a theological outgrowth of the deity of God the Father, God the Son, and God the Holy Spirit. The Father is God; the Son is God; the Holy Spirit is God. The Father is not the Son; the Father is not the Holy Spirit; the Son is not the Holy Sprit. God is one in essence; God is three in person.

[37] There are numerous sources on Creationism and Intelligent design such as James Porter Moreland, *The Creation Hypothesis: Scientific Evidence for an Intelligent Designer* (Downers Grove: Intervarsity Press, 1994).

[38] The original source of these categories is unknown.

[39] Glenda DeVries adapted from T.W. Hunt, *The Mind of Christ* (Nashville: Lifeway Christian Resources), 4, 5.

[40] Author unknown.

[41] This quote is credited James Thurber.

[42] Paul D. Stanley and J. Robert Clinton, *Connecting* (Colorado Springs NavPress, 1992), page 197.

[43] Linda Waite and Maggie Gallagher, *The Case for Marriage* (New York, New York: Broadway Books, 2000), 79.

[44] Ibid, 89.

[45] Ibid, 90.

[46] *The Book of Common Prayer*, 1552

[47] M. Peck, Scott, *The Different Drummer* (New York: Simon and Shuster, 1987).

[48] Jack O. Balswick and Judith K. Balswick, *The Family: A Christian Perspective on the Contemporary Home* (Grand Rapids, Michigan, 1991), 44-46.

[49] Ross Campbell, *How to Really Love Your Child* (Wheaton, Illinois: Victor Books, 1977).

[50] Various specialists on parenting employ similar categories or developmental stages. I have been unable to identify the source of these four categories.

[51] Howard Hendricks, *Marriage and Family Classnotes*, Dallas Theological Seminary, 1983.

[52] William Barclay, *The Letters to the Galatians and Ephesians The Daily Bible Study Series* rev. ed. (Philadelphia, PA: Westminister, 1976), 149.

[53] Balswick and Balswick, 105-107.

[54] J. Robert Clinton, *Leadership in the Nineties: Six Factors to Consider* (Altadena, California: Barnabus, 1992).

[55] Gordon McDonald, *Mentoring Leaders Classnotes*, Willow Creek Community Church, 2007.

[56] See Stephen R. Covey, *The Seven Habits of Highly Effective People* (New York, New York: Simon and Schuster, 1989) and related Seven Habits resource materials.

[57] Ibid.

[58] James F. Engel and Wilbert Norton, *What's Gone Wrong With The Harvest?* (Grand Rapids, Mich.: Zondervan, 1975).

[59] I am indebted to Lon Anderson for his stimulation here. These initial observations were made at an Arrow Leadership seminar, 1999.

[60] Paul Brand and Phil Yancey, *Fearfully and Wonderfully Made* (Grand Rapids, Michigan: Zondervan, 1980), 60.

[61] R. Paul Stevens and Phil Collins, *The Equipping Pastor: A Systems Approach to Congregational Leadership* (New York: Baker Books, 1996), xxi.

[62] Ibid.

[63] Ibid.

[64] Stevens and Collins, xvii, xviii.

[65] John Crowe, "Church Health: An Organic, Doctrinal, Systems Approach," 9, April 2000, http://www.gbgm-umc.org/gibsonmemorial/health.htm.d (January 18, 2001), 6.

[66] Peter L. Steinke, *Healthy Congregations: A Systems Approach.* New York, New York: The Alban Institute, 1996), vii.

[67] Rick Warren, "Comprehensive Health Plan" *Leadership Journal*, Vol. 18, No 3,
Summer 1997, 24.

[68] Arndt and Gingrich, 418, 419.

[69] Barclay, *Galatians and Ephesians*, 149.

[70] Cordeiro, 126.

[71] George Barna, *The Power of Vision* (Ventura, California: Regal, 1992), 159.

[72] Cordeiro, 150.

[73] Ibid.

[74] Ibid, 153.

[75] James M. Kouzes and Barry Z. Posner, *The Leadership Challenge* (San Francisco: Jossey-Bass Publishers, 1987), 123, 124.

[76] Max De Pree, *Leadership Jazz* (New York: Doubleday, 1992), 8-9.

[77] George Cladis, *Leading the Team-Based Church* (San Francisco: Jossey-Bass Publishers, 1999), 89.

[78] Jon R. Katzenbach, and Douglas K. Smith, *The Wisdom of Teams* (New York, New York: HarperCollins, 1994), 214.

[79] Fred Smith, "Learning to Lead" *Christianity Today* (1986): 93.

[80] Adapted from George Cladis, *Leading the Team-Based Church* (San Francisco, California: Jossey-Bass Publishers, 1999).

[81] John C. Maxwell, Developing the Leader Within You (Nashville, Tennessee: Thomas Nelson, 1993), 55.

[82] Lee G. Bolman and Terrence E. Deal, *Reframing Organizations* (San Francisco: Jossey-Bass Publishers, 1997), 22-24.

[83] Ibid., page 25.

[84] Max Depree, *Leadership is an Art,* (New York, New York: Bantam Doubleday Dell Publishing, 1990).

[85] Albert Humphrey of Stanford University is credited with this model.

[86] Adapted from C. C. Ryrie, *The Ryrie Study Bible* (Chicago: Moody Press, 1994), 227.

[87] I am indebted to Wayne Goodwin for provoking some of these leadership burdens. Wayne Goodwin, *Doctor of Ministry Classnotes* (Gordon-Conwell Theological Seminary, Summer 1999).

[88] J. Robert Clinton, *The Making of a Leader* (Colorado Springs, Colorado: Navpress, 1988).